Lecture Notes of the Institute
for Computer Sciences, Social-Informatics
and Telecommunications Engineering   34

Editorial Board

Ozgur Akan
    Middle East Technical University, Ankara, Turkey
Paolo Bellavista
    University of Bologna, Italy
Jiannong Cao
    Hong Kong Polytechnic University, Hong Kong
Falko Dressler
    University of Erlangen, Germany
Domenico Ferrari
    Università Cattolica Piacenza, Italy
Mario Gerla
    UCLA, USA
Hisashi Kobayashi
    Princeton University, USA
Sergio Palazzo
    University of Catania, Italy
Sartaj Sahni
    University of Florida, USA
Xuemin (Sherman) Shen
    University of Waterloo, Canada
Mircea Stan
    University of Virginia, USA
Jia Xiaohua
    City University of Hong Kong, Hong Kong
Albert Zomaya
    University of Sydney, Australia
Geoffrey Coulson
    Lancaster University, UK

Preface

Welcome to the proceedings of CloudComp 2009.

A computing cloud is more than a collection of computer resources, because it provides mechanisms to manage those resources. In a cloud computing platform, software is migrating from the desktop to the "clouds," promising users, at any time and anywhere, access to their programs and data.

This year, 44 academic, industrial and student papers from all over the world were submitted, of which 17 were accepted as regular long papers. Additionally, three were included as short papers on hot topics. The Program Committee appreciates the time and effort all of the researchers put into preparing their papers. Many thanks also to the members of the Program Committee and the external reviewers for all of their hard work in reading, evaluating, and providing detailed feedback. Without the contributions of both of these groups, CloudComp would not have been such a lively symposium.

The symposium featured keynote addresses by Jesús Villasante, Head of Unit, European Commission, Dane Walther, Director of Custom Engineering, Akamai Technologies Inc. Cambridge, MA, USA, Greg Malewicz, Google, Mountain View, CA, USA, and Mauro Campanella, Consortium GARR, Italy.

A scientific visit of the Leibniz Supercomputer Centre (LRZ), Bavarian Academy of Science, Garching (Munich), was organized during the conference. The visit was hosted by Prof. A. Bode.

We feel that the symposium will grow and develop in its service to the research community within both academia and industry.

D. R. Avresky
Michel Diaz
Bruno Ciciani
Arndt Bode
Eliezer Dekel
Javier Alonso

Organization

Steering Committee Chair

I. Chlamtac   CreateNet Research Consortium, Trento, Italy
D. Avresky   International Research Institute on Autonomic Network
       Computing (IRIANC), Munich, Germany

General Chairs

D. Avresky   IRIANC, Munich, Germany

Program Co-chairs

M. Diaz   LAAS, CNRS, Toulouse, France
B. Ciciani   University of Rome, Italy
A. Bode   Technical University of Munich, Germany
E. Dekel   IBM Research Laboratory in Haifa, Israel

Publicity Chair

J. Alonso   Technical University of Catalonia – Barcelona
       Supercompting Center, Spain

Conference Coordinator

Gabriella Magyar   ICST, Brussels, Belgium

Technical Program Committee

J. Arlat   LAAS, CNRS, Toulouse, France
A. Bode   Technical University of Munich, Germany
F. Cappello   INRIA, France
M. Colajanni   University of Modena, Italy
G. Cooperman   Northeastern University, USA
T. Coupaye   France Telecom Orange Labs, France
J. Dongarra   University of Tennessee, USA
G. Deconinck   University of Leuven, Belgium
M. Dacier   Symantec, Europe
J.C. Fabre   LAAS,CNRS/ INP-ENSEEIHT, Toulouse, France
S. Fallis   British Telecomm Innovate, UK
P. Felber   University of Neuchatel, Switzerland

A. Ferreira   INRIA, Sofia Antipolis, France
M. Gerndt   Technical University of Munich, Germany
H. Hellwagner   Klagenfurt University, Austria
W. Juling   Karlsruhe Institute of Technology, Germany
G. Malewicz   Google, USA
E. Maehle   University of Luebeck, Germany
F. Quaglia   University of Rome, Italy
A. Puliafito   University of Messina, Italy
C. Pampu   Huawei Technologies Research, Berlin, Germany
S. Papavassiliou   National Technical University of Athens, Greece
K. Pentikousis   VTT, Oulu, Finland
J. Schopf   National Science Foundation (NSF), USA
H. Schmeck   Karlsruhe Institute of Technology, Germany
H. Schwefel   Aalborg University, Denmark
L. Silva   University of Coimbra, Portugal
V. Strumpen   IBM Research, Austin, USA
J. Torres   Technical University of Catalonia - BSC, Spain
C. Trinitis   Technical University of Munich, Germany
M. Vouk   North Carolina State University, USA

Table of Contents

Cloud Computing Infrastructure Track Session 3

Cloud Computing Platforms Track Session 2

Cloud Computing Platforms Track Session 3

Cloud Computing Platforms Track Session 4

Cloud Computing Applications Track Session 1

The FEDERICA Project:
Creating Cloud Infrastructures

Mauro Campanella

Consortium GARR,
Via dei Tizii 6, 00185 Roma, Italy
Mauro.Campanella@garr.it

Abstract. FEDERICA is a European project started in January 2008 that created a scalable, Europe-wide, clean slate, infrastructure to support experiments on Future Internet. The key architectural principle is virtualization both in computer systems and in network equipment and circuits. The project "slices" its substrate to offer "virtual infrastructures" (slices) made of computing elements and network resources to researchers. The user may fully configure the resources, including the slice topology. The slices can be seen as "cloud infrastructures", generalizing the concept of "cloud computing" and enhancing that of "Infrastructure as a Service". A section elaborates on the main open issues: reproducibility, resource description, monitoring and mapping of virtual resources to the physical substrate.

Keywords: NREN, virtualization, Future Internet, FIRE, GEANT.

1 Introduction

The FEDERICA project [1] has been devised to provide support and research on current and Future Internet technologies and architectures. The project is linked to the European FIRE initiative [2] and the European Future Internet Assembly [3]. Other similar initiatives exists worldwide, e.g. GENI [4] in the United Stated in Europe and AKARI [5] in Japan.

Such experimentation requires new environments that combine flexibility, a minimum set of constraint and full control of the environment for the researchers. A clean-slate approach has been advocated by the GENI, which initially planned to build a dedicated, new infrastructure.

The constant developments of technology in computing and in networks, coupled with the virtualization capabilities allow a new approach, which leverage existing infrastructures to create new ones. FEDERICA is built on top of the National Research and Education Networks (NREN [6]) in Europe, which In the last years created a strong multidomain hybrid network infrastructure with advanced capabilities. Virtualization technologies allow creating on this large physical footprint more than one infrastructure and each of them appearing independent and isolated, eventually to the wavelength level.

The project adds to the basic network resource (capacity) and network functionalities (e.g. switching, routing) computing elements to create virtual infrastructures with rich functionalities.

The paper describes the project architecture, its implementation and the challenges posed with particular emphasis to "cloud computing" developments.

2 The FEDERICA Project

The project [1] partners include a wide range of stakeholders on network research, European National Research and Education Networks (NRENs), DANTE, TERENA, academic and industrial research groups and vendors. In the following the architecture will be described as well as its current implementation.

2.1 Project Goals and Objectives

The FEDERICA project scope, as defined in the description of work, is to:

- Create an e-Infrastructure for researchers on Future Internet allowing researchers a complete control of set of resources in a "slice", enabling disruptive experiments
- Support research in virtualization of e-Infrastructures integrating network resources and nodes capable of virtualization (V-Nodes). In particular on multi-(virtual)-domain control, management and monitoring, including virtualization services and user oriented control in a federated environment.
- Facilitate technical discussions amongst specialists, in particular arising from experimental results and disseminating knowledge and NREN experience of meeting users' requirements.
- Contribute with real test cases and results to standardization bodies, e.g. IETF, ITU-T, OIF, IPsphere.

2.2 Architecture

2.2.1 Requirements

As the scope is focused on a research environment on new technologies, the following set of requirements for the infrastructure have been assumed:

- Be technology agnostic and neutral (transparent) to allow disruptive and novel testing, as to not impose constraints to researchers. The requirement is valid for all networking layers, not just the application layer and extends to the operating system used.
- Ensure reproducibility of the experiments, i.e. given the same initial conditions, the results of an experiment are the same. This requirement is considered of particular importance.
- Provide to the user complete control and configuration capabilities within the assigned resources
- Allow more than one user group to run experiments at the same time, without interference.
- Open to interconnect / federate with other e-Infrastructures and Internet. This last requirement plans for interoperability and migration testing.

2.2.2 Framework and Design

The requirements suggest two key framework choices for the infrastructure, which are at the core of design:

- The simultaneous presence of computing and network physical resources. These resources form the substrate of the infrastructure.
- The use of virtualization technologies applied both to computing and network resources. Virtualization will allow creating virtual, un-configured resources.

Virtualization is defined as the capability to create a virtual version of a physical resource, both in the computing and network environment. The virtual resources (e.g. a virtual circuit, a disk partition, a virtual computer) are usually created by segmenting a physical resource. Virtualization may create un-configured (clean) virtual resources, e.g. an image of the hardware of a computing element on which (almost) any operating system can be installed, a point-to-point network circuit, a portion of disk space. Those resources can be then tailored to various needs and even moved from a virtualization-aware platform to another.

Such framework brings to a design in which the infrastructure is considered made of two in two distinct levels (see for a pictorial representation):

1. The virtualization substrate. The physical infrastructure which contains all the hardware and software capable to create the virtual resources;
2. The level containing all virtual infrastructures. Each containing the virtual resources and the initial network topology connecting them.

The virtualization substrate is a single administrative domain. The virtual infrastructures (VI or "slices") may be in principle unlimited, in practice a large number, restricted by the physical resources available and the requested characteristics for the slice.

Two basic resource entities are defined:

1. Connectivity. In form of a point to point circuit with or without assured capacity guarantees and with or without a data link protocol (a "bit pipe")
2. A computing element, offering the equivalent of a computer hardware containing at least RAM, CPU and one network interface, mass storage is optional, although usually available. The computing element is capable of hosting various operating systems and perform also perform functionalities (e.g. routing)

To minimize the load on the physical resources and the interference between virtual resources, the network topology has a high level of meshing. Where virtualization is not available in hardware, as on most of network interfaces for computers, more hardware is installed. As a design principle, the infrastructure would favour testing of functionalities, protocols and new ideas, rather than providing a laboratory for very high performance studies.

Following the framework outlined above, FEDERICA is designed in two layers. The lower layer is the substrate an it's made of physical resources, both network and computing elements, each capable of creating "virtual" resources of their kind. The resource sets, or slices, managed by the user, compose the upper layer.

Given the sophisticated NREN network architecture, a distributed infrastructure can be engineered, with various Points of Presence on the top of the GÉANT [7] backbone, interconnecting several NRENs in Europe. Figure 1 depicts pictorially the design of the infrastructure built on top of the existing NREN and GÉANT production environment. The virtual infrastructures (slices) are shown on the top of the picture. More than one slice is active at the same time.

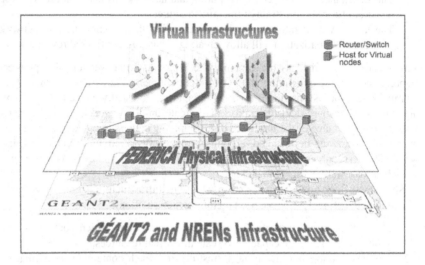

Fig. 1. Pictorial representation of FEDERICA

The figure represents the slice in vertical format for sake of clarity and to show that there is no dependency or hierarchy between them. Each slice may contain a virtual resource coming from any part of the substrate. The same physical node, as an example, can provide virtual systems to more than one slice. A virtual router can be created in a Juniper node (ensuring complete independence between the virtual routers) or by a virtual system running the routing suite.

3 The Infrastructure Implementation

The infrastructure is built using:

- A mesh of one Gigabit Ethernet circuits provided by the GEANT2 backbone. The circuits are initially at one Gbps as this capacity allows slicing to still high-speed links and it is still affordable as contribution by the participating NRENs. Most of the circuits are created over SDH using generic framing procedure and virtual concatenation. Figure 2 represents the current topology
- Network equipment. Programmable high-end routers/switches: Juniper Networks MX480 with dual CPU and 1 line card with 32 ports at 1Gb Ethernet. The MC functionalities include virtual and logical routing, MPLS, VLANs, IPv4, IPv6. The MX 480are installed in four core Points of Presence and 2 MX480 are equipped with Ethernet line cards with hardware QoS capabilities. Smaller multi-protocol switches (Juniper EX series) are installed in non-core PoPs.

-   Computing equipment. PC-based nodes (V-Nodes) running virtualization software, capable of implementing e.g., open source software routers and emulating end-user nodes. Each PC contains 2 x Quad core AMD running at 2 GHz, 32GB RAM, 8 network interfaces, 2x500GB disks. The V-Nodes are connected to the Juniper routers.

The initial choice of the virtualization software for the V-nodes is VMware [8], the free version of ESXi. This choice has been done after a review of other virtualization software (e.g. XEN). In particular it has been evaluated the Application Programming Interface, the availability of usage examples and expertise and an upgrade path to better management using not-for-free version of the software. The capabilities and performance of the free version have been adequate for the current requirements.

These building blocks of the substrate pose very few constraints to the user. In the current status of the infrastructure the most significant one is that the data link layer is fixed to Ethernet framing. Future development of FEDERICA may permit access to optical equipment to overcome this limitation.

2.3.1 Topology

The topology is composed of 13 physical sites. Of these points of presence (PoP) a full mesh of four is equipped with MX router/switches and it is considered the core. The 9 non-core nodes are equipped by EX switches. The core nodes are equipped by 2 V-Nodes the non-core PoPs host one node each. The FEDERICA physical topology is depicted in Figure 2.

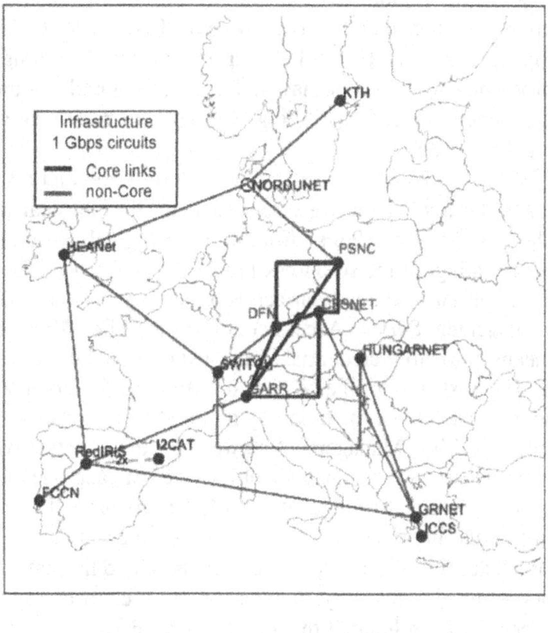

The design placed particular importance on the resiliency and load balancing of the network, based on GEANT2's infrastructure, and resources availability at partners' locations.

The FEDERICA sub-

Fig. 2. FEDERICA topology on a map of Europe

strate is configured as an IPv4 and IPv6 Autonomous System with both public and private addresses. The infrastructure is connected to Internet using the Border Gateway Protocol and receives full routing tables in the four core PoPs.

The infrastructure is centrally managed and monitored by a Network Operation Centre. The NOC has also the task to create the slices. The infrastructure (substrate) is a single domain that contains all the physical resources (point to point circuits, nodes) in all PoPs. The domain does not contain the optical equipment of GÉANT used to transport the circuits between PoPs.

2.3.2 Resource Virtualization and Slice Creation

The process to create a virtual system is rather straightforward and can be based on an image provided by the user or on template of various operating systems. The virtualization capabilities in the network are also evolving, as described in [9]. The article reviews the current research in a Network Virtualization Environment (NVE) and the many challenges associated. The initial choice in FEDERICA is to use VLANs and use QoS techniques for circuit virtualization; MPLS may be applied when needed.

The slice creation procedure definition is constantly developed and may change slightly to incorporate the feedback received after the first user feedback. The slice creation includes a manual step to map the virtual resources to the physical substrate. The step is manual to ensure that the mapping ensures the best reproducibility of the behaviour of the virtual resources.

The current slice creation process consists of the following steps. First, the researcher that wants to perform an experiment over the FEDERICA infrastructure is required to provide the NOC with the desired topology, including requirements for the nodes and the network (each V-node RAM size, CPU power, mass storage space, topology and bandwidth between the V-Nodes, routing or switching functionalities, protocols). The request may be for un-configured resources, that the user will configure directly, even substituting protocols, or resources with a n initial configuration, e.g. IP routing.

Once the NOC receives the slice description and resource requirements, the NOC maps the logical topology requested on the physical topology of the substrate and chooses the sites (PoPs) from which physical resources will be allocated. Besides instantiating all the resources requested by the user, the NOC needs to instantiate an extra virtual machine, that act as a gateway between Internet and the slice: the Slice Management Server. Access control of the Slice Management Server is performed by means of identity credentials managed by a RADIUS server.

The next step for the NOC is to instantiate Ethernet VLANs to connect the slice resources and create the topology required by the researcher. Finally, the NOC needs to setup the Slice Management network for the user that will connect the Slice Management Server to the management interface of each one of the managed resources in the slice (V-Nodes, logical routers, software routers). The connection is performed creating virtual interfaces in all resources and one in the Management Server in the same IP subnet (usually private) and creating an additional VLAN linking them. This subnet is initially the only IP path for the user to connect to the slice resources when accessing from Internet the Management server.

2.3.3 User Access and Support

When the NOC has finished the slice creation process, they inform the researchers that the slice is ready to use. The following information needs to be included: the public IP address of the Virtual Slice Management Server plus the credentials to access it, the credentials for accessing the Juniper logical routers and/or the software routers, and finally the IP addressing scheme of the Virtual Slice Management Network. Now the user is ready to access his slice through the Virtual Slice Management Server.

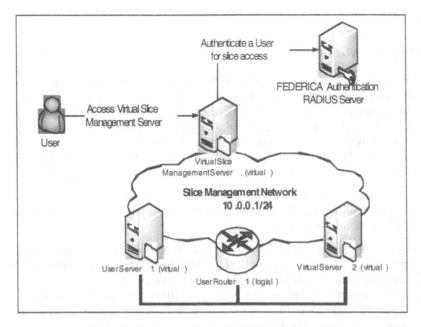

Fig. 3. Researcher accessing a simple FEDERICA slice

In the example in Figure 3 the user has requested a simple slice consisting of two virtual servers connected through a Juniper logical router. The NOC has already setup these three resources, connected them through a VLAN (black line at the bottom of the Figure), instantiated the Virtual Slice Management Server and created the Slice Management Network (cloud at the centre of the Figure). The researcher connects to the Virtual Slice Management Server using the credentials provided by the NOC, and is authenticated against the FEDERICA Authentication RADIUS Server. If the authentication is successful, the user can access all his/her nodes via the management IP interfaces.

Besides remote access to the resources, another complimentary mechanism is under investigation. VMware virtual machines can be configured to be accessed through remote VNC connections (the virtual machine clients would connect to a special port of the physical machine where VMware is installed). By exploiting this mechanism users would have access to the console of their virtual servers, but they would also be able to interact with graphical user interfaces and to even access the BIOS of the server; i.e. they would have full control of the virtual machine.

During the initial FEDERICA operation, all the steps explained in these two sections will be performed either manually or using a heterogeneous set of tools (web portal for users, VMware Infrastructures application, the remote console of the devices, VNC clients, monitoring tools). However, a tool bench that provides a unified environment to operate the FEDERICA infrastructure and use the FEDERICA slices is being developed, and will be progressively deployed and used by the NOC and the FEDERICA users.

3 Challenges

3.1 Real vs. Virtual

The reproducibility and the stability of the behaviour of the virtual resources is a fundamental requirement for quantitative evaluations of new ideas. As an example, a virtual circuit may not be capable of offering a constant, fixed amount of bit per second, and a virtual computer image may not provide a constant CPU usage.

The quality of a virtual resource can then be defined as a function of the difference between the behaviour of the virtual and the physical resource. The difference is due to two main independent causes:

- Sharing of the physical resource with other virtual resources
- The virtualization technology itself, usually a layer placed between the physical resources and the virtual ones

Hardware assistance for virtualization has been introduced recently to reduce such a difference. Since 2005 the main CPU manufacturers have added virtualization-friendly extensions, in particular related to protection rings.

QoS is considered in both resource types: connectivity and computing element.

Computing elements in FEDERICA have been chosen to provide specific functionalities in hardware, like virtualization-aware CPUs. Some circuits are connected to Quality of Service capable line cards in the Juniper MX. In other cases, where hardware was not available, the resources have been adequately increased, to avoid any overbooking and minimize contention. It is possible then to create a slice with a set of resources, which exhibits, singularly, a known behaviour in all conditions.

Virtual resource performance measurements are ongoing in FEDERICA.

Assuring the QoS of a set of connected resources is more complex and under evaluation. While for a single virtual computer or link it is possible to carefully configure its performance, the complexity increases with the number of resources involved. The classic problem of guaranteeing an end-to-end quality of service of an IP flow exemplifies the issue. In case of virtual infrastructures, as in the case of Internet traffic, probably most of the resources do not require strict guarantees, but rather "best effort" behaviour.

In the particular case of a geographically distributed set of resources, the resource synchronization is more complex due to the longer delay, making the issue harder to solve.

3.2 Virtualization Service Definition and Automation of Procedures

A service to create "virtual infrastructures" (i.e. slices) needs more dynamic and automated procedures. Such a service opens the possibility to federate with other infrastructures and to develop new business models with the user virtual infrastructure extending in many domains. To achieve these goals a standardisation of resource description is required. The design of FEDERICA identified two basic entities (computer and point-to-point circuit) each with a set of characteristics and a set of relationship between them.

The most complex step in automating the service is the definition of the logic and the rules to map virtual resources to physical resources in such a way that the use of the substrate is fair and that the resources comply with a service level agreement, when requested.

3.3 Complexity

The complexity of the systems based on virtualization, in particular when coupling network and computing resources, increases fast with the increase of number of resources. The complexity may actually reduce the reliability and the quality of the system, increasing its operational cost for management and problem resolution.

It is worth underling that virtualization is not restricted to a single layer, but allows recursivity. Multiple virtual networks stacked on the same physical infrastructure may be recursively created, as an example. Such advances require better ad-hoc support in the hardware and the development of new standards for virtual resource interaction. In particular the need is for a more rich information system, which tracks the relationships between entities (virtual or real).

4 Conclusions and Next Steps

An infrastructure substrate based on virtualization both on computing and network resources is a novel approach to provide an ideal environment for innovative research and services. The substrate can create virtual infrastructures containing any combination of the basic, "raw" fundamental virtual resources in arbitrary topologies and hosting any operating system and application type. Such virtual infrastructures are decoupled from their physical location, albeit exhibiting the requested functionalities, appearing as "cloud infrastructures".

The initial experience of the FEDERICA project with its users is that:

- There are very few constraints, except the amount of physical resources available in the substrate when reproducibility is requested.
- It's possible to easily interconnect the slices with the current Internet. Two "cloud infrastructures" can be connect through Internet to validate the behaviour of application in real-life environment;
- A slice may allow the user to fully control and configure almost all communication and computing layers;
- A "Cloud Infrastructure" can be reconfigured in a very short time, even manually. Resources can be added, subtracted or restarted also in a short time.
- The presence of computing capabilities in the infrastructure enables new usage models and service. In particular increases resiliency, as functionalities and even whole "infrastructures" may move in the substrate continuing to work.

The main challenges are related to the reproducibility of the behaviour of the virtual resources and to the complexity of the overall system, in particular the substrate. The current size of FEDERICA is still well manageable and does not present issues. Management and control of distributed, parallel, virtual infrastructures, which may communicate among them and with the open Internet, are also key functions in the next generation networks. The FEDERICA project will continue to develop experience and draft a model for managing and using virtual infrastructures as a combination of networks and systems.

Acknowledgments

The FP7 project FEDERICA is partially supported by the European Commission under the Grant Agreement No.: RI- 213107. The author acknowledges the fundamental contribution of all project partners.

References

1. FEDERICA, Federated E-infrastructure DEdicated to Researchers Innovating in Computing Architectures, European Commission co-funded in the 7th Framework Work Programme, project n. RI-213107, http://www.fp7-federica.eu/ and documents therein
2. Future Internet Research and Experimentation,
   http://cordis.europa.eu/fp7/ict/fire/
3. Future Internet Assembly, http://www.future-internet.eu/
4. Global Environment for Network Innovation, http://www.geni.net
5. AKARI Architecture Design Project, http://akari-project.nict.go.jp/eng/index2.htm
6. For a detailed analysis of NRENs in Europe and their role, see the documents (in particular the TERENA compendium), http://www.terena.org/publications/
7. GÉANT2, the European Research and Education backbone, http://www.geant2.net
8. VMware, http://www.wmware.com
9. Chowdhury, N.M.M.K., Boutaba, R.: Network Virtualization: State of the Art and Research Challenges. IEEE Communications Magazine, 20–26 (July 2009)

Akamai and Cloud Computing

Dane S. Walther

Akamai Technologies,
8 Cambridge Center, Cambridge, MA, 02139, USA
dsw@akamai.com

Abstract. Since 1999, Akamai has built a reliable, Internet-scale, globally distributed system with 50,000+ servers spread across 900+ networks and 70+
countries. Akamai's technology has transformed the Internet into a predictable,
scalable, secure, and high-performance platform for anyone doing business
online. Cloud computing proposes to transform the way IT is consumed and
managed with promises of improved cost efficiencies, accelerated innovation,
faster time-to-market, and the ability to scale applications on demand. However,
as companies begin to implement cloud solutions, the reality of the cloud comes
to bear. Most cloud computing services are accessed over the Internet, and thus
fundamentally rely on an inherently unpredictable and insecure medium. In order for companies to realize the potential of cloud computing, they will need to
overcome the performance, reliability, and scalability challenges the Internet
presents. This talk will take a look at the cloud computing arena today, several
issues that impact applications running over the Internet, and the techniques that
Akamai uses for optimization of the cloud. The talk will describe technologies,
and their underlying architecture, such as route, protocol, and application
optimization that are used by Akamai to enhance the speed and reliability of
applications and services delivered across the Internet. The talk will also delve
into the design principles that guide Akamai's development and deployment
strategies. These guidelines enable Akamai to efficiently operate a globally
distributed system within the cloud.

Models of Computation in the Cloud

Grzegorz Malewicz

Google, Inc., Mountain View, CA 94043, USA
malewicz@google.com

Abstract. Many companies, including Google, operate datacenters consisting of networked commodity computers. Solving practical computational problems on such datacenters can be difficult because of several challenges. Input data can be significantly imbalanced, resulting in hotspots. Individual computers can fail. Even in the absence of failure computers can work at varying paces, introducing delays. Many models of computation have complicated semantics, making programming difficult, and some theoretical models do not have any scalable and efficient realization that is suitable for industrial use.

Google has introduced several models of computation that meet these challenges. The best known example is MapReduce [Dean, J., and Ghemawat, S.: MapReduce: Simplified Data Processing on Large Clusters. OSDI, p137–150 (2004)] where input records are transformed and intermediate records are grouped by key and passed to a reduce operation. Other example is Pregel [Malewicz, G., Austern, M. H., Bik, A. J. C., Dehnert, J. C., Horn, I., Leiser, N., and Czajkowski, G.: Pregel: A System for Large-Scale Graph Processing. PODC, p6 (2009)], a graph computing system where vertices send messages to one another in a series of iterations separated by synchronization barriers. Despite the simplicity of these models, many useful algorithms can easily be expressed in them.

In this talk I will describe these models, the challenges in implementing them, and the techniques that led to the first successful sort of 1PB of data in 6h 2m [Sorting 1PB with MapReduce, http://googleblog. blogspot. com/2008/11/sorting-1pb-with-mapreduce.html (2008)].

Keywords: models of computation, cloud computing, distributed systems, high-performance computing.

Cloud Computing Enabling the Future Internet

Jesús Villasante

European Commission, DG Information Society and Media, Unit D.3
BU25 3/134, 1049 Brussels, Belgium
Jesus.Villasante@ec.europa.eu

Abstract. The Future of the Internet is nowadays a hot topic for researchers and technology developers worldwide. The structural limitations of today's Internet in terms of scalability, flexibility, mobility, security and robustness of networks and services are increasingly being recognised world-wide. Much research and development is underway, aiming to avoid the current network limitations and to develop new online services and applications that meet the increased expectations among users, businesses and governments.

Cloud Computing is expected to become one of the drivers for the take up of online services and applications. It helps to meet the emerging demands of open innovation and flexibility required for global service platforms. There is already a lot of commercial activity around Cloud Computing, and current solutions have demonstrated significant results and also the potential of the technologies. On the other hand, important improvements are still required before Cloud Computing becomes a mature technology; major issues still being security, interoperability, cross-border data protection or running very complex legacy applications.

Europe can seize the opportunity, through its research programmes for the Future Internet, and provide solutions to the limitations of the current technologies. In addition, an adequate policy and regulatory framework can drive the growth of the software sector and facilitate the necessary transformations in the European software industry.

Cloud Computing Infrastructure

Track Session 1

Executing Distributed Applications on Virtualized Infrastructures Specified with the VXDL Language and Managed by the HIPerNET Framework

Guilherme Koslovski[1], Tram Truong Huu[2],
Johan Montagnat[3], and Pascale Vicat-Blanc Primet[1]

[1] INRIA - University of Lyon
guilherme.koslovski@ens-lyon.fr, pascale.primet@inria.fr
[2] University of Nice - I3S
tram@polytech.unice.fr
[3] CNRS - I3S
johan@i3s.unice.fr

Abstract. With the convergence of computing and communication, and the expansion of cloud computing, new models and tools are needed to allow users to define, create, and exploit on-demand virtual infrastructures within wide area distributed environments. Optimally designing customized virtual execution-infrastructure and executing them on a physical substrate remains a complex problem. This paper presents the VXDL language, a language for specifying and describing virtual infrastructures and the HIPerNET framework to manage them. Based on the example of a specific biomedical application and workflow engine, this paper illustrates how VXDL enables to specify different customized virtual infrastructures and the HIPerNET framework to execute them on a distributed substrate. The paper presents experiments of the deployment and execution of this application on different virtual infrastructures managed by our HIPerNet system. All the experiments are performed on the Grid'5000 testbed substrate.

Keywords: Virtual Infrastructure as a service, resource virtualization, application mapping, graph embedding problem, workflow language, topology language.

1 Introduction

The convergence of communication and computation portrays a new vision of the Internet. It is becoming a worldwide cloud increasingly embedding the computational and storage resources that are able to meet the requirements of emerging applications. This resulting vision of a global facility, that brings together distributed resources to build large-scale computing environments, recalls and extends the promising vision of Grid computing, enabling both data-intensive and computing-intensive applications. In this context, the concept of virtualization is a powerful abstraction. It enables an efficient separation between the

D.R. Avresky et al. (Eds.): Cloudcomp 2009, LNICST 34, pp. 3–19, 2010.
© Institute for Computer Sciences, Social-Informatics and Telecommunications Engineering 2010

service and application layers on one hand and the physical resources layer on the other hand. The OS-level virtual machines paradigm is becoming a key feature of servers, distributed systems, and grids. It simplifies the management of resources and offers a greater flexibility in resource usage. Each Virtual Machine (VM) a) provides a confined environment where non-trusted applications can be run, b) allows establishing limits in hardware-resource access and usage, through isolation techniques, c) allows adapting the runtime environment to the application instead of porting the application to the runtime environment (this enhances application portability), d) allows using dedicated or optimized OS mechanisms (scheduler, virtual-memory management, network protocol) for each application, e) enables applications and processes running within a VM to be managed as a whole. Extending these properties to network resources (links and equipments) through the concept of "virtual infrastructure", the abstraction of the hardware enables the creation of multiple, isolated, and protected organized aggregates on the same set of physical resources by sharing them in time and space. The virtual infrastructures are logically isolated by virtualization. The isolation also provides a high security level for each infrastructure. Moreover, virtualizing routers and switching equipments enables the customization of packet routing, packet scheduling, and traffic engineering for each virtual network crossing it.

However, programming applications on large-scale distributed environments is difficult. Defining the optimal infrastructure to execute them is another issue. The flexibility offered by virtual infrastructures could make the problem even more complex. Promising work on workflow has been done in the area of application development to optimize their usage of distributed environments. This paper proposes to explore how this work can also benefit to the composition of virtual infrastructures.

The rest of the paper is structured as follows. In section 2, we define our model of customized *Virtual Private eXecution Infrastructures* named VPXI. To specify these VPXIs we define a description language for VPXI specification and modeling, *Virtual eXecution Description Language*, VXDL. Section 3 details the process for mapping an application on physical resources in a virtualized-infrastructure context. In section 4 we illustrate the application mapping through an example with the Bronze Standard workflow. In section 5, we develop our combined network and system virtualization approach embedded in the HIPer-Net software and report the experiments on a real-scale testbed using the medical image analysis application. Section 6 discusses related works. Finally, conclusions and perspectives are developed in section 7.

2 The Virtual Private eXecution Infrastructure Concept

2.1 The VPXI Concept

We define the *Virtual Private eXecution Infrastructure* (VPXI) concept as a time-limited interconnection of virtual computing resources through a virtual private overlay network. Ideally, any user of a VPXI has the illusion that he is using his own distributed system, while in reality he is using multiple systems, part of the global system. The resulting virtual instances are kept isolated from each others. The members of a VPXI have a consistent view of a single private TCP/IP overlay, independently from the underlying physical topology. A VPXI can span multiple networks belonging to disparate administrative domains. Users can join from any location, deploying and using the same TCP/IP applications they were using on the Internet or their intranet.

A VPXI can be formally represented as a graph in which a vertex is in charge of active data-processing functions and an edge is in charge of moving the data between vertices. A VPXI has a life time and can be requested online or reserved in advance. It is described and submitted as a request by a user. Then, if accepted by the operating framework, it exists as a descriptor and has an entry in a VPXI table until its release time. During the activation phase, the VPXI runs in the data plane and is represented in the control plane of each allocated equipment.

2.2   VXDL: VPXI Description Language

A VPXI specification comprises the recursive description of: a) individual end resources or resource aggregates (clusters) involved, b) performance attributes for each resource element (capacity), c) security attributes, d) commercial attributes, e) temporal attributes, f) elementary functions, which can be attributed to a single resource or a cluster (e.g. request of *computing* nodes, *storage* nodes, *visualization* nodes, or *routing* nodes), g) specific services to be provided by the resource (software), h) the virtual-network's topology, including the performance characteristics (typically bandwidth and latency), as well as the security, commercial, and temporal attributes of the virtual channels. Figure 1 illustrates this concept, representing a virtual infrastructure composed by the aggregation of virtual machines interconnected via virtual channels. It shows two virtual routers (vertices $r_v A$ and $r_v B$) which are used to interconnect and perform the bandwidth control among the other virtual resources (vertices r_v 1 to 8). The virtual routers can independently forward the traffic of the different virtual infrastructures which share the same physical network. Each edge represents a virtual link (as $l_v 1$ and $l_v 2$) with different configurations, used to interconnect a pair of virtual resources.

To enable the specifications and the manipulation of these VPXI entities we propose the VXDL (Virtual Infrastructure Description Language) [9]. It allows the description not only of the end resources, but also of the virtual network's topology, including virtual routers and timeline representation. Implemented with the XML standard, VXDL helps users and applications to create or change VPXI specifications[1]. The VXDL grammar is divided in *Virtual Resources description*, *Virtual Network Topology description*, and *Virtual Timeline description*. A key aspect of this language is that these descriptions are partially optional: it is possible to specify a simple communication infrastructure (a virtual private overlay network) or a simple aggregate of end ressources without any

---

[1] More information about VXDL is provided on
http://www.ens-lyon.fr/LIP/RESO/Software/vxdl

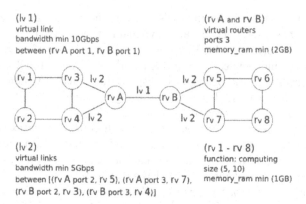

(lv 1)
virtual link
bandwidth min 10Gbps
between (rv A port 1, rv B port 1)

(rv A and rv B)
virtual routers
ports 3
memory_ram min (2GB)

(lv 2)
virtual links
bandwidth min 5Gbps
between [(rv A port 2, rv 5), (rv A port 3, rv 7),
(rv B port 2, rv 3), (rv B port 3, rv 4)]

(rv 1 - rv 8)
function: computing
size (5, 10)
memory_ram min (1GB)

Fig. 1. Example of a VPXI composition using graph representation

network topology description (a virtual cluster or grid). Below, we detail the key aspects of this language.

Virtual Resources Description: This part of VXDL grammar enables users and applications to describe, in a simple and abstract way, all the required end hosts and host groups. VXDL allows the basic resource parametrization (e.g. minimum and maximum acceptable values for RAM memory and CPU frequency). An important feature of VXDL is that it proposes cross-layer parameters. With the specification of *anchor* and *the number of virtual machines allocated per physical host* users can directly interact with lower layers and transmit application-specific information. The *anchor* parameters corresponds to a physical allocation constraint of a VPXI. Indeed, in theory a VPXI can be allocated anywhere in a virtualized substrate, but sometimes it is desirable that a virtual end host (or group) be positioned in a given physical location (e.g. a site or a machine - URL, IP) for an application-specific reason. On the other hand, in a virtualized substrate, multiple virtual machines can be allocated in the same physical host, sharing the real resources. VXDL enables the definition of a maximum number of virtual machines that must be allocated in a physical host, enabling users to interact directly with the allocation algorithm.

Virtual Network Topology Description: VXDL brings two original aspects within the network's topology description: I) the joined specification of network elements and computing elements and II) the link-organization concept, which permits a simple and abstract description of complex structures. Links can define connections between end hosts, between end hosts and groups, inside groups, between groups and VXrouters, and between VXrouters. In VXDL grammar, the definition of *source - destination pairs* for each link is proposed. The same link definition can be applied to different pairs, simplifying the specification of complex infrastructures. For example, links used to interconnect all components of an homogeneous group, as a cluster, can all be defined in a same link description. Each link can be defined by attributes such as latency, bandwidth, and direction. Latency and bandwidth can be defined by the maximum and minimum values.

Virtual Timeline Description: Any VPXI can be permanent, semi-permanent, or temporary. The VPXI are allocated for a defined lifetime in time slots. Time-slot duration is specific to the substrate-management framework and consequently this parameter is configured by the manager of the environment. Often the VPXI components are not used simultaneously or all along the VPXI lifetime. Thus, the specification of an internal timeline for each VPXI can help optimizing the allocation, scheduling, and provisioning processes. Periods are delimited by temporal marks. A period can start after the end of another period or after an event.

2.3   VPXI Embedding Problem

Using the VXDL language, users can specify the desirable configuration and network composition of a VPXI. A VPXI request must then be interpreted, and the corresponding virtual resources have to be reserved and provisioned on available physical resources. This virtual-infrastructure allocation corresponds to a classical graph embedding problem, where the graph describing the virtual infrastructure must be mapped the physical substrate graph.

Virtual and physical graphs are of the form $G(V, E)$ where vertices V are a set of resources interconnected by a set of links (edges represented by E). Each resource or link can have a capacity represented by c_v and c_p for virtual and physical components respectively. Capacities can be interpreted as configuration of bandwidth or latency for links, and as memory size or CPU speed for resources/nodes. The information about virtual resources allocation are represented in a map notation. Each virtual component allocated in a physical one is represented as a line of map, containing the reserved capacity (c_v) and the utilization period (Δt). This time notation enables the representation of different time periods in the same VPXI, where virtual resources and links can be used in disjoined time windows, in accordance with the *timeline description* proposed by VXDL.

This embedding problem is extremely challenging and has been proved to be NP-hard. Embedding heuristics taking into account the substrate characteristics to simplify the allocation have been proposed [12,13]. These proposals aim at maximizing the resources usage or at minimizing the maximum link load. To complement these works, we examine the virtual infrastructure description and embedding problem from the application perspective.

3   Application-Mapping Principles

In our model, the application-mapping process is separated in three steps:

I) workflow generation: the workflow is generated using information extracted from the application, such as benchmarks results, data input description, data transfer in each module, and the number of nodes required to perform a satisfactory execution.

II) workflow translation into VXDL: taking into account the application's requirements (RAM configuration, CPU speed, and storage size), users can develop a VXDL description, asking for the desirable configuration of the VPXI.

At this point users can also declare that some components must be allocated in a specific location as well as define the virtual network topology specifying the proximity (latency configuration) of the components and the needed bandwidth.

III) VPXI allocation: in this step VPXI management framework will allocate the virtual components respecting the configuration expressed by the user (such as parametrizations and time periods organization). In a second phase, the software configuration (OS, programming and communication tools), extracted directly from the application and described using VXDL, will be deployed within the virtual machines that compose the VPXI.

3.1 Workflow Language

Complex applications able to exploit large scale distributed environments are generally described with workflows. These workflows are interpreted by engines that convert the description of work in execution scripts.

Several workflow languages have been proposed in the literature. On grid-based infrastructures, Directed Acyclic Graph (DAG)-based languages such as the MA-DAG language, part of the DIET middleware [3], have often been used. They provide a explicit, static graph of all computing tasks to be performed. To ease definition of grid applications with a complex logic to be represented, more abstract language have been introduced. For instance, Scufl was introduced within the myGrid project[2] to present data flows enacted through the Taverna workflow engine [10]. It is one of the first grid-oriented data flow languages that focuses on the application data flow rather than on the generated graph of tasks. The *GWENDIA* language[3] considered in this paper is a data-flow oriented language that aims at easing the description of the complex application data flows from a user point of view while ensuring good application performances and grid resources usage. An example of a graphic representation of workflow description is given in figure 2. In this figure *Floating* and *Reference* are representing data unit to be processed and *CrestLines, CrestMatch, PFMatchICP, PFRegister, Yasmina* and *Baladin* are processing units. *Floating* and *Reference* represent groups of data items to be processed: processing units will be invoked as many time as needed to process all data items received. The user describing the application focus on the data processing logic rather than on the execution schedule. The structural application workflow is transformed into an execution schedule dynamically, while the workflow engine is being executed.

GWENDIA is represented in XML using the tags and syntax defined below:

Types: values flowing through the workflow are typed. Basic types are `integer`, `double`, `string` and `file`.

Processors: a `processor` is a data production unit. A regular processor invokes a service through a known interface. Special processors are workflow `input` (a processor with no inbound connectivity, delivering a list of externally defined

---

[2] myGrid UK e-Science project: `www.mygrid.org`
[3] GWENDIA is defined in the context of the ANR-06-MDCA-009 GWENDIA project: `http://gwendia.polytech.unice.fr`

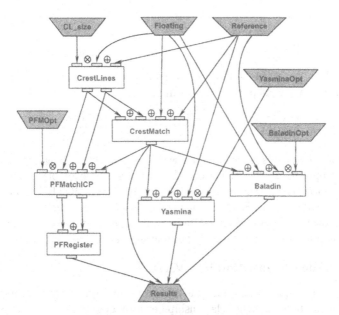

Fig. 2. Bronze Standard workflow

data values), `sink` (a processor with no outbound connectivity, receiving some workflow output) and `constant` (a processor delivering a single, constant value).

Processor ports: processor input and output ports are named and declared. A port may be an input (`<in>` tag), an output (`<out>` tag) or both an input/output value (`<inout>` tag). The input ports also define iteration strategies that control the number of invocation of the processor as a function of its inputs.

A simple example is given below:

```
<workflow>
  <interface>
    <constant name="parameter" type="interger">
      <value>50</value>
    </constant>
    <source name="reals" type="double"/>
    <sink name="results" type="file"/>
  </interface>
  <processors>
    <processor name="docking" type="webservice">
      <wsdl url="http://localhost/docking.wsdl" operation="dock"/>
      <in name="param" type="integer"/>
      <in name="input" type="file"/>
      <out name="result" type="double"/>
      <iterationstrategy>
        <cross>
          <port name="param"/>
          <port name="input"/>
        </cross>
      </iterationstrategy>
    </processor>
    <processor name="statisticaltest" type="diet">
      <service path="weightedaverage"/>
      <in name="weights" type="double"/>
      <in name="values" type="list(integer)"/>
      <in name="coefficient" type="double"/>
      <out name="result" type="file"/>
      <iterationstrategy>
        <cross>
          <port name="coefficient"/>
          <match tag="patient">
            <port name="values"/>
            <port name="weights"/>
```

```
    </match>
   </cross>
  </iterationstrategy>
 </processor>
</processors>
</workflow>
```

Data link: a data link is a simple connection between a processor output port and a processor input port as exemplified below:

```
<links>
 <link from="reals" to="statisticaltest:coefficient"/>
 <link from="docking:result" to="statisticaltest:weights"/>
 <link from="statisticaltest:result" to="results"/>
</links>
```

Workflow managers are associated with these workflow language and are in charge of optimizing the execution of workflows. For example, MOTEUR [6] is a data-intensive grid-interfaced workflow manager. MOTEUR can enact a workflow represented in Scufl language or in GWENDIA language and submits the workflow tasks to a grid infrastructure. To optimize the execution, it enables three levels of parallelism: workflow parallelism, data parallelism and pipelining.

3.2 Workflow Translation into VXDL

A workflow description represents the input/output data, the processors (a data-processing module), and the relationship between an application's processors. In our model, the workflow description will be translated in a VPXI description, specified in VXDL. Generally, to execute a complex application in a virtualized infrastructure, one has to consider that a middleware has to supervise the execution of the different tasks. In our example, the workflow engine (MOTEUR) and a specific task scheduler are executed for every application on independent computing resources. Input data and the intermediate results also require the presence of a file server. Therefore the VXDL description of any VPXI executing an application controled by the MOTEUR engine will contain a *generic* part describing these 3 nodes.

The *variable* part of the VPXI description directly depends on the information extracted from the workflow such as input data, the number of processors, and the links between the processors. The computation time, the data volume and the number of invocations of each module is another information that can be extracted from the workflow. Given p the number of processors (modules) of an application, the user can naively request n virtual computing resource and evenly split the set of resources among the workflow processors. Each module therefore has n/p resources. This will of course be sub-optimal since the processors have different execution times. A first variant of this naive strategy could take into account extra information on the benchmarked execution time of each module.

4   Medical Application Example

Let us illustrate this VPXI description and embedding problem through a complex, real-scale medical-image analysis application known as *bronze standard.*

The bronze standard [7] technique tackles the difficult problem of validating procedures for medical-image analysis. As there is usually no reference, or *gold standard*, to validate the result of the computation in the field of medical-image processing, it is very difficult to objectively assess the results' quality. The statistical analysis of images enables the quantitative measurement of computation errors. The bronze standard technique statistically quantifies the maximal error resulting from widely used *image registration algorithms*. The larger the sample image database and the number of registration algorithms to compare with, the most accurate the method. This procedure is therefore very scalable and it requires to compose a complex application workflow including different registration-computation services with data transfer inter-dependencies.

Bronze standard's workflow is enacted with the data-intensive grid-interfaced MOTEUR workflow manager [6] designed to optimize the execution of data-parallel flows. It submits the workflow tasks to the VPXI infrastructure through the DIET middleware [3], a scalable grid scheduler based on a hierarchy of agents communicating through CORBA.

The estimated algorithm performance is valid for a typical database image. In the experiments reported below, we use a clinical database of 32 pairs of patient images to be registered by the different algorithms involved in the workflow. For each run, the processing of the complete image database results in the generation of approximately 200 computing tasks. As illustrated in figure 2, the workflow of the application has a completely deterministic pattern. All processors of this application have the same number of invocations. The execution time and the data volume transferred of each processor have been mesured in initial microbenchmarks reported in table 1.

Table 1. Execution time and processed data volume for each module of bronze standard

Module	Execution time	Data volume
CrestLines	35s	32MB
CrestMatch	4s	36MB
PFMatchICP	14s	10MB
PFRegister	1s	0.5MB
Yasmina	62s	22MB
Baladin	250s	25MB

Let us now consider a request for a VPXI composed of 35 nodes to execute Bronze Standard's workflow. Three nodes will be dedicated to the *generic* part: 1 node for MOTEUR, 1 node for the middleware server and 1 node for the database server. The 32 nodes left are distributed and allocated proportionally to the execution time of the workflow processors : 3 nodes for CrestLines, 1 node for CrestMatch, 1 node for PFMatchIP, 1 node for PFRegister, 22 nodes for Baladin, and 4 nodes for Yasmina. Then, for this same computing-resources set, several variants of VPXI descriptions with different network topologies can be expressed. We exemplify developing two different VPXI descriptions.

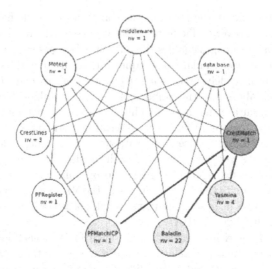

Fig. 3. VPXI description of the bronze standard's workflow

The listing below presents a VXDL description of a virtual node (MOTEUR) and a computing cluster (Baladin).

```
<vxdl:resource>
 <vxdl:id>Moteur</vxdl:id>
 <vxdl:ramMemory>
    <vxdl:min>4</vxdl:min>
    <vxdl:minUnit>GB</vxdl:minUnit>
 </vxdl:ramMemory>
</vxdl:resource>
<vxdl:group>
 <vxdl:id>Cluster_Baladin</vxdl:id>
 <vxdl:function>
    <vxdl:id>computing</vxdl:id>
 </vxdl:function>
 <vxdl:size>
    <vxdl:min>22</vxdl:min>
 </vxdl:size>
 <vxdl:resource>
    <vxdl:id>Node_Cluster_Baladin</vxdl:id>
    <vxdl:ramMemory>
       <vxdl:min>2</vxdl:min>
       <vxdl:minUnit>GB</vxdl:minUnit>
    </vxdl:ramMemory>
 </vxdl:resource>
</vxdl:group>
```

Figure 3 illustrates the description of a VPXI using graphs. All components and network links required to execute bronze standard's workflow are represented. We developed two descriptions considering this scenario: in **VPXI 1** the network is composed by two links type, one with low latency intra cluster and the other one with a maximum latency of 10 ms to interconnect the clusters. In **VPXI 2** the network comprises three virtual links: one with a low intra-cluster latency (maximum latency of 0.200 ms), another one with a latency of 10 ms interconnecting the components except one asking for a maximum latency of 0.200 ms to interconnect CrestMatch (dark blue) with the components

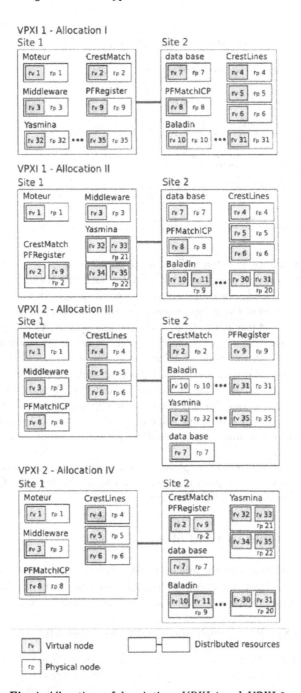

Fig. 4. Allocations of descriptions *VPXI-1* and *VPXI-2*

PFMatchICP, Yasmina and Baladin (blue in the figure). Listing below shows the VXDL description of this communication-intensive link.

```
<vxdl:link>
  <vxdl:id>Communication Intensive</vxdl:id>
  <vxdl:direction>bi</vxdl:direction>
  <vxdl:latency>
    <vxdl:max>0.200</vxdl:max>
    <vxdl:maxUnit>ms</vxdl:maxUnit>
  </vxdl:latency>
  <vxdl:pair>
    <vxdl:source>Cluster_CrestMatch</vxdl:source>
    <vxdl:destination>Cluster_Baladin</vxdl:destination>
  </vxdl:pair>
  <vxdl:pair>
    <vxdl:source>Cluster_CrestMatch</vxdl:source>
    <vxdl:destination>Cluster_Yasmina</vxdl:destination>
  </vxdl:pair>
  <vxdl:pair>
    <vxdl:source>Cluster_CrestMatch</vxdl:source>
    <vxdl:destination>Cluster_PFMatchICP</vxdl:destination>
  </vxdl:pair>
  <vxdl:pair>
    <vxdl:source>Database</vxdl:source>
    <vxdl:destination>Cluster_CrestMatch</vxdl:destination>
  </vxdl:pair>
</vxdl:link>
```

Let us now illustrate how each VPXI description can be embedded in a physical substrate. We propose two different solutions for both VPXI, which correspond to four different physical allocations as represented in figure 4. In this example, *Site 1* and *Site 2* represent two geographically-distributed-resources sets.

In **VPXI 1 - Allocation I**, intra-cluster link specification enables the allocation of loosely connected resources. In this embedding solution, 1 virtual machine per each physical node is allocated.

In **VPXI 1 - Allocation II** each physical node in clusters CrestMatch, PFRegister, Yasmina, and Baladin are allocated 2 virtual machines.

The **VPXI 2 - Allocation III** respects the required interconnection allocating corresponding resources in the same physical set of resources (such as a site in a grid). This embedding solution explores the allocation of 1 virtual machine per physical node.

VPXI 2 - Allocation IV explores the same physical components as *Allocation III* but allocates 2 virtual machines per physical node in the CrestMatch, PFRegister, Yasmina, and Baladin clusters.

5   Experiments in Grid'5000

To have a better insight on the influence of VPXI description, we deploy different virtual infrastructures for executing the proposed workflow in the Grid'5000 physical substrate managed and operated by the HIPerNET framework.

5.1   HIPerNet Framework and Grid'5000 Substrate

The HIPerNET software[4] [11] aims to provide a framework to build and manage private, dynamic, predictable and large-scale virtual computing environments, that high-end challenging applications, like biomedical or bioinformatic applications, can use with traditional APIs: standard POSIX calls, sockets and Message

---

[4] http://www.ens-lyon.fr/LP/RESO/software/HIPerNET

Passing (MPI, OpenMP) communication libraries. With this framwork, a user preempt and interconnect virtually, for a given timeframe, a pool of virtual resources from a distributed physical substrate in order to execute his application. The originality of HIPerNet is to combine system and networking virtualization technologies with crypto-based security, bandwidth sharing and advance reservation mechanisms.

The HIPerNet substrate is transparent to all types of upper layers: upper layer protocols (e.g. TCP, UDP), APIs (e.g. sockets), middleware (e.g. Globus, Diet), applications, services and users. Hence, the HIPerNet model maintains backward compatibility with existing APIs, Middlewares and Applications which were designed for UNIX and TCP/IP APIs. Therefore, users do not need to learn new tools, developers do not need to port applications, legacy user authentication can still be used to enroll a user into a VPXI.

The HIPerNet framework aims at partitionning a distributed physical infrastructure (computers, disks, networks) into dedicated virtual private computing environment dynamically composed. When a new machine joins the physical resource set, HIPerNet prepares its operating system to enable several virtual machines (VMs) to be instantiated dynamically when required. This set of potential virtual machines is called an HIPerSpace and it is represented in the HIPerSpace Database. The HIPerSpace is the only entity that see the physical entities. A resource, volunteer to join the resource pool, is automatically initiated and registered in the HIPerSpace database. The discovery of all the devices of the physical node is also automatic. An image of the specific HIPerNet operating system is deployed on it. In our current HIPerNet implementation, the operating system image contains basically the Xen Hypervisor and its domain of administration called domain 0 (Dom 0). The HIPerSpace registrar (Operational HIPerVisor) collects and stores persistently data and manages accounts (e.g., the authentication database). It is therefore hosted by a physical machine outside of the HIPerSpace itself. For the sake of robustness and scalability, HIPerSpace registrar can be replicated or even distributed.

We run the application within several virtual infrastructures created and managed by our HIPerNet software within the Grid'5000 testbed[4]. Grid'5000 enables user to request, reconfigure and access physical machines belonging to 9 sites distributed in France. In our experiment, we reserve several Grid'5000 nodes to compose a pool of physical resources that we initialize to form an HIPerSpace. To instanciate an HIPerSpace, specific tools provided by the hosted Grid are used. This is the only part aware of the physical infrastructure of the HIPerNet Software. All the other parts are independant of the physical resources because they use them indirectly through the services provided by HIPerNet. In Grid'5000, the HIPerSpace appears like a set of ordinary jobs scheduled by OAR with the use of a specific operating system image deployed by kadeploy.

5.2   Medical Imaging Application Deployment on the Testbed

For testing VPXIs, a system image containing the operating system based on a standard Linux distribution Debian *Etch* with a kernel version 2.6.18-8 for

AMD64, the domain-specific image processing services and the middleware components (MOTEUR and DIET) was created. The experiments on the VPXIs described in the section 4 were performed. In each experiment, we repeated the application 10 times to measure the average and standard deviation of the application makespan, the data transfer and task execution time. The physical infrastructure is reserved on the Grid'5000 clusters: *capricorne* (Lyon), *bordemer* (Bordeaux) and *azur* (Sophia) which CPUs are 2.0 GHz dual-cores Opterons. The distance between clusters is 500km and they are connected through 10Gbps links. Each VPXI is composed of 35 nodes divided in *generic* and *variable* part: 3 nodes are dedicated to *generic* part (MOTEUR, DIET, file server) using 1 CPU per node and the remaining 32 nodes of the *variable* part are allocated dependently on the VPXIs (*VPXI 1 - Allocation I* and *VPXI 2 - Allocation III* used 1 CPU per node while *VPXI 1 - Allocation II* and *VPXI 2 - Allocation IV* used 1 CPU core per node).

Coallocating resources on one grid site: the application's makespan on the *VPXI 2 - Allocation III* and *VPXI 2 - Allocation IV* is 11min 44s (±49s) and 12min 3s (±50s) respectively. This corresponds to a +3.8% makespan increase, due to the execution overhead when there are two virtual machines collocated on the same physical resource. Indeed, we present in the table 2 the average execution time of application services on the *VPXI 2 - Allocations III and IV*. We can observe that the average execution overhead is 5.17% (10.53% in the worst case and 1.28% in the best case).

Table 2. Execution time on VPXI 2 - Allocations III and IV and 4

Services	Allocation III	Allocation IV	variation
CrestLines	34.12 ± 0.34	36.84 ± 5.78	+7.97%
CrestMatch	3.61 ± 0.48	3.99 ± 0.63	+10.53%
PFMatchICP	11.93 ± 2.76	12.75 ± 5.35	+6.87%
PFRegister	0.78 ± 0.18	0.79 ± 0.18	+1.28%
Yasmina	59.72 ± 14.08	61.53 ± 13.98	+3.03%
Baladin	244.68 ± 16.68	247.99 ± 19.51	+1.35%

Resources distributed over 2 sites: when porting the application from a local infrastructure to a large scale infrastructure, the data transfer increases. Table 3 presents the data transfer time (s) of the application services on *VPXI 2 - Allocation IV* (local) and *VPXI 1 - Allocation II* (distributed over 2 sites). The measured overhead is 150% in the worst case. Conversely, some local transfers may be slightly reduced. In the case of our application however, this overhead has little impact on the application makespan since it is compensated for by the parallel data transfer and computations. Indeed, the makespan is 12min (±12s) and 12min 11s (±20s) on *VPXI 1 - Allocation I* and *VPXI 1 - Allocation II* respectively, very similar to the performance of *VPXI 2 - Allocation IV*.

Resources distributed over 3 sites: further distributing computational resources causes an additional increase of the data-transfer overheads. An

Table 3. Data transfer time on the local VPXI 2 - Allocation IV and large scale VPXI 1 - Allocation II infrastructure

Services	Allocation IV	Allocation II	variation
CrestLines	2 ± 0.45	3.01 ± 1.6	+50.5%
CrestMatch	1.99 ± 0.34	1.83 ± 0.36	-8.04%
PFMatchICP	1.3 ± 0.4	3.25 ± 0.13	+150%
PFRegister	0.51 ± 0.23	0.43 ± 0.09	-15.69%
Yasmina	1.19 ± 0.27	1.16 ± 0.21	-2.52%
Baladin	1.17 ± 0.38	1.81 ± 1.03	+54.7%

additional experiment with *VPXI 1 - Allocation II* the *generic* part of which is located in Lyon while the *variable* part is randomly distributed in Lyon, Bordeaux and Sophia leads to a makespan of 12min 13s (± 30s) with a data-transfer overhead of 176% in the worst case.

6   Related Work

In this section, we briefly describe related works which explore a virtual- infrastructure composition on distributed resources, as well as the mapping process.

In [8] the authors propose the use of virtual grids to simplify application scheduling. Their descriptive language, vgDL, enables users to specify an initial description of the desirable resources, resulting in a pre-selected virtual grid corresponding to a simple vgDL description. vgDL proposes three aggregation types to specify the interconnection network: LooseBag, TightBag and Cluster. The approach proposed in VXDL is more comprehensive and allows the definition of the infrastructure's shape through the description and configuration of virtual links.

The approach of controlled virtual network infrastructures, running in parallel over a shared physical network is an emerging idea offering a variety of new features for the network. Cabo [5] proposes to exploit virtual networks for Internet Service Providers, distinguishing them from the physical infrastructure providers, and giving them end-to-end control. HIPerNET shares the same vision but focuses more on distributed computing application and proposes a language to express the infrastructure requirements in capacity, time, and space.

In [2], the authors propose VINI, a virtual network infrastructure that allows several virtual networks to share a single physical infrastructure, in a similar way to HIPerNET. VINI makes the network transparent to the user, representing each component of the network. This being one of our main interests, HIPerNET provides a language, VXDL, to specify the topology of those components. The GENI project [1] aims to build a shared infrastructure for hosting multiple types of network experiments. VXDL can help in the description of slices and HIPerNET is an orchestration framework that suits GENI's requirements.

7   Conclusion and Perspectives

This paper proposed the VXDL language to specify virtual infrastructures and the HIPerNET framework to deploy and execute them. It illustrated the usage of these combined tools by a real application. In particular it developed the process of translating an applicaton's workflow into a VXDL description of a virtual private execution-infrastructure. This paper detailed the description of several virtual infrastructures for executing the same medical applications that require a high quality of service and a scalable infrastructure. Experimental results of the deployment and execution of this application in different virtual infrastructures using the HIPerNET framework within the Grid'5000 substrate assess the pertinence of the VXDL language and of the HIPerNET framework. Based on these promising results, our future works will explore an approach to automate the translation of the workflow in a VXDL description, with the aim of capitalising on the expertise of application and workflow developers to ease the embedding process while improving end-user satisfaction as well as infrastructure usage.

Acknowledgments

This work has been funded by the ANR CIS HIPCAL grant (contract ANR06-CIS-005), the French ministry of Education and Research, INRIA, and CNRS, via ACI GRID's Grid'5000 project and Aladdin ADT.

References

1. Geni design principles. Computer 39(9), 102–105 (2006)
2. Bavier, A., Feamster, N., Huang, M., Peterson, L., Rexford, J.: VINI Veritas: Realistic and Controlled Network Experimentation. ACM SIGCOMM Computer Communication Review (CCR) 36(4), 3–14 (2006)
3. Caron, E., Desprez, F.: DIET: A Scalable Toolbox to Build Network Enabled Servers on the Grid. Int. Journal of High Performance Computing Applications 20(3), 335–352 (2006)
4. Cappello, F., Primet, P., et al.: Grid 5000: A large scale and highly reconfigurable grid experimental testbed. In: GRID 2005: Proceedings of the 6th IEEE/ACM International Workshop on Grid Computing, pp. 99–106. IEEE Computer Society, Los Alamitos (2005)
5. Feamster, N., Gao, L., Rexford, J.: How to lease the internet in your spare time. SIGCOMM Comput. Commun. Rev. 37(1), 61–64 (2007)
6. Glatard, T., Montagnat, J., Lingrand, D., Pennec, X.: Flexible and efficient workflow deployement of data-intensive applications on grids with MOTEUR. Int. Journal of High Performance Computing and Applications (IJHPCA) 22(3), 347–360 (2008)
7. Glatard, T., Pennec, X., Montagnat, J.: Performance evaluation of grid-enabled registration algorithms using bronze-standards. In: Larsen, R., Nielsen, M., Sporring, J. (eds.) MICCAI 2006. LNCS, vol. 4191, pp. 152–160. Springer, Heidelberg (2006)

8. Huang, R., Casanova, H., Chien, A.A.: Using virtual grids to simplify application scheduling. In: 20th International Parallel and Distributed Processing Symposium, IPDPS 2006, April 2006, p. 10 (2006)
9. Koslovski, G., Primet, P.V.-B., Charão, A.S.: VXDL: Virtual Resources and Interconnection Networks Description Language. In: GridNets 2008 (October 2008)
10. Oinn, T., Li, P., Kell, D.B., Goble, C., Gooderis, A., Greenwood, M., Hull, D., Stevens, R., Turi, D., Zhao, J.: Taverna/myGrid: Aligning a Workflow System with the Life Sciences Community, ch. 19, pp. 300–319. Springer, Heidelberg (2007)
11. Primet, P.V.-B., Gelas, J.-P., Mornard, O., Koslovski, G., Roca, V., Giraud, L., Montagnat, J., Huu, T.T.: A scalable security model for enabling dynamic virtual private execution infrastructures on the internet. In: IEEE International Conference on Cluster Computing and the Grid CCGrid 2009, Shanghai (May 2009)
12. Yu, M., Yi, Y., Rexford, J., Chiang, M.: Rethinking virtual network embedding: substrate support for path splitting and migration. SIGCOMM Comput. Commun. Rev. 38(2), 17–29 (2008)
13. Zhu, Y., Ammar, M.: Algorithms for assigning substrate network resources to virtual network components. In: INFOCOM 2006. 25th IEEE International Conference on Computer Communications. Proceedings, April 2006, pp. 1–12 (2006)

High Performance Parallel Computing with Clouds and Cloud Technologies

Jaliya Ekanayake and Geoffrey Fox

School of Informatics and Computing,
Indiana University, Bloomington, IN 47405, USA
{jekanaya,gcf}@indiana.edu

Abstract. Infrastructure services (Infrastructure-as-a-service), provided by cloud vendors, allow any user to provision a large number of compute instances fairly easily. Whether leased from public clouds or allocated from private clouds, utilizing these virtual resources to perform data/compute intensive analyses requires employing different parallel runtimes to implement such applications. Among many parallelizable problems, most "pleasingly parallel" applications can be performed using MapReduce technologies such as Hadoop, CGL-MapReduce, and Dryad, in a fairly easy manner. However, many scientific applications, which have complex communication patterns, still require low latency communication mechanisms and rich set of communication constructs offered by runtimes such as MPI. In this paper, we first discuss large scale data analysis using different MapReduce implementations and then, we present a performance analysis of high performance parallel applications on virtualized resources.

Keywords: Cloud, Virtualization, MapReduce, Dryad, Parallel Computing.

1 Introduction

The introduction of commercial cloud infrastructure services such as Amazon EC2/S3 [1-2] and GoGrid[3] allow users to provision compute clusters fairly easily and quickly by paying a monetary value only for the duration of the usage of resources. The provisioning of resources happens in minutes as opposed to the hours and days required in the case of traditional queue-based job scheduling systems. In addition, the use of such virtualized resources allows the user to completely customize the Virtual Machine (VM) images and use them with root/administrative privileges, which is another feature that is hard to achieve with traditional infrastructures.

The availability of open source cloud infrastructure software such as Nimbus [4] and Eucalyptus [5], and the open source virtualization software stacks such as Xen Hypervisor[6], allows organizations to build private clouds to improve the resource utilization of the available computation facilities. The possibility of dynamically provisioning additional resources by leasing from commercial cloud infrastructures makes the use of private clouds more promising.

With all the above promising features of cloud, we can assume that the accessibility to computation power is no longer a barrier for the users who need to perform large

D.R. Avresky et al. (Eds.): Cloudcomp 2009, LNICST 34, pp. 20–38, 2010.
© Institute for Computer Sciences, Social-Informatics and Telecommunications Engineering 2010

scale data/compute intensive applications. However, to perform such computations, two major pre-conditions need to be satisfied: (i) the application should be parallelizable to utilize the available resources; and (ii) there should be an appropriate parallel runtime support to implement it.

We have applied several cloud technologies such as Hadoop[7], Dryad and Dryad-LINQ[8,9], and CGL-MapReduce[10], to various scientific applications wiz: (i) Cap3[11] data analysis; (ii) High Energy Physics(HEP) data analysis; (iv) Kmeans clustering[12]; and, (v) Matrix Multiplication. The streaming based MapReduce [13] runtime - CGL-MapReduce- developed by us extends the MapReduce model to iterative MapReduce domain as well. Our experience suggests that although most "pleasingly parallel" applications can be performed using cloud technologies such as Hadoop, CGL-MapReduce, and Dryad, in a fairly easy manner, scientific applications, which require complex communication patterns, still require more efficient runtime support such as MPI[14].

In order to understand the performance implications of virtualized resources on MPI applications, we performed an extensive analysis using Eucalyptus based private cloud infrastructure. The use of a private cloud gives us complete control over both VMs and bare-metal nodes, a feature that is impossible to achieve in commercial cloud infrastructures. It also assures a fixed network topology and bandwidth with the nodes deployed in the same geographical location, improving the reliability of our results. For this analysis, we used several MPI applications with different communication/computation characteristics, namely Matrix Multiplication, Kmeans Clustering, and Concurrent Wave Equation Solver and performed them on several VM configurations. Instead of measuring individual characteristics such as bandwidth and latency using micro benchmarks we used real applications to understand the effect of virtualized resources for such applications, which makes our results unique.

In the sections that follow, we first present the work related to our research followed by a brief introduction to the data analysis applications we used. Section 4 presents the results of our evaluations on cloud technologies and a discussion. In section 5, we discuss an approach with which to evaluate the performance implications of using virtualized resources for high performance parallel computing. Section 6 presents the results of this evaluation along with a discussion of the results. In the final section we give our conclusions and we discuss implications for future work.

2   Related Work

Traditionally, most parallel applications achieve fine grained parallelism using message passing infrastructures such as PVM [15] and MPI. Applications achieve coarse-grained parallelism using workflow frameworks such as Kepler [16] and Taverna [17], where the individual tasks could themselves be parallel applications written in MPI. Software systems such as Falkon [18], SWARM [19], and DAGMan [20] can be used to schedule applications which comprise of a collection of a large number of individual sub tasks.

Once these applications are developed, in the traditional approach, they are executed on compute clusters, super computers, or Grid infrastructures [21] where the focus on allocating resources is heavily biased by the availability of computational power. The application and the data both need to be moved to the available computational power in order for them to be executed. Although these infrastructures are highly efficient in performing compute intensive parallel applications, when the volumes of data accessed by an application increases, the overall efficiency decreases due to the inevitable data movement.

Cloud technologies such as Google MapReduce, Google File System (GFS) [22], Hadoop and Hadoop Distributed File System (HDFS) [7], Microsoft Dryad, and CGL-MapReduce adopt a more data-centered approach to parallel runtimes. In these frameworks, the data is staged in data/compute nodes of clusters or large-scale data centers, such as in the case of Google. The computations move to the data in order to perform data processing. Distributed file systems such as GFS and HDFS allow Google MapReduce and Hadoop to access data via distributed storage systems built on heterogeneous compute nodes, while Dryad and CGL-MapReduce support reading data from local disks. The simplicity in the programming model enables better support for quality of services such as fault tolerance and monitoring. Table 1 highlights the features of three cloud technologies that we used.

Table 1. Comparison of features supported by different cloud technologies

Feature	Hadoop	Dryad & DryadLINQ	CGL-MapReduce
Programming Model	MapReduce	DAG based execution flows	MapReduce with *Combine* phase
Data Handling	HDFS	Shared directories/ Local disks	Shared file system / Local disks
Intermediate Data Communication	HDFS/ Point-to-point via HTTP	Files/TCP pipes/ Shared memory FIFO	Content Distribution Network (NaradaBrokering[23])
Scheduling	Data locality/ Rack aware	Data locality/ Network topology based run time graph optimizations	Data locality
Failure Handling	Persistence via HDFS Re-execution of map and reduce tasks	Re-execution of vertices	Currently not implemented (Re-executing map tasks, redundant reduce tasks)
Monitoring	Monitoring support of HDFS, Monitoring MapReduce computations	Monitoring support for execution graphs	Programming interface to monitor the progress of jobs
Language Support	Implemented using Java Other languages are supported via Hadoop Streaming	Programmable via C# DryadLINQ provides LINQ programming API for Dryad	Implemented using Java Other languages are supported via Java wrappers

Y. Gu, et al., present Sphere [24] architecture, a framework which can be used to execute user-defined functions on data stored in a storage framework named Sector, in parallel. Sphere can also perform MapReduce style programs and the authors compare the performance with Hadoop for tera-sort application. Sphere stores intermediate data on files, and hence is susceptible to higher overheads for iterative applications.

All-Paris [25] is an abstraction that can be used to solve a common problem of comparing all the elements in a data set with all the elements in another data set by applying a given function. This problem can be implemented using typical MapReduce frameworks such as Hadoop, however for large data sets, the implementation will not be efficient, because all map tasks need to access all the elements of one of the data sets. We can develop an efficient iterative MapReduce implementation using CGL-MapReduce to solve this problem. The algorithm is similar to the matrix multiplication algorithm we will explain in section 3.

Lamia Youseff, et al., presents an evaluation on the performance impact of Xen on MPI [26]. According to their evaluations, the Xen does not impose considerable overheads for HPC applications. However, our results indicate that the applications that are more sensitive to latencies (smaller messages, lower communication to computation ratios) experience higher overheads under virtualized resources, and this overhead increases as more and more VMs are deployed per hardware node. From their evaluations it is not clear how many VMs they deployed on the hardware nodes, or how many MPI processes were used in each VM. According to our results, these factors cause significant changes in results. Running 1-VM per hardware node produces a VM instance with a similar number of CPU cores as in a bare-metal node. However, our results indicate that, even in this approach, if the parallel processes inside the node communicate via the network, the virtualization may produce higher overheads under the current VM architectures.

C. Evangelinos and C. Hill discuss [27] the details of their analysis on the performance of HPC benchmarks on EC2 cloud infrastructure. One of the key observations noted in their paper is that both the OpenMPI and the MPICH2-nemsis show extremely large latencies, while the LAM MPI, the GridMPI, and the MPICH2-scok show smaller smoother latencies. However, they did not explain the reason for this behavior in the paper. We also observed similar characteristics and a detailed explanation of this behavior and related issues are given in section 5.

Edward Walker presents benchmark results of performing HPC applications using "high CPU extra large" instances provided by EC2 and on a similar set of local hardware nodes [28]. The local nodes are connected using infiniband switches while Amazon EC2 network technology is unknown. The results indicate about 40%-1000% performance degradation on EC2 resources compared to the local cluster. Since the differences in operating systems and the compiler versions between VMs and bare-metal nodes may cause variations in results, for our analysis we used a cloud infrastructure that we have complete control. In addition we used exactly similar software environments in both VMs and bare-metal nodes. In our results, we noticed that applications that are more susceptible to latencies experience higher performance degradation (around 40%) under virtualized resources. The bandwidth does not seem to be a consideration in private cloud infrastructures.

Ada Gavrilvska, et al., discuss several improvements over the current virtualization architecture to support HPC applications such as HPC hypervisors (sidecore) and self-virtualized I/O devices [29]. We notice the importance of such improvements and research. In our experimental results, we used hardware nodes with 8 cores and we deployed and tested up to 8VMs per node in these systems. Our results show that the virtualization overhead increases with the number of VMs deployed on a hardware node. These characteristics will have a larger impact on systems having more CPU cores per node. A node with 32 cores running 32 VM instances may produce very large overheads under the current VM architectures.

3 Data Analysis Applications

The applications we implemented using cloud technologies can be categorized into three classes, depending on the communication topologies wiz: (i) Map-only; (ii) MapReduce; and (iii) Iterative/Complex. In our previous papers [10,30], we have presented details of MapReduce style applications and a Kmeans clustering application that we developed using cloud technologies, and the challenges we faced in developing these applications. Therefore, in this paper, we simply highlight the characteristics of these applications in table 2 and present the results. The two new applications that we developed, Cap3 and matrix multiplication, are explained in more detail in this section.

Table 2. Map-Only and MapReduce style applications

Feature	Map-only	MapReduce
Program/data flow	Cap3 Analysis application implemented as a map-only operation. Each map task processed a single input data file and produces a set of output data files.	HEP data analysis application implemented using MapReduce programming model (ROOT is an object-oriented data analysis framework).
More Examples	Converting a collection of documents to different formats, processing a collection of medical images, and Brute force searches in cryptography	*Histogramming* operations, distributed search, and distributed sorting.

3.1 Cap3

Cap3 is a sequence assembly program that operates on a collection of gene sequence files which produce several output files. In parallel implementations, the input files are processed concurrently and the outputs are saved in a predefined location. For our analysis, we have implemented this application using Hadoop, CGL-MapReduce and DryadLINQ.

3.2 Iterative/Complex Style Applications

Parallel applications implemented using message passing runtimes can utilize various communication constructs to build diverse communication topologies. For example, a matrix multiplication application that implements Cannon's Algorithm [31] assumes parallel processes to be in a rectangular grid. Each parallel process in the gird communicates with its left and top neighbors as shown in Fig. 1(left). The current cloud runtimes, which are based on data flow models such as MapReduce and Dryad, do not support this behavior, where the peer nodes communicate with each other. Therefore, implementing the above type of parallel applications using MapReduce or Dryad models requires adopting different algorithms.

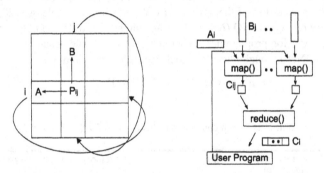

Fig. 1. Communication topology of matrix multiplication applications implemented using Cannon's algorithm (left) and MapReduce programming model (right)

We have implemented matrix multiplication applications using Hadoop and CGL-MapReduce by adopting a row/column decomposition approach to split the matrices. To clarify our algorithm, let's consider an example where two input matrices A and B produce matrix C, as the result of the multiplication process. We split the matrix B into a set of column blocks and the matrix A into a set of row blocks. In each iteration, all the map tasks consume two inputs: (i) a column block of matrix B, and (ii) a row block of matrix A; collectively, they produce a row block of the resultant matrix C. The column block associated with a particular map task is fixed throughout the computation while the row blocks are changed in each iteration. However, in Hadoop's programming model (typical MapReduce model), there is no way to specify this behavior and hence, it loads both the column block and the row block in each iteration of the computation. CGL-MapReduce supports the notion of long running map/reduce tasks where these tasks are allowed to retain static data in memory across invocations, yielding better performance for iterative MapReduce computations. The communication pattern of this application is shown in Fig. 1(right).

4 Evaluations and Analysis

For our evaluations, we used two different compute clusters (details are shown in Table 3). DryadLINQ applications are run on the cluster Ref A while Hadoop, CGL-MapReduce, and MPI applications are run on the cluster Ref B. We measured the performance (average running time with varying input sizes) of these applications and then we calculated the overhead introduced by different parallel runtimes using the following formula, in which P denotes the number of parallel processes (map tasks) used and T denotes time as a function of the number of parallel processes used. T(1) is the time it takes when the task is executed using a single process. T(P) denotes the time when an application is executed using P number of parallel processes (For the results in Fig. 2 to Fig. 5, we used 64 CPU cores and hence the P=64). The results of these analyses are shown in Fig. 2 –5. Most applications have running times in minutes range and we noticed that the fluctuations in running time are less than 5% for most cloud runtimes. The average times shown in figures are calculated using the results of 5 repeated runs of the applications. We used Hadoop release 0.20, the academic release of DryadLINQ (Note: The academic release of Dryad only exposes the DryadLINQ API for programmers. Therefore, all our implementations are written using DryadLINQ although it uses Dryad as the underlying runtime).

$$\text{Overhead} = [P * T(P) - T(1)]/T(1). \qquad (1)$$

Table 3. Different computation clusters used for the analyses

Cluster Ref	# Nodes used /Total CPU cores	CPU	Memory	Operating System
Ref A	8/64	2x Intel(R) Xeon(R) CPU L5420 2.50GHz	16GB	Windows Server 2008 – 64 bit HPC Edition (Service Pack 1)
Ref B	8/64	2 x Intel(R) Xeon(R) CPU L5420 2.50GHz	32GB	Red Hat Enterprise Linux Server release 5.3 - 64 bit

All three cloud runtimes work competitively well for the CAP3 application. In the Hadoop implementation of HEP data analysis, we kept the input data in a high performance parallel file system rather than in the HDFS because the analysis scripts written in ROOT could not access data from HDFS. This causes Hadoop's *map* tasks to access data remotely resulting lower performance compared to DryadLINQ and CGL-MapReduce implementations, which access input files from local disks. Both DryadLINQ and Hadoop show higher overheads for Kmeans clustering application,

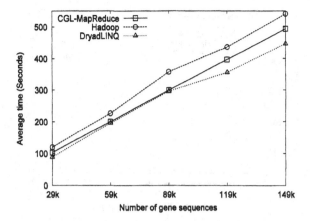

Fig. 2. Performance of the Cap3 application

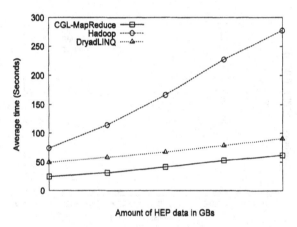

Fig. 3. Performance of HEP data analysis applications

and Hadoop shows higher overheads for the Matrix multiplication application. CGL-MapReduce shows a close performance to the MPI for large data sets in the case of Kmeans clustering and matrix multiplication applications, highlighting the benefits of supporting iterative computations and the faster data communication mechanism in the CGL-MapReduce.

From these results, it is clearly evident that the cloud runtimes perform competitively well for both the *Map-only* and the *MapReduce style* applications. However, for iterative and complex classes of applications, cloud runtimes show considerably high overheads compared to the MPI versions of the same applications, implying that, for these types of applications, we still need to use high performance parallel runtimes or use alternative approaches. (Note: The negative overheads observed in the matrix multiplication application are due to the better utilization of a cache by the parallel application than the single process version). These observations lead us to the next phase of our research.

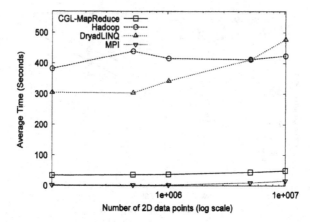

Fig. 4. Performance of different implementations of Kmeans Clustering application (Note: X axis is in log scale)

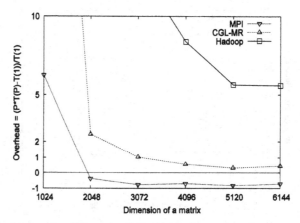

Fig. 5. Overhead induced by different parallel programming runtimes for the matrix multiplication application (8 nodes are used)

5   Performance of MPI on Clouds

After the previous observations, we analyzed the performance implications of cloud for parallel applications implemented using MPI. Specifically, we were trying to find the overhead of virtualized resources, and understand how applications with different communication-to-computation (C/C) ratios perform on cloud resources. We also evaluated different CPU core assignment strategies for VMs in order to understand the performance of VMs on multi-core nodes.

Commercial cloud infrastructures do not allow users to access the bare hardware nodes, in which the VMs are deployed, a must-have requirement for our analysis. Therefore, we used a Eucalyptus-based cloud infrastructure deployed at our university for this analysis. With this cloud infrastructure, we have complete access to both virtual machine instances and the underlying bare-metal nodes, as well as the help of the administrators; as a result, we could deploy different VM configurations allocating different CPU cores to each VM. Therefore, we selected the above cloud infrastructure as our main test bed.

For our evaluations, we selected three MPI applications with different communication and computation requirements, namely, (i) the Matrix multiplication, (ii) Kmeans clustering, and (iii) the Concurrent Wave Equation solver. Table 4 highlights the key characteristics of the programs that we used for benchmarking.

Table 4. Computation and communication complexities of the different MPI applications used

Application	Matrix multiplication	Kmeans Clustering	Concurrent Wave Equation
Description	Implements Cannon's Algorithm Assume a rectangular process grid (Fig.1- left)	Implements Kmeans Clustering Algorithm Fixed number of iterations are performed in each test	A vibrating string is decomposed (split) into points, and each MPI process is responsible for updating the amplitude of a number of points over time.
Grain size (n)	Number of points in a matrix block handled by each MPI process	Number of data points handled by a single MPI process	Number of points handled by each MPI process
Communication Pattern	Each MPI process communicates with its neighbors in both row wise and column wise	All MPI processes send partial clusters to one MPI process (rank 0). Rank 0 distribute the new cluster centers to all the nodes	In each iteration, each MPI process exchanges boundary points with its nearest neighbors
Computation per MPI process	$O((\sqrt{n})^3)$	$O((\sqrt{n})^3)$	$O(n)$
Communication per MPI process	$O((\sqrt{n})^2)$	$O(1)$	$O(1)$
C/C	$O\left(\frac{1}{\sqrt{n}}\right)$	$O\left(\frac{1}{n}\right)$	$O\left(\frac{1}{n}\right)$
Message Size	$(\sqrt{n})^2 = n$	D – Where D is the number of cluster centers.	Each message contains a double value
Communication routines used	$MPI\_Sendrecv\_replace()$	$MPI\_Reduce()$ $MPI\_Bcast()$	$MPI\_Sendrecv()$

6 Benchmarks and Results

The Eucalyptus (version 1.4) infrastructure we used is deployed on 16 nodes of an iDataplex cluster, each of which has 2 Quad Core Intel Xeon processors (for a total of 8 CPU cores) and 32 GB of memory. In the bare-metal version, each node runs a Red Hat Enterprise Linux Server release 5.2 (Tikanga) operating system. We used OpenMPI version 1.3.2 with gcc version 4.1.2. We then created a VM image from this hardware configuration, so that we have a similar software environment on the VMs once they are deployed. The virtualization is based on Xen hypervisor (version 3.0.3). Both bare-metal and virtualized resources utilize giga-bit Ethernet connections.

When VMs are deployed using Eucalyptus, it allows configuring the number of CPU cores assigned to each VM image. For example, with 8 core systems, the CPU core allocation per VM can range from 8 cores to 1 core per VM, resulting in several different CPU core assignment strategies. In Amazon EC2 infrastructure, the standard instance type has ½ a CPU per VM instance [28]. In the current version of Eucalyptus, the minimum number of cores that we can assign for a particular VM instance is 1; hence, we selected five CPU core assignment strategies (including the bare-metal test) listed in Table 5.

Table 5. Different hardware/virtual machine configurations used for performance evaluations

Ref	Description	Number of CPU cores accessible to the virtual or bare-metal node	Amount of memory (GB) accessible to the virtual or bare-metal node	Number of virtual or bare-metal nodes deployed
BM	Bare-metal node	8	32	16
1-VM-8-core	1 VM instance per bare-metal node	8	30 (2GB is reserved for Dom0)	16
2-VM-4-core	2 VM instances per bare-metal node	4	15	32
4-VM-2-core	4 VM instances per bare-metal node	2	7.5	64
8-VM-1-core	8 VM instances per bare-metal node	1	3.75	128

We ran all the MPI tests, on all 5 hardware/VM configurations, and measured the performance and calculated speed-ups and overheads. We calculated two types of overheads for each application using formula (1). The total overhead induced by the virtualization and the parallel processing is calculated using the bare-metal single process time as $T(1)$ in the formula (1). The parallel overhead is calculated using the single process time from a corresponding VM as $T(1)$ in formula (1). The average times shown in figures are obtained using 60 repeated runs for each and every measurement.

In all the MPI tests we performed, we used the following invariant to select the number of parallel processes (MPI processes) for a given application.

$$\textit{Number of MPI processes} = \textit{Number of CPU cores used.} \qquad (2)$$

For example, for the matrix multiplication application, we used only half the number of nodes (bare-metal or VMs) available to us, so that we have 64 MPI processes = 64 CPU cores. (This is mainly because the matrix multiplication application expects the MPI processes to be in a square grid, in contrast to a rectangular grid). For Kmeans clustering, we used all the nodes, resulting in a total of 128 MPI processes utilizing all 128 CPU cores. Some of the results of our analysis highlighting different characterizes we observe are shown in Fig. 6 through 13.

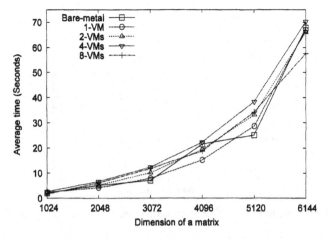

Fig. 6. Performance of the matrix multiplication application (Number of MPI processes = 64)

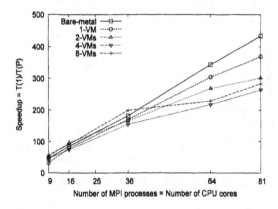

Fig. 7. Speed-up of the matrix multiplication application (Matrix size = 5184x5184)

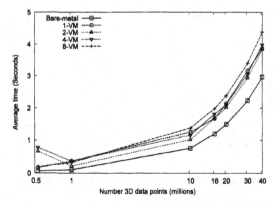

Fig. 8. Performance of Kmeans clustering (Number of MPI Processes = 128)

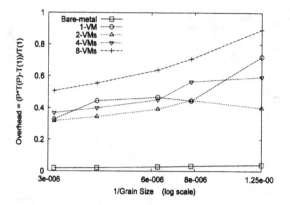

Fig. 9. Total overhead of the Kmeans clustering (Number of MPI Processes = 128)

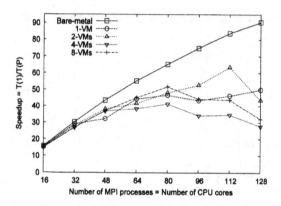

Fig. 10. Speed-up of the Kmeans clustering (Number of data points = 860160)

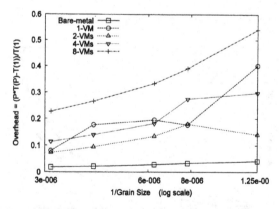

Fig. 11. Parallel overhead of the Kmeans clustering (Number of MPI Processes = 128)

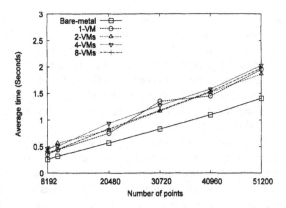

Fig. 12. Performance of the Concurrent Wave Solver (Number of MPI Processes = 128)

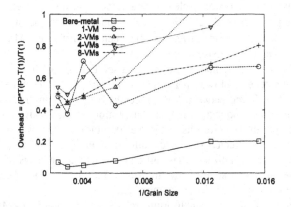

Fig. 13. Total overhead of the Concurrent Wave Solver (Number of MPI Processes = 128)

For the matrix multiplication, the graphs show very close performance characteristics in all the different hardware/VM configurations. As we expected, the bare-metal has the best performance and the speedup values, compared to the VM configurations (apart from the region close to the matrix size of 4096x4096 where the VM perform better than the bare-metal. We have performed multiple tests at this point, and found that it is a due to cache performances of the bare-metal node). After the bare-metal, the next best performance and speed-ups are recorded in the case of 1-VM per bare-metal node configuration, in which the performance difference is mainly due to the overhead induced by the virtualization. However, as we increase the number of VMs per bare-metal node, the overhead increases. At the 81 processes, 8-VMs per node configuration shows about a 34% decrease in speed-up compared to the bare-metal results.

In Kmeans clustering, the effect of virtualized resources is much clearer than in the case of the matrix multiplication. All VM configurations show a lower performance compared to the bare-metal configuration. In this application, the amount of data transferred between MPI processes is extremely low compared to the amount of data processed by each MPI process, and also, in relation to the amount of computations performed. Fig. 9 and Fig. 11 show the total overhead and the parallel overhead for

Kmeans clustering under different VM configurations. From these two calculations, we found that, for VM configurations, the overheads are extremely large for data set sizes of less than 10 million points, for which the bare-metal overhead remains less than 1 (<1 for all the cases). For larger data sets such as 40 million points, all overheads reached less than 0.5. The slower speed-up of the VM configurations (shown in Fig. 10) is due to the use of a smaller data set (~800K points) to calculate the speed-ups. The overheads are extremely large for this region of the data sizes, and hence, it resulted in lower speed-ups for the VMs.

Concurrent wave equation splits a number of points into a set of parallel processes, and each parallel process updates its portion of the points in some number of steps. An increase in the number of points increases the amount of the computations performed. Since we fixed the number of steps in which the points are updated, we obtained a constant amount of communication in all the test cases, resulting in a C/C ratio of $O(1/n)$. In this application also, the difference in performance between the VMs and the bare-metal version is clearer, and at the highest grain size the total overhead of 8-VMs per node is about 7 times higher than the overhead of the bare-metal configuration. The performance differences between the different VM configurations become smaller with the increase in grain size.

From the above experimental results, we can see that the applications with lower C/C ratios experience a slower performance in virtualized resources. When the amount of data transferred between MPI processes is large, as in the case of the matrix multiplication, the application is more susceptible to the bandwidth than the latency. From the performance results of the matrix multiplication, we can see that the virtualization has not affected the bandwidth considerably. However, all the other results show that the virtualization has caused considerable latencies for parallel applications, especially with smaller data transfer requirements. The effect on latency increases as we use more VMs in a bare-metal node.

According to the Xen para-virtualization architecture [6], *domU*s (VMs that run on top of Xen para-virtualization) are not capable of performing I/O operations by themselves. Instead, they communicate with *dom0* (privileged OS) via an event channel (interrupts) and the shared memory, and then the *dom0* performs the I/O operations on behalf of the *domU*s. Although the data is not copied between *domU*s and *dom0*, the *dom0* needs to schedule the I/O operations on behalf of the *domU*s. Fig. 14(top) and Fig. 14 (bottom) shows this behavior in 1-VM per node and 8-VMs per node configurations we used.

In all the above parallel applications we tested, the timing figures measured correspond to the time for computation and communication inside the applications. Therefore, all the I/O operations performed by the applications are network-dependent. From Fig. 14 (bottom), it is clear that *Dom0* needs to handle 8 event channels when there are 8-VM instances deployed on a single bare-metal node. Although the 8 MPI processes run on a single bare-metal node, since they are in different virtualized resources, each of them can only communicate via *Dom0*. This explains the higher overhead in our results for 8-VMs per node configuration. The architecture reveals another important feature as well - that is, in the case of 1-VM per node configuration, when multiple processes (MPI or other) that run in the same VM communicate with

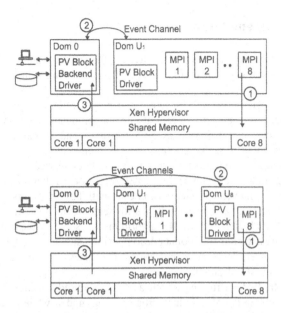

Fig. 14. Communication between dom0 and domU when 1-VM per node is deployed (top). Communication between dom0 and domUs when 8-VMs per node are deployed (bottom).

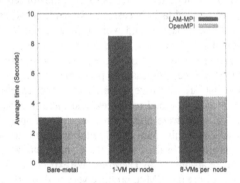

Fig. 15. LAM vs. OpenMPI (OMPI) under different VM configurations

each other via the network, all the communications must be scheduled by the *dom0*. This results higher latencies. We could verify this by running the above tests with LAM MPI (a predecessor of OpenMPI, which does not have improved support for in-node communications for multi-core nodes). Our results indicate that, with LAM MPI, the worst performance for all the test occurred when 1-VM per node is used. For example, Fig. 15 shows the performance of Kmeans clustering under bare-metal, 1-VM, and 8-VMs per node configurations. This observation suggests that, when using VMs with multiple CPUs allocated to each of them for parallel processing, it is better to utilize parallel runtimes, which have better support for in-node communication.

7 Conclusions and Future Work

From all the experiments we have conducted and the results obtained, we can come to the following conclusions on performing parallel computing using cloud and cloud technologies.

Cloud technologies work well for most pleasingly-parallel problems. Their support for handling large data sets, the concept of moving computation to data, and the better quality of services provided such as fault tolerance and monitoring, simplify the implementation details of such problems over the traditional systems.

Although cloud technologies provide better quality of services such fault tolerance and monitoring, their overheads are extremely high for parallel applications that require complex communication patterns and even with large data sets, and these overheads limit the usage of cloud technologies for such applications. It may be possible to find more "cloud friendly" parallel algorithms for some of these applications by adopting more coarse grained task/data decomposition strategies and different parallel algorithms. However, for other applications, the sheer performance of MPI style parallel runtimes is still desirable.

Enhanced MapReduce runtimes such as CGL-MapReduce allows iterative style applications to utilize the MapReduce programming model, while incurring minimal overheads compared to the other runtimes such as Hadoop and Dryad.

Handling large data sets using cloud technologies on cloud resources is an area that needs more research. Most cloud technologies support the concept of moving computation to data where the parallel tasks access data stored in local disks. Currently, it is not clear to us how this approach would work well with the VM instances that are leased only for the duration of use. A possible approach is to stage the original data in high performance parallel file systems or Amazon S3 type storage services, and then move to the VMs each time they are leased to perform computations.

MPI applications that are sensitive to latencies experience moderate-to-higher overheads when performed on cloud resources, and these overheads increase as the number of VMs per bare-hardware node increases. For example, in Kmeans clustering, 1-VM per node shows a minimum of 8% total overhead, while 8-VMs per node shows at least 22% overhead. In the case of the Concurrent Wave Equation Solver, both these overheads are around 50%. Therefore, we expect the CPU core assignment strategies such as ½ of a core per VM to produce very high overheads for applications that are sensitive to latencies.

Improved virtualization architectures that support better I/O capabilities, and the use of more latency insensitive algorithms would ameliorate the higher overheads in some of the applications. The former is more important as it is natural to run many VMs on future many core CPU architectures.

Applications those are not susceptible to latencies, such as applications that perform large data transfers and/or higher Communication/Computation ratios, show minimal total overheads in both bare-metal and VM configurations. Therefore, we expect that the applications developed using cloud technologies will work fine with cloud resources, because the milliseconds-to-seconds latencies that they already have under the MapReduce model will not be affected by the additional overheads introduced by the virtualization. This is also an area we are currently investigating. We are also building applications (biological DNA sequencing) whose end to end implementation from data processing to filtering (data-mining) involves an integration of MapReduce and MPI.

Acknowledgements

We would like to thank Joe Rinkovsky and Jenett Tillotson from IU UITS for their dedicated support in setting up a private cloud infrastructure and helping us with various configurations associated with our evaluations.

References

1. Amazon Elastic Compute Cloud (EC2), http://aws.amazon.com/ec2/
2. Amazon Simple Storage Service (S3), http://aws.amazon.com/s3/
3. GoGrid Cloud Hosting, http://www.gogrid.com/
4. Keahey, K., Foster, I., Freeman, T., Zhang, X.: Virtual Workspaces: Achieving Quality of Service and Quality of Life in the Grid. Scientific Programming Journal 13(4), 265–276 (2005); Special Issue: Dynamic Grids and Worldwide Computing
5. Nurmi, D., Wolski, R., Grzegorczyk, C., Obertelli, G., Soman, S., Youseff, L., Zagorodnov, D.: The Eucalyptus Open-source Cloud-computing System. In: CCGrid 2009: the 9th IEEE International Symposium on Cluster Computing and the Grid, Shanghai, China (2009)
6. Barham, P., Dragovic, B., Fraser, K., Hand, S., Harris, T., Ho, A., Neugebauer, R., Pratt, I., Warfield, A.: Xen and the art of virtualization. In: Proceedings of the Nineteenth ACM Symposium on Operating Systems Principles, SOSP 2003, pp. 164–177. ACM, New York (2003), http://doi.acm.org/10.1145/945445.945462
7. Apache Hadoop, http://hadoop.apache.org/core/
8. Isard, M., Budiu, M., Yu, Y., Birrell, A., Fetterly, D.: Dryad: Distributed data-parallel programs from sequential building blocks. In: European Conference on Computer Systems (2007)
9. Yu, Y., Isard, M., Fetterly, D., Budiu, M., Erlingsson, U., Gunda, P., Currey, J.: Dryad-LINQ: A System for General-Purpose Distributed Data-Parallel Computing Using a High-Level Language. In: Symposium on Operating System Design and Implementation (OSDI), San Diego, CA (2008)
10. Ekanayake, J., Pallickara, S., Fox, G.: MapReduce for Data Intensive Scientific Analysis. In: Fourth IEEE International Conference on eScience, Indianapolis, pp. 277–284 (2008)
11. Huang, X., Madan, A.: CAP3: A DNA Sequence Assembly Program. Genome Research 9(9), 868–877 (1999)
12. Hartigan, J.: Clustering Algorithms. Wiley, Chichester (1975)
13. Dean, J., Ghemawat, S.: Mapreduce: Simplified data processing on large clusters. ACM Commun. 51, 107–113 (2008)
14. MPI (Message Passing Interface), http://www-unix.mcs.anl.gov/mpi/
15. Dongarra, J., Geist, A., Manchek, R., Sunderam, V.: Integrated PVM framework supports heterogeneous network computing. Computers in Physics 7(2), 166–175 (1993)
16. Ludäscher, B., Altintas, I., Berkley, C., Higgins, D., Jaeger-Frank, E., Jones, M., Lee, E., Tao, J., Zhao, Y.: Scientific Workflow Management and the Kepler System. Concurrency and Computation: Practice & Experience (2005)

17. Hull, D., Wolstencroft, K., Stevens, R., Goble, C., Pocock, M., Li, P., Oinn, T.: Taverna: a tool for building and running workflows of services. Nucleic Acids Research (Web Server issue), W729 (2006)
18. Raicu, I., Zhao, Y., Dumitrescu, C., Foster, I., Wilde, M.: Falkon: a Fast and Light-weight tasK executiON framework. In: Proceedings of the ACM/IEEE Conference on Supercomputing, SC 2007, Nevada, ACM, New York (2007), http://doi.acm.org/10.1145/1362622.1362680
19. Pallickara, S., Pierce, M.: SWARM: Scheduling Large-Scale Jobs over the Loosely-Coupled HPC Clusters. In: Fourth IEEE International Conference on eScience, pp. 285–292 (2008)
20. Frey, J.: Condor DAGMan: Handling Inter-Job Dependencies, http://www.bo.infn.it/calcolo/condor/dagman/
21. Foster, I.: The Anatomy of the Grid: Enabling Scalable Virtual Organizations. In: Proceedings of the 7th international Euro-Par Conference Manchester on Parallel Processing (2001)
22. Ghemawat, S., Gobioff, H., Leung, S.: The Google file system. SIGOPS Oper. Syst. Rev. 37(5), 29–43 (2003), http://doi.acm.org/10.1145/1165389.945450
23. Pallickara, S., Fox, G.: NaradaBrokering: A Distributed Middleware Framework and Architecture for Enabling Durable Peer-to-Peer Grids. In: Endler, M., Schmidt, D.C. (eds.) Middleware 2003. LNCS, vol. 2672, pp. 41–61. Springer, Heidelberg (2003)
24. Gu, Y., Grossman, R.: Sector and Sphere: The Design and Implementation of a High Performance Data Cloud. Philosophical Transactions A Special Issue associated with the UK e-Science All Hands Meeting (2008)
25. Moretti, C., Bui, H., Hollingsworth, K., Rich, B., Flynn, P., Thain, D.: All-Pairs: An Abstraction for Data Intensive Computing on Campus Grids. IEEE Transactions on Parallel and Distributed Systems (2009)
26. Youseff, L., Wolski, R., Gorda, B., Krintz, C.: Evaluating the Performance Impact of Xen on MPI and Process Execution For HPC Systems. In: Proceedings of the 2nd international Workshop on Virtualization Technology in Distributed Computing. IEEE Computer Society, Washington (2006), http://dx.doi.org/10.1109/VTDC.2006.4
27. Constantinos, E., Hill, N.: Cloud Computing for parallel Scientific HPC Applications: Feasibility of Running Coupled Atmosphere-Ocean Climate Models on Amazon's EC2. In: Cloud Computing and Its Applications, Chicago, IL (2008)
28. Walker, E.: benchmarking Amazon EC2 for high-performance scientific computing, http://www.usenix.org/publications/login/2008-10/openpdfs/walker.pdf
29. Gavrilovska, A., Kumar, S., Raj, K., Gupta, V., Nathuji, R., Niranjan, A., Saraiya, P.: High-Performance Hypervisor Architectures: Virtualization in HPC Systems. In: 1st Workshop on System-level Virtualization for High Performance Computing (2007)
30. Fox, G., Bae, S., Ekanayake, J., Qiu, X., Yuan, H.: Parallel Data Mining from Multicore to Cloudy Grids. In: High Performance Computing and Grids workshop (2008)
31. Johnsson, S., Harris, T., Mathur, K.: Matrix multiplication on the connection machine. In: Proceedings of the 1989 ACM/IEEE Conference on Supercomputing, Supercomputing 1989, pp. 326–332. ACM, New York (1989), http://doi.acm.org/10.1145/76263.76298

Cloud Computing Platforms

Track Session 1

Cloud@Home on Top of RESERVOIR

Vincenzo D. Cunsolo, Salvatore Distefano, and Antonio Puliafito*

University of Messina,
Contrada di Dio, S. Agata, 98166 Messina, Italy
{vdcunsolo,sdistefano,apuliafito}@unime.it

Abstract. Cloud computing is the emerging technology in distributed, autonomic, service-oriented, on-demand, trusted computing. The fact that several Cloud solutions have been implemented so far, such as Amazon EC^2 and S^3, IBM's Blue Cloud, Sun Network.com, Microsoft Azure Services Platform, etc., is evidence of the great success already achieved by this computing paradigm. On the other hand, an increasing number of research projects focus on Cloud (Nimbus, OpenNEbula, Eucalyptus, OpenQRM, RESERVOIR, etc.) thus confirming that the topic is really hot, attracts investments and funds, and involves more and more researchers.

Our idea of Cloud has been synthesized into *Cloud@Home*, a computing paradigm that supports both open and commercial communities. Starting from the contribution philosophy at the basis of the Volunteer computing paradigm, we imagine a Cloud built on off the shelf, independent, network-connected resources and devices owned and managed by different users. Such users can both sell and/or buy their resources to/from Cloud providers or, alternatively, they can share them with other users establishing open interoperable Clouds.

Being aware of the crucial and driving role played by the RESERVOIR project in defining and implementing a reference architecture for Cloud computing, in this paper we focus on how to adapt and use the results of such project in the Cloud@Home specification. Starting from the RESERVOIR architecture, we discuss and detail how the Cloud@Home paradigm can be implemented on top of it, individuating components and modules to be integrated in a new reference architecture which allows to extend RESERVOIR towards the Volunteer contributing paradigm, improving SLA management and federation issues and, at the same time, enhancing virtualization and resources management in Cloud@Home.

Keywords: Cloud computing, Volunteer computing, cross-platform interoperability, RESERVOIR.

1 Introduction and Motivation

Cloud computing is a *distributed/network* computing paradigm that mixes aspects and goals of several other paradigms such as: *Grid computing* (*"... hardware*

---

* The research leading to these results is partially supported by the European Community's Seventh Framework Programme (FP7/2001-2013) under grant agreement n 215605.

© Institute for Computer Sciences, Social-Informatics and Telecommunications Engineering 2010

and software infrastructure that provides dependable, consistent, pervasive, and inexpensive access to high-end computational capabilities" [1]), *Internet computing* ("... a computing platform geographically distributed across the Internet" [2]), *Utility computing* ("a collection of technologies and business practices that enables computing to be delivered seamlessly and reliably across multiple computers, ... available as needed and billed according to usage, much like water and electricity are today" [3]) *Autonomic computing* ("computing systems that can manage themselves given high-level objectives from administrators" [4]), *Edge computing* ("... provides a generic template facility for any type of application to spread its execution across a dedicated grid, balancing the load ..." [5]) *Green computing* (a new frontier of *Ethical computing* starting from the assumption that in next future energy costs will be related to the environment pollution [6]) and *Trusted computing* ("... a Trusted platform is a computing platform that has a trusted component, probably in the form of built-in hardware, which it uses to create a foundation of trust for software processes." [7]).

Cloud computing is a distributed computing paradigm derived from the *service-centric perspective* that is quickly and widely spreading on the IT world. From this perspective, all capabilities and resources of a Cloud (usually geographically distributed) are provided to users *as a service*, to be accessed through the Internet without any specific knowledge of, expertise with, or control over the underlying technology infrastructure that supports them. Cloud computing provides *on-demand service provision*, *QoS guaranteed offer*, and *autonomous system* for managing hardware, software and data transparently to users [8].

In order to achieve such goals it is necessary to implement a level of abstraction of physical resources, uniforming their interfaces and providing means for their management, adaptively to user requirements. The development and the success of Cloud computing is due to the maturity reached by the hardware and software *virtualization* and Web technologies.

A great interest on Cloud computing has been manifested as demonstrated by the numerous projects proposed by both industry and academia. In commercial contexts, among the others we highlight: Amazon Elastic Compute Cloud [9], IBMs Blue Cloud [10], Sun Microsystems Network.com [11], Microsoft Azure Services Platform [12], Google App Engine [13], Dell Cloud computing solutions [14]. Some scientific activities worth of mention are: RESERVOIR [15], Nimbus-Stratus-Wispy-Kupa [16], Eucalyptus [17], OpenQRM [18] and OpenNEbula [19]. All of them support and provide an on-demand computing paradigm: a user submits his/her requests to the Cloud that remotely processes them and gives back the results. This client-server model well fits aims and scopes of commercial Clouds: the business. But, on the other hand, it represents a restriction for scientific Clouds, that have an open view [20,21], closer to that of *Volunteer computing*. Volunteer computing (also called *Peer-to-Peer computing*, *Global computing* or *Public computing*) uses computers volunteered by their owners as a source of computing power and storage to provide distributed scientific computing [22]. It is behind the *"@home"* philosophy of sharing/donating network connected resources for supporting distributed scientific computing.

In [23] we introduced *Cloud@Home*, a more "democratic" form of Cloud computing in which the resources of the users accessing the Cloud can be shared in order to contribute to the computing infrastructure. The proposed solution allows to overcome both hardware and software compatibility problems of Volunteer computing and, in commercial contexts, it can establish an *open computing-utility market* where users can both buy and sell their services. Since the computing power can be described by a "long-tailed" distribution, in which a high-amplitude population (Cloud providers and commercial data centers) is followed by a low-amplitude population (small data centers and private users) which gradually "tails off" asymptotically, Cloud@Home can catch the *Long Tail* effect [24], providing similar or higher computing capabilities than commercial providers' data centers, by grouping small computing resources from many single contributors.

In order to make real such vision of Cloud, we decide to base a possible implementation on a riper architecture. Since from the infrastructure point of view one of the most important activity on Cloud is carried on by the RESERVOIR project, as above introduced, we choose to start from such architecture in order to develop the Cloud@Home infrastructure. More specifically, in this paper we investigate how to implement Cloud@Home starting from the RESERVOIR architecture, mainly building an extra layer on top of it.

Thus, in section 2 we describe the architecture of both the RESERVOIR and the Cloud@Home infrastructures, comparing the two architectures in the following section 3. Section 4 describes the implementation of Cloud@Home on top of RESERVOIR. Finally, section 5 summarizes the paper also discussing about challenges and future work.

2 Background

In this section we summarize the RESERVOIR (subsection 2.1) and the Cloud@Home (subsection 2.2) projects and the corresponding architectures.

2.1 RESERVOIR

RESERVOIR (*REsources and SERvices VirtualizatiOn wIthout baRriers*) [15,25] is an European Union FP7 funded project that will enable massive scale deployment and management of complex IT services across different administrative domains, IT platforms and geographies. The project will provide a foundation for a service-based online economy, where - using virtualization technologies - resources and services are transparently provisioned and managed on an on-demand basis at competitive costs with high quality of service.

The RESERVOIR vision is to enable on-demand delivery of IT services at competitive costs, without requiring a large capital investment in infrastructure. The model is inspired by a strong desire to liken the delivery of IT services to the delivery of common utilities. It starts from the consideration that no single provider can serve all customers at all times, thus, next-generation

Cloud computing infrastructure should support a model where multiple independent providers can cooperate seamlessly to maximize their benefit. In their vision, to truly fulfill the promise of Cloud computing, there should be technological capabilities to *federate* disparate data centers, including those owned by separate organizations. Only through *federation* and *interoperability* infrastructure providers can take advantage of their aggregated capabilities to provide a seemingly infinite service computing utility. This view is totally shared by the Cloud@Home project.

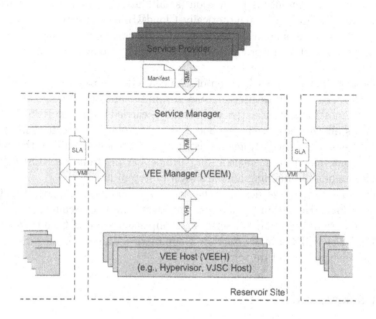

Fig. 1. RESERVOIR Architecture

The RESERVOIR architecture depicted in Fig. 1 is designed to provide a clean separation of concerns among the layers operating at different levels of abstraction. The rationale behind this particular layering is to keep a clear separation of concerns and responsibilities and to hide low level infrastructure details and decisions from high-level management and service providers. The *Service Manager* is the highest level of abstraction, interacting with the service providers to receive their *Service Manifests*, negotiate pricing, and handle billing. Its two most complex tasks are: 1) deploying and provisioning VEEs based on the Service Manifest, and 2) monitoring and enforcing SLA compliance by throttling a service application's capacity. The Service Manager is also responsible for monitoring the deployed services and adjusting their capacity, i.e., the number of VEE instances as well as their resource allocation (memory, CPU, etc.), to ensure SLA compliance and alignment with high-level business goals (e.g., cost-effectiveness). Finally, the Service Manager is responsible for accounting and billing.

The *Virtual Execution Environment Manager* (VEEM) is the next level of abstraction, interacting with the Service Manager above, VEE Hosts below, and VEE Managers at other sites to enable federation. The VEEM is responsible for the optimal placement of VEEs into VEE hosts subject to constraints determined by the Service Manager. The VEEM is free to place and move VEEs anywhere, even on the remote sites (subject to overall cross-site agreements), as long as the placement satisfies the constraints. Thus, in addition to serving local requests (from the local Service Manager), VEEM is responsible for the federation of remote sites. At the VEEM level a service is provided as a set of inter-related VEEs (a VEE Group), and hence it should be managed as a whole.

The *Virtual Execution Environment Host* (VEEH) is the lowest level of abstraction, interacting with the VEE Manager to realize its IT management decisions onto a set of virtualization platforms. The VEEH is responsible for the basic control and monitoring of VEEs and their resources (e.g., creating a VEE, allocating additional resources to a VEE, monitoring a VEE, migrating a VEE, creating a virtual network and storage pool, etc.). Each VEEH type encapsulates a particular type of virtualization technology, and all VEEH types expose a common interface such that VEEM can issue generic commands to manage the life-cycle of VEEs. The receiving VEEH is responsible for translating these commands into commands specific to the virtualization platform being abstracted.

The layered design stresses the use of standard, open, and generic protocols and interfaces to support vertical and horizontal interoperability between layers. Different implementations of each layer will be able to interact with each other. The *Service Management Interface* (SMI) with its service manifest exposes a standardized interface into the RESERVOIR Cloud for service providers. The service provider may then choose among RESERVOIR cloud providers knowing that they share a common language to express their business requirements. The *VEE Management Interface* (VMI) simplifies the introduction of different and independent IT optimization strategies without disrupting other layers or peer VEEMs. Further, VMI's support of VEEM-to-VEEM communication simplifies cloud federation by limiting the horizontal interoperability to one layer of the stack. The *VEE Host Interface* (VHI) will support plugging-in of new virtualization platforms (e.g., hypervisors), without requiring VEEM recompilation or restart.

2.2 Cloud@Home

Cloud@Home intends to reuse *"domestic"* computing resources to build voluntary contributors' Clouds that can interoperate each other and with external commercial Clouds, such as Amazon EC^2, IBM Blue Cloud, Microsoft Azure Services Platform, and so on. With Cloud@Home, anyone can experience the power of Cloud computing, both actively providing his/her own resources and services, and passively submitting his/her applications.

In Cloud@Home both the commercial/business and the volunteer/scientific viewpoints coexist: in the former case the end-user orientation of Cloud is extended to a collaborative two-way Cloud in which users can buy and/or sell their resources/services; in the latter case, the Grid philosophy of few but large computing requests is extended and enhanced to *open* Virtual Organizations. In both cases QoS requirements could be specified, introducing both in the Grid and in the Volunteer philosophy (*best effort*) the concept of quality.

Cloud@Home can be also considered as a generalization and a maturation of the @home philosophy: a context in which users voluntarily share their resources without any compatibility problem. This allows to knock down both hardware (processor bits, endianness, architecture, network) and software (operating systems, libraries, compilers, applications, middlewares) barriers of Grid and Volunteer computing, into a service oriented architecture.

On the other hand, Cloud@Home can be considered as the enhancement of the Grid-Utility vision of Cloud computing. In this new paradigm, users' hosts are not passive interfaces to Cloud services, but they can be actively involved in computing. Single nodes and services can be enrolled by the Cloud@Home middleware, in order to build own-private Cloud infrastructures that can (for free or by charge) interact with other Clouds.

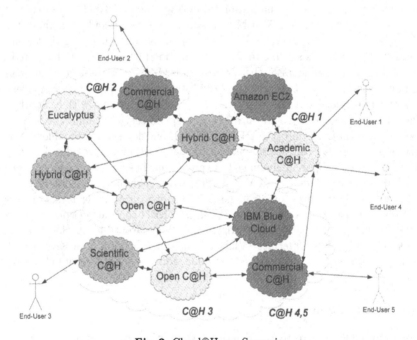

Fig. 2. Cloud@Home Scenario

The key points of Cloud@Home are on one hand the *volunteer contribution* and on the other the *interoperability* among Clouds. Well-known problems for the parallel, distributed and network computing communities have to be addressed regarding security, QoS, SLA, resource enrollment and management, heterogeneity of hw and sw, virtualization, etc. All of them must be contextualized into an highly dynamic environment in which nodes and resources can frequently change state, instantaneously becoming available/unavailable. Problems that are also partially shared and faced by the RESERVOIR project, in particular with regard to virtualization, resource management and interoperability. This motivates our choice of developing the Cloud@Home architecture on top of the RESERVOIR architecture above introduced.

The Cloud@Home idea can be pictorially depicted in Fig. 2, where several different Clouds, also built on volunteered resources (open Clouds), can interact and can provide resources and services to the other federated Clouds. They are characterized as: *open* if identify open environments operating for free Volunteer computing; *commercial* if they represent entities or companies selling their computing resources for business; *hybrid* if they can both sell or give for free their services. Both open and hybrid Clouds can interoperate with any other Clouds, also commercial, while these latter can interoperate each other if and only if the two commercial Clouds are mutually *recognized*. In this way it is possible to make *federations* of Clouds working together on the same project. Thus, a user interacting with a specific Cloud can use resources from different other Clouds, implementing different access points for a unique, global computing infrastructure. Such a form of computing, in which workloads and requests can be spread among different interoperable Cloud infrastructures, can be ideally associated to a fluid, giving rise to a new concept of computing we can identify as *fluid computing*.

The Cloud@Home logic architecture [23] by which we try to implement such idea is shown in Fig. 3, where three hierarchical layers can be identified:

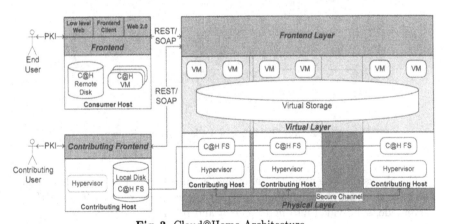

Fig. 3. Cloud@Home Architecture

– The *Frontend Layer* that globally manages resources and services (coordination, discovery, enrollment, etc), implements the user interface for accessing the Cloud (ensuring security reliability and interoperability), and provides QoS and business models and policies management facilities.
– The *Virtual Layer* that implements a homogeneous view of the distributed Cloud system offered to the higher frontend layer (and therefore to users)

in form of two main basic services: the *execution service* that allows to set up a virtual machine, and the *storage service* that implements a distributed storage Cloud to store data and files as a remote disk, locally mounted or accessed via Web.
- The bottom *Physical Layer* that provides both the physical resources for elaborating incoming requests and the software for locally managing such resources.

According to this view the Cloud is composed of several *contributing hosts* that share their resources. A user can interact with the Cloud through the *consumer host* after authenticating him/herself into the system. One of the main enhancement of Cloud@Home is that a host can be at the same time both contributing and consumer host, establishing a symbiotic mutual interaction with the Cloud.

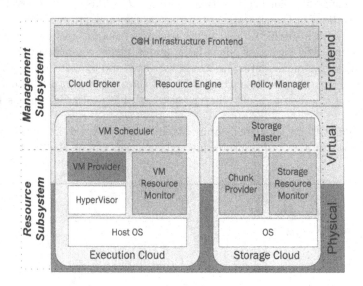

Fig. 4. Core Structure of a Cloud@Home Server

The blocks implementing the functional architecture of Fig. 3, are depicted in the layered model of Fig. 4, that reports the core structure of the Cloud@Home server-side, subdivided into *management* and *resource subsystems*:

- *Management subsystem* - is the backbone of the overall system management and coordination composed of six blocks: the *C@H infrastructure frontend*, the *Cloud broker*, the *resource engine*, the *policy manager*, the VM scheduler and the storage master.
- *Resource subsystem* - provides primitives for locally managing the resources (distributed operations), offering different services over the same resources: the *execution Cloud* and the *storage Cloud*.

The two subsystems are strictly interconnected: the management subsystem implements the upper layer of the functional architecture, while the resource subsystem implements the lower level functionalities.

The infrastructure frontend provides tools for Cloud@Home-service provider interactions, forwarding the incoming requests to the lower level blocks. The Cloud broker collects and manages information about the available Clouds and the services they provide (both *functional* and *non-functional* parameters, such as QoS, costs, reliability, *request formats' specifications* for Cloud@Home-foreign Clouds translations, etc). The policy manager provides and implements the Cloud's access facilities. This task falls into the security scope of identification, authentication, permission and identity management.

The resource engine is the hearth of Cloud@Home. It is responsible for the resources' management, the equivalent of a Grid *resource broker* in a broader Cloud environment. To meet this goal, the resource engine applies a hierarchical policy. It operates at higher level, in a centralized way, indexing all the resources of the Cloud. Incoming requests are delegated to *VM schedulers* or *storage masters* that, in a distributed fashion, manage the computing or storage resources respectively, coordinated by the resource engine. In order to manage QoS policies and to perform the resources discovery, the resource engine collaborates with both the Cloud broker and the policy manager at higher level, locally monitored and managed by schedulers and masters through the hosts' resource monitors.

The VM provider, the resource monitor and the hypervisor are responsible for managing a VM locally to a physical resource of an execution Cloud.

Chunk providers physically store the data into a storage Cloud, that are encrypted in order to achieve the confidentiality goal.

3   RESERVOIR vs. Cloud@Home

In order to adapt the Cloud@Home architecture to the RESERVOIR one, it is necessary to in depth investigate the two architectures, individuating points in common and differences. Let's start with the points in common. The first regards the architecture. Both RESERVOIR and Cloud@Home specify layered architectures decomposed in three levels, but the decomposition approach applied in the two contexts differs. In RESERVOIR the decomposition resulting in Fig. 1 is made on implementative issues. Specifically, in the RESERVOIR architecture there is a correspondence between layers and physical nodes implementing them. In Cloud@Home, the layered model of Fig. 3 describes a more abstract functional characterization, whose implementation, detailed in Fig. 4, does not establishes a direct 1:1 correspondence between functions, blocks and physical nodes. In order to implement Cloud@Home starting from the RESERVOIR architecture it is necessary to adapt the former architecture to the latter, and so to establish the correspondence between layers and blocks to physical nodes.

Another important point in common to both projects are the federation and the interoperability goals. Both projects share these goals providing different architectural solutions: RESERVOIR implements Cloud federations by providing vertical interoperability to service providers through a standardized SMI interface, and limiting the horizontal interoperability to one layer of the stack, the VEEM, achieving VEEM-to-VEEM communication through VMI. Due to the choice of defining a logical-functional architecture, Cloud@Home unifies both vertical and horizontal interoperability into a unique block specifically conceived and devoted to interoperability and federation tasks: the Cloud broker.

As in RESERVOIR, we believe that the best solution to achieve interoperability among different Clouds is the standardization way, opinion validated by several significant initiatives and efforts towards Cloud standardizations [20,26,21]. It is needed a clear, unambiguous and widely accepted standard allowing automatic Cloud discovery and communications setup. But, since at now Cloud infrastructures are mainly commercial, the question wether the involved corporations will accept to conform to a standard is an open problem not so obvious. So we think it could be necessary to provide means for bridging or translating between different interfaces in order to reach the interoperability goal in Cloud. The Cloud broker accomplishes this task with regard to Cloud@Home.

With regard to interoperability, another important problem to face is the *Cloud discovery*: how a Cloud knows about the existence of other Clouds and the services they provide? While RESERVOIR not so clearly identifies such topic problem, Cloud@Home deals with the Cloud discovery by delegating such task to the Cloud broker. Both centralized and distributed solutions are possible for addressing the Cloud discovery task, but we retain to follow a trade-off between the two approaches in order to take advantage from both [23].

A significant difference between RESERVOIR and Cloud@Home regards resource management. RESERVOIR concentrates all the resource management functions into the VEEM. This centralized solution allows to simplify the resource management but, on the other hand, it cannot easily manage great quantities of hosts (VEEH) implementing the Cloud infrastructure, since a unique manager does not scale when the number of hosts increases. Cloud@Home instead proposes a hierarchical approach, by which the resource management is coordinated at high level by a resource engine, and implemented at lower level by schedulers or masters that could be also hierarchical. This solution allows to reduce the workload incoming to the resource engine moving it toward the VM schedulers. A distributed-hierarchical approach is further motivated by the fact that the context in which Cloud@Home operates includes volunteer contributions. Such environment is highly dynamic, since resources can be "plugged" in or out the infrastructure autonomously, therefore the system must be able to manage such dynamics, quickly adapting to variations. For this reason to address the problem we think about autonomic approaches [23], able to quickly reconfigure after changes occur.

With regard to SLA and QoS issues, RESERVOIR splits the task of SLA in two parts: the *vertical SLA* towards Service Provider is managed by the Service Manager; the *horizontal SLA* among VEEM of different infrastructures due to the dynamic federation of infrastructure providers. The functional architecture of Cloud@Home individuates a specific block to which assign QoS and SLA challenges, the policy manager. In combination with the resource engine, the policy manager manages the vertical SLA with service providers, locally monitoring the resources through a resource monitor active for each host. The resource information are kept locally to the corresponding VM scheduler or storage master, accessed by the resource engine in the SLA discovery and checking/monitoring phases. The policy manager also provides tools for the horizontal SLA. In such case the SLA process is managed in combination with the Cloud broker that performs the Cloud discovery.

An important topic to adequately take into the right consideration is security, particularly felt in high dynamic and interoperable-distributed environments. Security issues are only partially covered into RESERVOIR, mainly delegated to underlying technologies such as virtualization isolation and OpenNEbula security. Cloud@Home faces several security issues in its architecture. Authentication is implemented through PKI infrastructure and X509 certificates, and it is managed by the policy manager. Starting from the Grid experience, credential delegation and Single Sign-On (SSO) mechanisms can be used in order to manage the identity into a Cloud. The problem of identity management in Cloud@Home is further complicated by the interoperability goal, since it is necessary that interoperable Clouds must mutually trust each other. Also in such case it is strongly recommended to specify and use widely accepted standards in the topic of authentication and identity management.

In the context thus individuated, we think it is necessary to build up an *identity provider* which provides tools and mechanisms for univocal/single-users and mutual-Clouds authentications. In order to implement such identity provider we think about a distributed technique as the *eXtensible Resource Identifier* (XRI) [27] and the OpenID [28] approaches.

Information security in Cloud@Home is achieved through encryption techniques [29]. The information stored in a Cloud@Home infrastructure are always encrypted, while information in clear are transferred through a secure channel such as SSH, TSL, IPSEC, SSL, XMPP, etc.

4   Synthesis: Implementing Cloud@Home on Top of RESERVOIR

The differences between RESERVOIR and Cloud@Home detailed in the previous section highlight that, in the corresponding architectures, there are parts in common and parts riper or better covered in one of them rather then in the other. This motivates our efforts in combining the two approaches into a Cloud architecture resulting as a trade-off between the existing ones.

From the above considerations we can observe that the main difference between the two approaches is that Cloud@Home adopts a higher abstraction level than RESERVOIR in the architecture specification. This impression is validated by the two architecture's implementations: RESERVOIR better focuses on low level aspects such as virtualization and centralized resource management, while Cloud@Home privileges higher level aspects mainly concerning the management of distributed resources, SLA and QoS, security and interoperability, maybe not yet well focused into RESERVOIR. Moreover, since the context of Cloud@Home, also including the volunteer contribution, can be wider than the RESERVOIR one, and also due to the experience and the knowhow reached by this latter project, we retain really practicable and feasible the idea of building a Cloud@Home architecture starting from the RESERVOIR one.

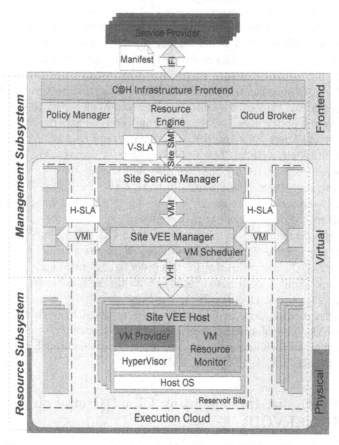

Fig. 5. Cloud@Home Architecture on top of RESERVOIR

More specifically, according to such interpretation, being RESERVOIR focused on lower level aspects than Cloud@Home, it is reasonable to think about an implementation of Cloud@Home on top of RESERVOIR. Such idea is formally represented into the architecture shown in Fig. 5, where concepts and parts of both the corresponding architectures are merged and integrated.

From a functional/higher-level perspective, the hierarchical distributed resources management, the interoperability among different Clouds and the high level security management are drawn from Cloud@Home. With regard to the resource management, at lower level, each site is organized according to the

RESERVOIR architecture, with a Site Manager that manages a pool of distributed network-connected resources, the Site VEEHs, constituting the site. In order to implement an adaptive and easy-to-scale solution, each site can manage a limited finite number of resources. Thus, the sites are hierarchically coordinated by the specific subsystems of the frontend layer (resource engine, policy manager and Cloud broker). This solution allows to also manage volunteer contributions: each time a new resource is offered to the infrastructure and must be enrolled into the Cloud, the resource engine has to select a site to which associate the resource. If no sites are available a new site is built up by aggregating the resources that are not yet associated to a site with the ones selected from other different sites, applying load balancing principle in the selection in order to avoid overloaded sites and resources.

In this new architecture, the SLA and QoS management solution is derived from both the original architectures: the characterization made in RESERVOIR, distinguishing between high level, vertical SLA (VSLA) and low level, horizontal SLA (HSLA) has been inherited by the new architecture. The high level VSLA is subdivided into two parts: the former between the service providers and the frontend, the latter between the frontend layer blocks and each site. The HSLA has the aim of making adaptive the infrastructure to external solicitations. Before asking to resource engine and policy manager, the single VEEM can autonomously try to discover resources when they cannot locally (on-site) satisfy the requirements, by asking to other VEEM. Otherwise, they recur to resource engine and policy manager, that must be always updated also in case of lower level reconfigurations. Such goal can be pursued by exploiting autonomic computing techniques.

Let's jump into details. Following a top-down approach, the service providers interact with the Cloud@Home infrastructure frontend through a specific *infrastructure frontend interface* (IFI) that forwards their service manifests to the lower level blocks. The information specified in the service manifests are translated into the local Cloud format by the Cloud@Home infrastructure frontend and therefore forwarded to the lower level blocks, as done in Cloud@Home. Thus the resource engine, in collaboration with the policy manager and, if required, with the Cloud broker, perform the VSLA with the service provider. This task requires the interposition of the infrastructure frontend, from one side, and of the site through the specific SMI interface from the other side.

Through the frontend, we can also adapt the SLA to interact (by the policy manager and the resource engine) with the VM Scheduler, which includes two RESERVOIR components: the Site Service Manager and the Site VEE Manager. According to the Cloud@Home architecture, the VM Scheduler uses and interacts with the VM Provider. To integrate this behavior within RESERVOIR, we can place the VM provider inside a Site VEEH, allowing the resource monitor to directly interact with VM scheduler.

Such requests are managed on-site by the site service manager, that negotiates the site SLA interacting with the lower VEEM layer, which manages the site resources and therefore monitors their status. Both such components implement the functions associated to the original Cloud@Home VM scheduler and therefore in Fig. 5 are encapsulated in this latter component.

A Cloud@Home site is also composed of a pool of VEEH physical nodes. Each VEEH contains a Cloud@Home VM provider and a VM resource monitor, and obviously has its own hypervisor and host OS, such as the one typically used in RESERVOIR (XEN, KVM hypervisors and Linux OS). A goal of Cloud@Home is to implement a cross-platform interface independent of hypervisor and host OS. This is a mandatory requirement in case Clouds interoperability is needed. Since this is not satisfied by the RESERVOIR architecture, we need to extend the RESERVOIR infrastructure in order to support other hypervisors. The best solution is the specification of a unique, standard VM format [26]. Another requirement is that the hypervisors have to be interoperable, independent of the host OS. Our idea to overcome this latter specific OS constraints, waiting for a standard VM format, is to include the support of VirtualBox [30] in the architecture.

5 Conclusions

Cloud computing provides *on-demand service provision*, *QoS guaranteed offer*, and *autonomous system* for managing hardware, software and data transparently to users. To such context, Cloud@Home adds the possibility of enrolling volunteer contributing resources merging aims and scopes of both Cloud and Volunteer computing paradigms. In order to implement Cloud@Home, instead of starting from scratch, we decided to exploit the existing work produced by the RESERVOIR project which is building a Cloud computing framework without barrier in a federated way for implementing large data center.

In this paper we propose how to merge the two approaches to introduce flexibility in RESERVOIR, improving SLA management and federation issues better covered in Cloud@Home. Moreover, the volunteer contribution feature allows to extend RESERVOIR Clouds with new available resources from academic, open communities and commercial organizations. On the other hand, Cloud@Home benefits from RESERVOIR, exploiting its riper infrastructure in terms of virtualization and site resources management.

References

1. Foster, I.: What is the grid? - a three point checklist. GRIDtoday 1(6) (July 2002)
2. Milenkovic, M., Robinson, S., Knauerhase, R., Barkai, D., Garg, S., Tewari, A., Anderson, T., Bowman, M.: Toward internet distributed computing. Computer 36(5), 38–46 (2003)
3. Ross, J.W., Westerman, G.: Preparing for utility computing: The role of it architecture and relationship management. IBM System Journal 43(1), 5–19 (2004)
4. Kephart, J.O., Chess, D.M.: The vision of autonomic computing. Computer 36(1), 41–50 (2003)

5. Davis, A., Parikh, J., Weihl, W.E.: Edgecomputing: extending enterprise applications to the edge of the internet. In: WWW Alt. 2004: Proceedings of the 13th international World Wide Web conference on Alternate track papers & posters, pp. 180–187. ACM, New York (2004)
6. Murugesan, S.: Harnessing green it: Principles and practices. IT Professional 10(1), 24–33 (2008)
7. Pearson, S.: Trusted Computing Platforms: TCPA Technology in Context. Prentice Hall PTR, Upper Saddle River (2002)
8. Wang, L., Tao, J., Kunze, M., Castellanos, A.C., Kramer, D., Karl, W.: Scientific Cloud Computing: Early Definition and Experience. In: HPCC 2008, pp. 825–830. IEEE Computer Society, Los Alamitos (2008)
9. Amazon Inc.: Elastic Compute Cloud [URL]. Amazon (2008),
   http://aws.amazon.com/ec2
10. IBM Inc.: Blue Cloud project. IBM (2008),
    http://www-03.ibm.com/press/us/en/pressrelease/22613.wss/
11. Sun Microsystem.: Network.com (SUN), http://www.network.com
12. Co., M.: (Azure services platform),
    http://www.microsoft.com/azure/default.mspx
13. Inc., G.: (Google application engine),
    http://code.google.com/intl/it-IT/appengine/
14. Dell: (Dell cloud computing solutions),
    http://www.dell.com/cloudcomputing
15. RESERVOIR Consortium: RESERVOIR Project (2009),
    http://www-03.ibm.com/press/us/en/pressrelease/23448.wss/
16. University of Chicago-University of Florida-Purdue University-Masaryk University: Nimbus-Stratus-Wispy-Kupa Projects (January 2009),
    http://workspace.globus.org/clouds/nimbus.html/,
    http://www.acis.ufl.edu/vws/,
    http://www.rcac.purdue.edu/teragrid/resources/#wispy,
    http://meta.cesnet.cz/cms/opencms/en/docs/clouds
17. Nurmi, D., Wolski, R., Grzegorczyk, C., Obertelli, G., Soman, S., Youseff, L., Zagorodnov, D.: The Eucalyptus Open-source Cloud-computing System. University of California Santa Barbara Computer Science (2009),
    http://open.eucalyptus.com/
18. OpenQRM: Open Source Data Management Platform (2009),
    http://www.openqrm.com/
19. Distributed Systems Architecture Research Group: OpenNEbula Project Universidad Complutense de Madrid (2009), http://www.opennebula.org/
20. Open Cloud Manifesto Organization: The Open Cloud Manifesto (Spring 2009),
    http://www.opencloudmanifesto.org/
21. Distributed Management Task Force, Inc.: Open Cloud Standards Incubator (2009), http://www.dmtf.org/about/cloud-incubator
22. Anderson, D.P., Fedak, G.: The computational and storage potential of volunteer computing. In: CCGRID 2006, Washington, DC, USA, pp. 73–80. IEEE Computer Society, Los Alamitos (2006)
23. Cunsolo, V.D., Distefano, S., Puliafito, A., Scarpa, M.: Volunteer Computing and Desktop Cloud: the Cloud@Home Paradigm. In: Proceedings of the 8th IEEE International Symposium on Network Computing and Applications (IEEE NCA 2009), July 9-11. IEEE, Los Alamitos (2009)
24. Anderson, C.: The Long Tail: How Endless Choice Is Creating Unlimited Demand. Random House Business Books (2006)

25. Rochwerger, B., Breitgand, D., Levy, E., Galis, A., Nagin, K., Llorente, I.M., Montero, R., Wolfsthal, Y., Elmroth, E., Caceres, J., Ben-Yehuda, M., Emmerich, W., Galan, F.: The reservoir model and architecture for open federated cloud computing. IBM Journal of Research and Development 53(4) (2009)
26. VMWare Inc., XEN Inc.: The Open Virtual Machine Format Whitepaper for OVF Specification (2007), http://www.vmware.com/appliances/learn/ovf.html
27. OASIS Extensible Resource Identifier (XRI) TC: Extensible Resource Identifier (XRI) (2009),
    http://www.oasis-open.org/committees/tc_home.php?wg_abbrev=xri
28. Reed, D., Chasen, L., Tan, W.: OpenID identity discovery with XRI and XRDS. In: IDtrust 2008: Proceedings of the 7th symposium on Identity and trust on the Internet, pp. 19–25. ACM, New York (2008)
29. Cunsolo, V.D., Distefano, S., Puliafito, A., Scarpa, M.: Implementing Data Security in Grid Environment. In: Proceedings of the IEEE Workshop on Emerging Technologies for Next Generation GRID (IEEE ETNGRID 2009), June 9 - July 11. IEEE, Los Alamitos (2009)
30. Sun Microsystems Inc.: VirtualBox (2009), http://www.virtualbox.org/

AppScale: Scalable and Open AppEngine Application Development and Deployment

Navraj Chohan, Chris Bunch, Sydney Pang, Chandra Krintz,
Nagy Mostafa, Sunil Soman, and Rich Wolski

Computer Science Department
University of California, Santa Barbara

Abstract. We present the design and implementation of AppScale, an open source extension to the Google AppEngine (GAE) Platform-as-a-Service (PaaS) cloud technology. Our extensions build upon the GAE SDK to facilitate distributed execution of GAE applications over virtualized cluster resources, including Infrastructure-as-a-Service (IaaS) cloud systems such as Amazon's AWS/EC2 and EUCALYPTUS. AppScale provides a framework with which researchers can investigate the interaction between PaaS and IaaS systems as well as the inner workings of, and new technologies for, PaaS cloud technologies using real GAE applications.

Keywords: Cloud Computing, PaaS, Open-Source, Fault Tolerance, Utility Computing, Distributed Systems.

1 Introduction

Cloud Computing is a term coined for a recent trend toward service-oriented cluster computing based on Service-Level Agreements (SLAs). Cloud computing simplifies the use of large-scale distributed systems through transparent and adaptive resource management. It provides simplification and automation for the configuration and deployment of an entire software stack. Moreover, cloud technology enables arbitrary users to employ potentially vast numbers of multi-core cluster resources that are not necessarily owned, managed, or controlled by the users themselves. Specific cloud offerings differ, but extant infrastructures share two common characteristics: they rely on operating system virtualization (e.g., Xen, VMWare, etc.) for functionality and/or performance isolation and they support per-user or per-application customization via a service interface typically implemented using high-level language technologies, APIs, and web services.

The three prevailing classes of cloud computing are Software-as-a-Service (SaaS), Platform-as-a-Service (PaaS), and Infrastructure-as-a-Service (IaaS). SaaS describes systems in which high-level functionality (e.g., SalesForce.com [24], which provides customer relationship management software as an on-demand service) is hosted by the cloud and exported to thin clients via the network. The main feature of SaaS systems is that the API offered to the cloud client is for a complete software service and not programming abstractions or

D.R. Avresky et al. (Eds.): Cloudcomp 2009, LNICST 34, pp. 57–70, 2010.
© Institute for Computer Sciences, Social-Informatics and Telecommunications Engineering 2010

resources. Commercial SaaS systems typically charge according to the number of users and application features.

PaaS refers to the availability of scalable abstractions through an interface from which restricted (e.g., HTTP(s)-only communication, limited resource consumption), network-accessible, applications written in high-level languages (e.g. Python, JavaScript, JVM and .Net languages) can be constructed. Two popular examples of PaaS systems are Google App Engine (GAE) [13] and Microsoft Azure [3]. Users typically test and debug their applications locally using a non-scalable development kit and then upload their programs to a proprietary, highly scalable PaaS cloud infrastructure (runtime services, database, distribution and scheduling system, etc.). Commercial offerings for both PaaS and IaaS systems charge a low pay-as-you-go price that is directly proportional to resource use (CPU, network bandwidth, and storage); these providers typically also offer trial or capped resource use options, free of charge.

IaaS describes a facility for provisioning virtualized operating system instances, storage abstractions, and network capacity under contract from a service provider. Clients fully configure and control their instances as root via ssh. The Amazon Web Services (AWS) which includes the Elastic Compute Cloud (EC2), Simple Storage System (S3), Elastic Block Store (EBS) and other APIs [1] is, at present, the most popular example of an IaaS-style computational cloud. Amazon charges per instance occupancy hour and for storage options at very competitive rates. Similar to those for PaaS systems, these rates are typically significantly less than the cost of owning and maintaining even a small subset of the resources that these commercial entities make available to users for application execution.

EUCALYPTUS [20] is an open-source IaaS system that implements the AWS interface. EUCALYPTUS is compatible with AWS to the extent that commercial tools designed to work with EC2 (e.g., Rightscale [22], Elastra [11], etc.) cannot differentiate between an Amazon and a EUCALYPTUS installation. EUCALYPTUS allows researchers to deploy, on their own cluster resources, an open-source web-service-based software infrastructure that presents a faithful reproduction of the AWS functionality in its default configuration. Furthermore, EUCALYPTUS provides a research framework for investigation of IaaS cloud technologies.

Such a framework is key to advancing the state of the art in scalable cloud computing software architectures and to enabling users to employ cloud technologies easily on their own local clusters. Yet, despite the popularity and wide-spread use of PaaS systems, there are no open-source implementations of PaaS systems or APIs. To address this need, we have designed and implemented an open-source *PaaS* cloud research framework, called *AppScale*. AppScale emulates the functionality of the popular GAE commercial cloud. Specifically, AppScale implements the Google App Engine open APIs and provides an infrastructure and toolset for distributed execution of GAE applications over virtualized clusters and IaaS systems (including EC2 and EUCALYPTUS). Moreover, by building on existing cloud and web-service technologies, AppScale is easy to use and able to execute real GAE applications using local and private cluster resources.

AppScale consists of multiple components that automate deployment, management, scaling, and fault tolerance of a GAE system. AppScale integrates, builds upon, and extends existing web service, high-level language, and cloud technologies to provide a system that researchers and developers can employ to investigate new cloud technologies or the behavior and performance of extant applications. Moreover, AppScale deployment requires no modifications to GAE applications. AppScale is not meant to compete with, outperform, or scale as well as, proprietary cloud systems, including GAE. Our intent is to provide a framework that enables researchers to investigate how such cloud systems operate, behave, and scale using real applications. Moreover, by facilitating application execution over important, lower-level cloud offerings such as EUCALYPTUS and EC2, AppScale also enables investigation of the interoperation and behavior of multiple cloud fabrics (PaaS and IaaS) in a single system. In the sections that follow, we describe the design, implementation, and a preliminary evaluation of AppScale.

2   Google App Engine

In April 2008, Google released a software framework for developing and hosting complete web service applications. This framework, called Google App Engine (GAE), enables users to write applications written in high-level programming languages and to deploy them on Google's proprietary and vast computing resources. The framework restricts the libraries that the application can use and limits the resources consumed by the program. This sandbox execution model limits application functionality in order to protect system stability, guarantee performance, and achieve scalability. The restrictions include communication limited to HTTP(S), program response to web requests within 30 seconds, no file system access except for files uploaded with the application, and persistent storage via simple in-memory or distributed key-value storage across requests.

Deployed GAE applications gain access to a high-quality, professionally maintained, and extremely scalable software infrastructure. This infrastructure is closed proprietary and includes the Google File System (GFS) [12], BigTable [8], MapReduce [9], Chubby [5] and Paxos [7]. GFS is a distributed, scalable, and reliable file system optimized for very large files and throughput-oriented applications. BigTable offers a distributed and highly available schema-free key-value store for fast access to structured data via a simple Datastore API. BigTable also integrates MapReduce for highly scalable concurrent execution of embarassingly parallel computations, such as data indexing and crunching for Google PageRank [4], Google Earth, and other applications. Chubby is a highly available naming service for GFS (that was originally designed as a locking service); the content of GFS are agreed upon using an optimized version of the original Paxos algorithm [15].

Google applications access these services through well-defined interfaces enabling the cloud to manage and controll resource usage very efficiently and scalably. GAE applications interoperate with other hosts via HTTP(S) using the

URL-Fetch API, manipulate images via the Images API, cache and store data via the Memcache and Datastore API, and access other Google applications via the Mail API and Accounts API. The web frontend of an application communicates via Remote Procedure Calls (RPC) with the datastore backend using protocol buffers [21] for fast and portable data serialization.

GAE developers write their web applications (webpage frontend, response computation, and data access) in Python using the GAE APIs, a subset of the Python libraries approved by Google, and the Django web framework [10] (or other similar and approved Python web framework). These frameworks significantly simplify and expedite common web development activities. Developers modify the data model in their programs to access the GAE Datastore API. In April 2009, Google made available a Java-based GAE framework. Developers employ the Java Servlet and Data Objects APIs and a subset of the Java libraries approved by Google to implement JVM-based GAE web applications.

Developers write a runtime configuration file for their application that identifies the program, specifies the versioning information, and identifies the handlers (code to execute or files to serve) for different URL accesses. Developers use a GAE software development kit (SDK) to test and execute their application locally and serially. The SDK implements the APIs using simple, slow, and non-scalable versions of the internal services. In particular, the SDK implements the Datastore API via a flat file (or very simple database). Once developers are ready to deploy their application on Google's resources, they do so by uploading a gzipped tar-ball of the code and configuration file to App Engine using an SDK tool. The developer also specifies and builds the indexes on the datastore for all queries that the application code can make, as part of the upload process.

The Google runtime system automatically load-balances the application according to user load. If the application exceeds its billable or fixed resource quota within a 24-hour period or 1-minute interval, the system returns a HTTP 403 Forbidden status until the resource is replenished. Application activities that are monitored by the Google system include CPU usage, network communication (bandwidth), requests (total and per minute), data storage, and emails sent.

In summary, Google App Engine provides access to vast and extreme scale resources for a very specific and well-defined web service application domain. Applications can be implemented and deployed into the clould quickly and easily using high-level languages, simple and well documented API's, and Google's SDK tools. Furthermore, the Google platform monitors and scales the applications. GAE thus enables a broad user base to develop web applications and deploy them without owning and managing sufficient cluster resources. The GAE APIs and the SDK carry open-source licenses but the internal, scalable, implementations are closed-source.

3   AppScale

To provide a platform for GAE application execution using local and private cluster resources, to investigate novel cloud services, and to faciliate research for

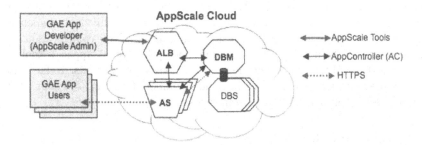

Fig. 1. Overview of the AppScale design. The AppScale cloud consists of an AppLoad-Balancer (ALB), a Database Master (DBM), one or more Database Slaves (DBS), and one or more AppServers (ASs). Users of GAE applications interact with ASs; the developer deploys AppScale and her GAE applications through the head node (i.e. the node on which the ALB is located) using the AppScale Tools. AppControllers (ACs) on each node interact with the other nodes in the system; ASs interact with the DBM via HTTPS.

the next-generation of cloud software and applications, we have implemented AppScale. AppScale is a multi-language, multi-component framework for executing GAE applications. Figure 1 overviews the AppScale design.

AppScale consists of a toolset (the AppScale Tools), three primary components, the AppServer (ASs), the database management system, and the AppLoadBalancer (ALB), and an AppController (AC) for inter-component communication. AppServers are the execution engines for GAE applications which interact with a Database Master (DBM) via HTTPS for data storage and access. Database Slaves (DBSs) facilitate distributed, scalable, and fault tolerant data management. The AppController is responsible for setup, initialization, and tear down of AppScale instances, as well as cross component interaction. In addition, the AppController facilitates deployment of and authentication for GAE applications. The ALB serves as the head node of an AppScale deployment and initiates connections to GAE applications running in ASs. The AC of the head node also monitors and manages the resource use and availability of the deployment. All communications across the system are encrypted via the secure socket layer (SSL).

A GAE application developer interacts with an AppScale instance (cloud) remotely using the AppScale Tools. Developers use these tools to deploy AppScale, to submit GAE applications to deployed AppScale instances, and to interact with and administer AppScale instances and deployed GAE applications. We distinguish developers from *users*; users are the clients/users of individual GAE applications.

An AppScale deployment consists of one or more virtualized operating system instances (guestVMs). GuestVMs are Linux systems (*nodes*) that execute over the Xen virtual machine monitor, the Kernel Virtual Machine (KVM) [25] or IaaS systems such as Amazon's EC2 and EUCALYPTUS. For each AppScale deployment, there is a single AppLoadBalancer (ALB) which we consider the head node, one or more AppServers (AS), one Database Master (DBM) and one or more Database Slaves (DBSs). A node can implement any individual component as well as any combination of these components; the AppScale configuration can be specified by the developer via command line options of an AppScale tool.

We next detail the implementation of each of these components. To facilitate this implementation we employ and extend a number of existing, successful, web service technologies and language frameworks.

3.1   AppController (AC)

The AppController (AC) is a SOAP client/server daemon written in Ruby. The AC executes on every node and starts automatically when the guestVM boots. The AC on the head node starts the ALB first and initiates deployment and boot of any other guestVM. This AC then contacts the ACs on the other guestVMs and spawns the components on each node. The head node AC first spawns the DBM (which then starts the DBSs) and then spawns the AppServers, configuring each with the IP of the DBM (to enable access to the database via HTTPS).

The AC on the head node also monitors the AppScale deployment for failed nodes and for opportunities to grow and shrink the AppScale deployment according to system demand and developer preferences. The AC periodically polls (currently every 10 seconds) the AC of every other node for a "heartbeat" and to collect per-application behavior and resource use (e.g. CPU and memory load). When a component fails, the AC restarts the component, respawning a node if necessary.

Although in this paper we evaluate the static default deployment of AppScale, we can also use this feedback mechanism to spawn and kill individual nodes of a deployment to respond to system load and performance. Killing nodes reduces resource consumption (and cost of resources are being paid for) and consists of stopping the components within a node and destroying the guestVM. We spawn nodes to add more AppServers or Database Slaves to the system. We are currently investigating various scheduling policies, feedback mechanisms, and capability to interact with the underlying cloud fabric to modify service level agreements. AppScale currently supports starting and stopping of any component in a node and automatic spawning and destroying nodes.

3.2   AppLoadBalancer (ALB)

The AppLoadBalancer is a Ruby on Rails [23] application that employs a simple HTTP server (nginx [19]) to select between three replicated Mongrel application servers [16] (for head-node load balancing). The ALB distributes initial requests from users to the AppServers (ASs) of GAE applications. Users initially contact the ALB to request a login to a GAE application. The ALB provides and/or authenticates this login and then selects an AS randomly. It then redirects the user request to the selected AS. The user, once redirected, continues to use the AppServer to which she was routed and does not interact further with the ALB unless she logs out or the AppServer she is using becomes unreachable.

3.3   AppServer (AS)

An AppServer is an extension to the development server distributed freely as part of the Google AppEngine SDK for GAE application execution. Our extensions to the development server enable fully automated execution of GAE applications on any virtualized cluster to which the developer has access, including EC2 and EUCALYPTUS. AppServers can also be used without virtualization which requires manual configuration. In addition, our extensions provide a generic datastore interface through which any database technology can be used. Currently we have implemented this interface to HBase and Hypertable, open-source implementations of Google's BigTable that execute over the distributed Hadoop File System (HDFS) [14]. We also have plugins for MySQL [17], Cassandra [6], and Voldemort [26].

We intercept the protocol buffer requests from the application and route them over HTTPS to/from the DBM front-end called the *PBServer*. The PBServer implements the interface to every datastore available and routes the requests to the appropriate datastore. The interaction is simple but fully supported by a number of different error conditions, and includes:

- Put: add a new item into the table (create table if non-existant)
- Get: retrieve an item by ID number
- Query: SQL-like query
- Delete: delete an item by ID number

Our other extensions facilitate automatic invocation of ASs and authentication of GAE users. The AC of the node sets the location of the datastore (passed in from a request from the head node AC), upon AS start. The AS also stores and verifies the cookie secret that we use to authenticate users and direct the component to authenticate using the local AppController (AC).

An AS executes a single GAE application at time. To host multiple GAE applications, AppScale uses additional ASs (one or more per GAE application) that it isolates within their own AppScale nodes or that it co-locates within other nodes containing other AppScale components.

3.4   Data Management

In front of the Database Master (DBM) sits the The PBServer is the front-end of the DBM. This Python program processes protocol buffers from a GAE application and makes requests on its behalf to read and write data to the datastore. As mentioned previously, AppScale currently supports HBase and Hypertable datastores. Both execute over HDFS within AppScale which performs replication, fault tolerance, and provides reliable service using distributed Database Slaves. The PBServer interfaces with HBase, Hypertable, Cassandra, and Voldemort using Thrift for cross-language interoperation.

The AC on the DBM node provides access to the datastore via these interfaces to the other ACs and the ALB of an AppScale system. The ALB stores uploaded GAE applications as well as user credentials in the database to authenticate the developer and users of GAE applications.

3.5   AppScale Tools

The developer employs the AppScale tools to setup an AppScale instance and to deploy GAE applications over AppScale. The toolset consists of a small number of Ruby scripts that we named in the spirit of Amazon's EC2 tools for AWS. The tools facilitate AppScale deployment on Xen-based clusters as well as EC2 and EUCALYPTUS. The latter two systems require credentials and service-level agreements (SLAs) for the use, allocation (killing and spawning of instances) of resources on behalf of a developer; the EC2 tools (for either IaaS system) generate, manage, distribute (to deployed instances), and authenticate the credentials throughout the cluster. The AppScale tools sit above these commands and make use of them for credential management in IaaS settings. In a Xen-only setting, no credential management is necessary; the tools employ ssh keys for cluster management. The tools enable developers to start an AppScale system, to deploy and tear down GAE applications, to query the state and performance of an AppScale deployment or application, and to manipulate the AppScale configuration and state. There is currently no limit on the number of uploaded applications.

3.6   Tolerating Failures

There are multiple ways in which AppScale is fault tolerant. The AppController executes on all nodes. If the AC fails on a node with an AS, that AS can no longer authenticate users for a particular GAE application but authenticated users proceed unimpeded. Users that contact an ALB to re-authenticate (acquire a cookie) are redirected to a node with a functioning AS/AC to continue accessing the application. If the AC fails on the node with the ALB, no new users can reach any GAE applications deployed in the AppScale instance and the developer is not able to upload additional GAE applications; extant users however, are unaffected. This scenario (AC on the ALB node failure) is similar to AC failure on the DBM node. In this scenario (AC on the DBM node failure), ASs and users are unaffected.

The database system continues to function as long as at least one DBS is available. Similarly, the system is tolerant to failure of the PBServer (DBM front-end). If the PBServer fails on the DBM, the ASs will temporarily be unable to reach the database until the AC on the node restarts the PBServer. The ASs are not able to continue to execute (GAE applications will fail) if the DBM goes down or becomes unreachable. In this scenario, the ALB will restart the DBM component but unless the data from the original DBM is available to restore, the restart is similar to restarting AppScale.

Although, coupling multiple components per node reduces the number of nodes (resource requirements) and potentially better utilizes underlying resources, it also increases the likelihood of failure. For example, if all components are located in a single node, node failure equals system failure. If the node containing the ALB and DBM fails, the system fails. In these scenarios, component failure does not equal node failure however; the AC in the head node will attempt to restart components as described previously. The DBM issues 3 replicas of tables for DBSs to

Table 1. Benchmarks Statistics. For each benchmark, Column 2 is its description and Column 3 is its number of lines of code (Python/JavaScript). Column 4 is the number of transactions in the Grinder user loop that we use to load the system in our experiments.

Benchmark	Description	LOC Python or JavaScript	Trans-actions in Loop
cccwiki	user-defined webpage creation	289/10948	74
guestbook	presents last 10 signatures on a page; users can sign as well	81/0	9
shell	an interactive Python shell via a webpage	308/6100	14
tasks	to-do list manipulation	485/1248	44

store, thus user data is available on failure of any individual DBS component. We are investigating the various failure scenarios and techniques for tolerating them within a deployed AppScale system as part of ongoing and future work.

We distribute AppScale as a single Linux image and the AppScale Toolset. The image contains the code for the implementation of all of the components and a 64-bit Linux kernel and Ubuntu distribution. The system is available from http://appscale.cs.ucsb.edu/; all new programs that we have contributed carry the Berkeley Software Distribution (BSD) License.

4   Evaluation

We next present the basic performance characteristics of AppScale default deployment. We note that we have not optimized AppScale in any way and that this study presents a baseline from which we will work to improve the performance and scalability of the system over time. Our goal with AppScale to provide a research framework for the community, thus, we and others will likely identify ways to improve its performance over time. We simply provide a framework with which to investigate existing open source GAE applications, services, and execution characteristics using local cluster resources.

4.1   Methodology

For our experimental methodology, we investigate four open source GAE applications made available as Google AppEngine Samples (http://code.google.com/p/google-app-engine-samples/). The applications are Python programs and Python/JavaScript programs. We overview them and their basic characteristics in Table 1. The cccwiki and tasks applications require the user to log in. Each application uses the AppScale datastore for all data manipulation. We record a user session that we replay for an increasing number of users repeatedly using the Grinder load testing framework (http://grinder.sourceforge.net) and its extensions [18].

For each experiment, we investigate two metrics, **(i) the total number of transactions completed over a five second interval**, and **(ii) the average**

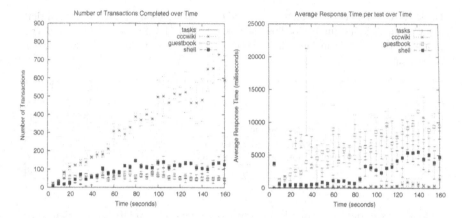

Fig. 2. Application performance under stress: Transactions over time (left) and average response time (right). The x-axis is time in seconds; Grinder introduces three additional users for load every 5 seconds. In the left graph each point is the number of transactions that completed in that interval, on average across five runs (y-axis). In the right graph, each point is the average response time across the transactions that began in that interval, on average across five runs (y-axis).

response time for transactions that start during the interval. Specifically, each *Grinder user* repeatedly executes a series of transactions (Table 1 Column 3). The *user* repeats this loop for 160 seconds. Grinder adds three users every five seconds to load the system.

For each five second interval in the 160 seconds of each test, we count the number of transactions that complete in that interval (for transactions completed per interval). For average response time, for each five second interval of the 160 seconds, we compute the average response time for the transactions that *started* in that interval. We repeat each experiment five times and compute the average and standard deviation for each interval across all of the runs.

Our cluster consists of quad-core 2.66GHz machines with 8GB RAM connected via gigabit Ethernet. We employ three of these machines for Grinder load generators. The machines are synchronized and each Grinder instance introduces a single user every five seconds. We specify the number of machines we use for the AppScale deployment with each experiment below.

4.2 Experimental Results

We first present data for each application, executed in isolation over App-Scale, over time and increasing load. For this experiment, we employ the default AppScale configuration: one head node (ALB+DBM) and three slave nodes (AS+DBS each) with each node/guestVM on its own machine. Each of the three Grinder machines accesses the AS of one slave node.

Figure 2 shows the results. The left graph is transactions over time (higher is better), the right graph is average response time (lower is better). Each graph

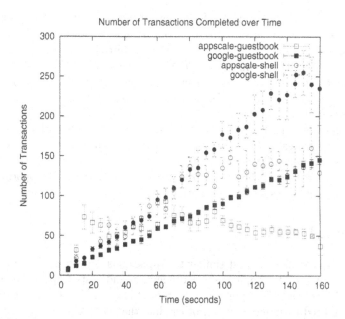

Fig. 3. Transactions over time under increasing load (3 users per 5 seconds) for two applications (guestbook and shell), when hosted by Google and AppScale

plots a point every five seconds. The x-axis is time and load: Grinder adds three additional users every 5 seconds. In the left graph each point, is the number of transactions that completed in that interval, on average across five runs (y-axis). In the right graph, each point is the average response time across the transactions that began in that interval, on average across five runs (y-axis).

All of the applications except guestbook tend to grow in the number of transactions as load increases. Guestbook's transaction count decreases after 100 seconds. This is because each guestbook posting increases the size of the database table. Our current (naive) implementation of database queries is to return the entire table to the node so that we can apply any filters at the GAE client side. As the database grows, each call is more expensive. We are currently extending our query process to return only the individual entries required, to address this issue. Cccwiki scales much better because each transaction only modifies an existing page, altering an entry in the table, as opposed to creating a new entry as guestbook does.

We also evaluated the difference between executing the four guestVMs on a single (quadcore) machine versus on individual machines. We find that we achieve very similar results for both for transactions completed and response time. This is interesting since it shows that the overhead of virtualization and co-location of virtual machines on these systems is not the performance bottleneck at this point. We find that in some cases the single machine case outperforms the distributed case due to network communication. This indicates that it may be beneficial to consider co-location of interoperating AppScale components for some behaviors and applications.

Finally, we investigate how AppScale performs relative to the Google proprietary infrastructure to better understand our baseline performance. We consider guestbook and shell applications since neither require the user to log in. We execute these applications using a Google AppEngine account. Figure 3 shows the results for transactions completed over time. AppScale transaction counts are more variable and do not scale for guestbook as load increases. Shell over AppScale scales up to a time/load of 80s. Google transaction counts scale perfectly. For response times (not shown) for guestbook Google consistently responds in 290-330ms regardless of load. For shell, Google's response time is more variable but still within a similar range. Shell performs more computation per request than guestbook. Google therefore starts to deny resources to the application at 150 seconds due to resource consumption limitations.

5   Related Work

The open-source offering most similar to AppScale is AppDrop [2]. AppDrop is a simple Ruby-on-Rails application that emulates and hosts AppEngine applications on Amazon's EC2. AppDrop is a proof-of-concept that GAE applications can be executed in an environment other than that of Google.

There are multiple differences between AppScale and AppDrop. First, AppDrop (and any GAE applications that execute using it) is hosted entirely using a single guestVM image, which places significant limitations on IaaS usage/accounting, performance, scalability, and fault tolerance. The AppDrop progenitor uses his own EC2 account to host GAE applications on behalf of GAE developers. Thus, AppDrop is responsible for all EC2 charges and resource use as well as any "bad behavior" by the GAE applications. Each AppScale instance and its GAE applications is deployed and "owned" by each individual GAE developer.

AppDrop implements the flat file database integrated in GAE SDK development server for its datastore. This system is not distributed, scalable, or fault tolerant. AppDrop also employs a secondary database (implemented using Rails ActiveRecord and PostGreSQL) to store and retrieve the user's session data. AppScale uses the same distributed and fault tolerant database infrastructure as it does for its GAE applications and facilitates any database to be "plugged into" AppScale. AppScale currently integrates HBase, Hypertable, MySQL, Cassandra, and Voldemort as distributed, fault tolerant datastore options.

6   Conclusions

We present AppScale, an open source PaaS cloud computing research framework that emulates the Google AppEngine-based cloud offering. AppScale is easy to use and to extend and automatically deploys itself and GAE applications over Xen-based cluster resources and IaaS clouds such as Amazon EC2 and EUCALYPTUS. AppScale implements a number of different components that facilitate deployment of GAE applications using local (non-proprietary resources).

Moreover, AppScale provides a framework with which cloud researchers and application developers can investigate new techniques (services, tools, schedulers, optimizations), and the performance and behavior of these techniques, and for real (GAE) applications.

References

1. Amazon Web Services, http://aws.amazon.com/
2. AppDrop, http://jchris.mfdz.com
3. Microsoft Azure Service Platform, http://www.microsoft.com/azure/
4. Brin, S., Page, L.: The anatomy of a large-scale hypertextual web search engine. In: Computer Networks and ISDN Systems, pp. 107–117 (1998)
5. Burrows, M.: The Chubby Lock Service for Loosely-Coupled Distributed Systems. In: OSDI 2006: Seventh Symposium on Operating System Design and Implementation (2006)
6. Cassandra, http://incubator.apache.org/cassandra/
7. Chandra, T., Griesemer, R., Redstone, J.: Paxos Made Live - An Engineering Perspective. In: PODC 2007: 26th ACM Symposium on Principles of Distributed Computing (2007)
8. Chang, F., Dean, J., Ghemawat, S., Hsieh, W., Wallach, D., Burrows, M., Chandra, T., Fikes, A., Gruber, R.: Bigtable: A Distributed Storage System for Structured Data. In: Proceedings of 7th Symposium on Operating System Design and Implementation (OSDI), pp. 205–218 (2006)
9. Dean, J., Ghemawat, S.: MapReduce: Simplified Data Processing on Large Clusters. In: Proceedings of 6th Symposium on Operating System Design and Implementation (OSDI), pp. 137–150 (2004)
10. Django, http://www.djangoproject.com/
11. Elastra Inc., http://www.elastra.com
12. Ghemawat, S., Gobioff, H., Leung, S.-T.: The Google File System. In: 19th ACM Symposium on Operating Systems Principles (2003)
13. Google AppEngine, http://code.google.com/appengine/
14. Hadoop, http://hadoop.apache.org/core/
15. Lamport, L.: The Part-Time Parliament. ACM Transactions on Computer Systems (1998)
16. Mongrel, http://mongrel.rubyforge.org
17. MySQL, http://www.mysql.com
18. Nagpurkar, P., Horn, W., Gopalakrishnan, U., Dubey, N., Jann, J., Pattnaik, P.: Workload characterization of selected jee-based web 2.0 applications. In: Workload Characterization, IISWC 2008. IEEE International Symposium on Workload Characterization (IISWC), September 2008, pp. 109–118 (2008)
19. Nginx, http://www.nginx.net
20. Nurmi, D., Wolski, R., Grzegorczyk, C., Obertelli, G., Soman, S., Youseff, L., Zagorodnov, D.: Eucalyptus: A technical report on an elastic utility computing architecture linking your programs to useful systems. UCSB Technical Report ID: 2008-10 (2008)
21. Protocol Buffers. Google's Data Interchange Format, http://code.google.com/p/protobuf

22. Rightscale Inc., http://www.rightscale.com/
23. Ruby on Rails, http://www.rubyonrails.org
24. Salesforce Customer Relationships Management (CRM) System,
    http://www.salesforce.com/
25. I. Sun Microsystems. White paper: Java(TM) 2 Platform Micro Edition
    (J2ME(TM)) Technology for Creating Mobile Devices (May 2000),
    http://java.sun.com/products/cldc/wp/KVMwp.pdf
26. Voldemort, http://project-voldemort.com/

Cloud Computing Infrastructure

Track Session 2

Mitigating Security Threats to Large-Scale Cross Border Virtualization Infrastructures[*]

Philippe Massonet[1], Syed Naqvi[1], Francesco Tusa[2], Massimo Villari[2], and Joseph Latanicki[3]

Centre d'Excellence en Technologies de l'Information et de la Communication
{Syed.Naqvi,Philippe.Massonet}@cetic.be
Università degli Studi di Messina, Facoltà di Ingegneria
{mvillari,ftusa}@unime.it
Thales
Joseph.Latanicki@thalesgroup.com

Abstract. Cloud Computing is being a computation resources platform where it is possible to make up an environment flexible and scalable able to host any kind of services. In Cloud Computing, virtualization technologies provide all the needful capabilities to deploy services and run applications in an easy way. Furthermore, large-scale cross border virtualization infrastructures present promising landscape to cope with the ever increasing requirements of modern scientific and business applications.

The large-scale cross border virtualization infrastructures can be seen as a federation of heterogeneous clouds. We present pragmatic analysis of the potential threats posed to the emerging large-scale cross border virtualization infrastructures. We have taken into consideration both *internal* and *external* threats to these infrastructures. We also drive the discussion considering a real model of cloud. In particular an *infrastructure cloud* is briefly presented; a useful scenario where to assess security threats and apply security solutions, that is the European Project, RESERVOIR.

Keywords: Cloud Computing, Security Architecture, Threats modelling, Virtualization infrastructure.

1 Introduction

Currently available cloud architectures do not strongly address security necessities [1,2]. Security has to be considered as an integral part of the development process rather than being later addressed as an add-on feature. The conception of a comprehensive security model requires a realistic threat model. Without such a threat model, security designers risk wasting time and effort implementing safeguards that do not address any realistic threat. Or, just as dangerously,

---

[*] The research leading to the results presented in this paper has received funding from the European Union's seventh framework programme (FP7 2007-2013) Project RESERVOIR under grant agreeement number 215605.

D.R. Avresky et al. (Eds.): Cloudcomp 2009, LNICST 34, pp. 73–82, 2010.
© Institute for Computer Sciences, Social-Informatics and Telecommunications Engineering 2010

they run the risk of concentrating their security measures on one threat while leaving the underlying architecture dangerously exposed to others.

In this paper, we drive the discussion considering a real model of cloud. In particular an *infrastructure cloud* is briefly presented, where it is possible to assess the security aspects through a meaningful scenario, that is the Resources and Services Virtualization without Barriers (RESERVOIR) [3]. The RESERVOIR platform presents concepts as virtualization infrastructure, VEEs, dynamic deployment, elastic and autonomic systems where all actions must to be performed in a secure way. Furthermore the dynamic management of computational resources among sites represents the main challenge to cope by the RESERVOIR cloud computing middleware.

Afterwords a brief description of RESERVOIR, we present a detailed analysis of the threats to large-scale cross border virtualization infrastructures. These threats are broadly classified into two major categories namely *internal threats* and *external threats* so as to complement the DolevYao threat model [4]. We also present some mitigating techniques to cope with these threats and position them with the existing solutions.

The paper is organised as follows: Section 2 surveys related works; Section 3 briefly covers RESERVOIR basic concepts, explaining its architecture, entities and stockholders involved. Section 4 presents all the threats that a cloud infrastructure may suffers by attackers. Sections 5 explains how to face the threats previously highlighted, providing some solutions, case by case. Section 6 finally concludes the dissertation.

2   Related Works

The term *Cloud Computing*, has recently become popular together with *Web 2.0*. Since such paradigm is mostly new, there are dozens of different definitions for Cloud Computing and there seems to be no consensus on what a Cloud is: the paper [5] aims to compare and contrast Cloud Computing with Grid Computing from various angles, explaining the essential characteristics of both. According to the authors, Cloud Computing is not completely a new concept; it has intricate connection to the existing Grid Computing paradigm and other relevant technologies. This paper offers a good starting point to identify the different kind of issues involved in cloud computing: the ones related to security represented a valid basis for our research.

Paper [6] refers to the threats analysis of those scenarios involving general computer systems: attackers and defenders both strive to gain complete control over them. To maximise their control, both attackers and defenders have migrated to low-level, operating system code. This paper assumes the perspective of the attacker, who is trying to run malicious software and avoid detection. By means of the proposed approach, the authors hope to help defenders to understand and defend against the threat posed by a new class of rootkit, called VMBR (Virtual Machine based rootkit), which install a virtual machine monitor underneath an existing operating system. As our main paper topic, the one of this work refers to the study of internal threats involved in the execution of virtual machines. Differently from our case, the study is not strictly related to Cloud Computing environments.

3   RESERVOIR - An Example of Large Scale Cross Border Virtualization Infrastructure

Nowadays, all the commercial cloud infrastructures do not provide any detail of whole components compounding their systems. As we already highlighted, in order to overcome to these limitations and survey however these type of cloud infrastructures, we performed our assessment on the RESERVOIR cloud scenario. In this section we briefly describe the RESERVOIR architecture (many more details are presented in [3]), hence we will opportunely address the security issues of a federation of infrastructure providers in the cloud computing context.

RESERVOIR will introduce an abstraction layer that will allow to develop a set of high level management components that are not tied to any specific environment. This abstraction involves a federation of heterogeneous physical infrastructures. As shown by Figure 1 (reference architecture), in RESERVOIR, more sites (site A and site B) can share physical infrastructure resources on which service applications can be executed. All the entities depicted by the picture are explained just below.

Every site is partitioned by a virtualization layer into virtual execution environments (VEEs). These environments are fully isolated runtime modules that abstract away the physical characteristics of the resource and enable sharing. The virtualized computational resources, alongside with the virtualization layer and

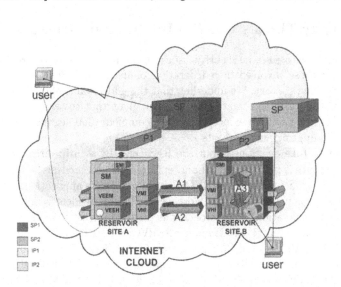

Fig. 1. RESERVOIR reference architecture: a federation of heterogeneous physical infrastructures

all the management enablement components, are referred to as the VEE Host. A service application is a set of software components which work to achieve a common goal. Each component of such service application is executed in a dedicated VEE. These VEEs are placed on the same or different VEE Hosts within the site, or even on different sites, according to automated placement policies that govern the site. Neither Service Provider (SP) nor final User are aware of the real mapping between service application and hardware resources. In RESERVOIR's model, there is a separation between SP (e.g. ebay, or Salesforce) and Infrastructure Providers (IP - Amazon, Google, Flexiscale, etc.). SP are the entities that understand the needs of particular business and offer service applications to address those needs. SPs do not have the computational resources needed by these service applications, instead, they lease resources from a cloud, which provides them with a seemingly infinite pool of computational resources.

RESERVOIR clouds installed on each site present three different layers (see Figure 1 RESERVOIR Site A) described as follows:

- Service Manager (SM): it is responsible for the instantiation of the service application by requesting the creation and configuration of VEEs for each service component, in agreement with SP performed with a shared manifest.
- Virtual Execution Environment Manager (VEEM): it is responsible for the placement of VEEs into VEE hosts.
- Virtual Execution Environment Host (VEEH): it represents a virtualized resource hosting a certain type of VEEs. VEEM issues generic commands to manage the lifecycle of VEEs, and VEEHs are responsible for translating these commands into commands specific to the virtualization platform abstracted by each VEEH.

4   Security Threats to RESERVOIR Infrastructure

In this section we assess the security issues raising in RESERVOIR architecture, highlighting those involved in a federation of infrastructure providers in the cloud computing context. We underline that the added value of our dissertation is not given by a simple threats classification, given that the work provides the gathering of more security concerns, with a complete (360 degrees) perspective of Cloud Computing environments.

In order to take decisions about the RESERVOIR security architecture, information security, policy creation and enforcement, an analysis of the various kinds of threats facing the RESERVOIR architecture, its applications, data and information systems is required. Moreover, in order to identify all the possible threats to federations of heterogeneous physical infrastructures, we provide a simple classification: 1) *within* a RESERVOIR site for all the interactions among VEEM, VEEH, and SM; 2) *across* the RESERVOIR sites for the SLA based VMI interactions between the VEEMs of different RESERVOIR sites; 3) *outside* the RESERVOIR sites for the interaction between SM and SP (SMI). Actually, the threats reported in item 1 and 2 are quite similar. The communication can be affected by the same type of threats. The vulnerability appears during the communication between entities and it is also present in all the network interfaces. The communications can be categorised as follows: *horizontal communication* (parallelepipeds P1 and P2, arrows A1 and A2); *vertical communication* (vertical arrow A3).

The endpoints in the horizontal communication are both SMs with SPs and RESERVOIR sites (i.e Site A and B), while in the vertical communication the entities involved are SMs, VEEMs and VEEH in each site (i.e Site A or B). Horizontal communication exposes endpoints toward External Threats. The communications occur throughout Internet since there is an high level of risk. Vertical communication is the subject of Internal Threats. The SMI, VMI and VHI interfaces are located in External Threats.

4.1   External Threats

The Internet represents the same origin of threats for the communication across the RESERVOIR sites (VMI-VHI interfaces) and outside the RESERVOIR sites for the SMI interface (e.g. injection, identity theft and spoofing).

All the interfaces could be also exposed different attacks (e.g. denial of service, flooding and buffer overflow). These kind of threats are aimed toward provoking a *system crash*, leading to the inability to perform ordinary functions. All the interfaces (SMI, VMI and VHI), are affected by the same issues, but we have to underline the solutions in some cases are different. Considering the VMI and VHI interfaces, the RESERVOIR system administrator has the full capability to manage security policies and to apply them on both the sides (endpoints of site A and site B). Hence in RESERVOIR it is possible to select an its own security framework. While in the case of communication between SM and SP (SMI), the RESERVOIR cloud has to use a common security framework shared with many different partners. Since, it is necessary to solve the same issues under two different perspective views.

4.2   Internal Threats

RESERVOIR site has a logical representation with three different layers, but these layers can be compounded by one or more hardware components. Figure 2 gives an overview of these entities and relative mapping with a simplified view of the hardware. First of all, it is possible to split the site in two different virtual zones: *control and execution zone*. In the *control zone* there are: Service Manager (SM), VEEM (in bridge configuration between control and execution zone), network components (router, switch, cable, etc.), SMI/VMI interfaces and VHI internal interface.

In the *execution zone* instead there are: VEEH, VEEM (in bridge configuration between control and execution zone), VHI internal interface: VHI, network components (router, switch, cable, etc.), network storage: NAS, databases, etc and VHI/User Internet access interfaces.

The *control zone* can be considered a trusted area. Some threats can appear through the interfaces SMI and VEEM, since they fall into the same cases of

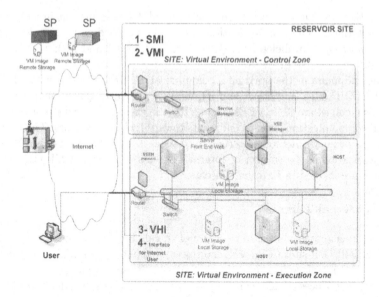

Fig. 2. RESERVOIR site: internal representation

external threats. The firewall located next to the router increases the trustworthiness. In this zone the weak ring of the chain is represented by the VEEM. It is the bridge between two areas, and it allows to exchange data among the zones. Figure 2 shows a firewall close to the VEEM, added to prevent any attacks from the execution area. The zone with high level of risk is represented by the *execution zone*. It can be considered as Demilitarised Zone (DMZ). This area shares has all the hardware components. The hypervisor (VEEH) uses the network, storage, CPU and ram (host) to load and execute all the VEEs. To better explain the role of each component it can be useful to evaluate chronologically all the phases necessary to execute a Virtual Execution Environment: VEEH, once all the requirements from VEEM are received, it downloads the VM Image from the SP, stores the Image into the NAS, it performs the setup configuration and executes the VM. The internal threats related with these phases can be classified as: 1) authentication/communication of SPs and other RESERVOIR site; 2) misbehaviour of service resource allocation due to malicious manifests; 3) data export control legislation: on an international cloud or between two clouds; 4) fake command for placement of VEEs and compromising data integrity of Distributed File System (NFS, SAMBA, CIFS); 5) Storage Data compromising (fake VEE image); 6) data privacy compromising; 7) hypervisor and OS security breaking; 8) data partitioning between VEE.

To avoid any fraudulent access, the VEEH has to verify *authentication/communication* of SPs and other RESERVOIR sites. Thus is the same behaviour analysed for all the communications in external threats. Relatively to later group of threats (3,4,5 - 6,7,8) RESERVOIR site has to guarantee different types of isolation, that is: runtime isolation, network isolation and storage isolation.

Runtime isolation resolves all the security problems with the underlying OS. The hypervisor has to provide all the solutions.

Network isolation is addressed via the dynamic configuration of network policies; virtual circuits that involve Routers and Switches (Virtual LAN) (See figure 2, there are more virtual circuits with different colours).

To avoid fake VEE image loading and do not compromise data privacy, *storage isolation* has to be performed and secure protocols has to be used. Protocols like NFS, SAMBA, CIFS are not secure. Virtual Execution Environment, downloaded from any generic SP, can expose the infrastructure toward back door threats, spoofing threats and malicious code execution (virus, worm and Trojan horse). The RESERVOIR site administrator needs to know at any time the state of threats, with a strong monitoring of the *execution zone*.

5   Mitigating Techniques for Security Threats

This section presents some security techniques that could be used to mitigate some of the security threats described in the previous section. It is by no means a complete and detailed description of the RESERVOIR security architecture that is required to cover all of the threats described in the previous section. This section does not argue on the isolation needed at hypervisor level (VEEH) (*runtime isolation*). These type of threats could meaningful compromise the whole architecture and they have to be treated in a careful way. Paragraph 5.6 highlights a possible solution able to reduce, and even remove all the risks related to *runtime isolation*.

5.1   Centralised or Decentralised PKI: Cross Certification?

One of the key security issue in a virtualized architecture is the identification/authentication of all the different elements which build up a Cloud. To be able to identify and authenticate such elements, one solution is to use a Private Key Infrastructure (PKI) based on certificates controlled by a Certification Authority (CA). But two solutions are available, a centralised or a distributed architecture. Another issue is raised by the fact that every architecture provider will have its own PKI. To solve this issues, one could use a cross certification process which will permit the use of every agreed CA certificates in the cloud, but this process is quit painful to run due to legal aspects. Another solution would be to create a root CA and then the PKI becomes fully centralised. This solution brings new issues such as, who is going to manage and run this root CA.

The choice of centralised or distributed PKI also depends on the centralised or decentralised cooperation between RESERVOIR sites. In the case of centralised cooperation a virtual organisation could be formed by relying on a unique certification authority. The virtual organisation could then provide authentication and access control for all RESERVOIR sites: cooperation would only be authorised between RESERVOIR sites that are members of the same virtual organisation.

However, in the case of decentralised cooperation between sites that form a loosely coupled federation, a distributed PKI architecture is more adequate. In this approach each site is responsible for establishing and managing trust relationships with other RESERVOIR sites. A potential security architecture for RESERVOIR could supports multiple certification authorities. This architecture introduces certification authorities (CA) and a new component for each site, an LDAP slave server. CA entities can be external, e.g. Verisign or Digital Signature Trust Company, some sites can have their own RESERVOIR certification authorities.

The LDAP server represents the entity where it is possible to publish certificates of service providers (SP1, SP2, SP3 etc. etc.), service managers (SM site A, SM site B, SM site C etc.), VEEM (VEEM site A, VEEM site B, VEEM site C etc.), as well as relationships between sites and VEEH (VEEH of site A, VEEH of site B, etc.) and relationships between VEE and service providers (VEE1 belong to SP1, VEE2 belong to SP2, VEE3 belong to SP3 etc.). In a Master/Slave configuration each site has a consistent copy of all information.

5.2   Ciphering: Communications, Data, Customer Data in the Management

One of the major threats in a virtualized architecture is about the communications and data confidentiality. Many technical solutions are available, such as Secure Socket Layer (SSL), IPSEC... One has to be careful to use the right algorithm and the right key length to be sure of the robustness to the solution. Speaking of keys, some issues raise. Who is delivering keys, how are they distributed? A good way is to use the TPM component which is mainly built for this purpose. It could be used also to generate keys to ciphered data, but what about the key recovery process issue. How to recover the key used to cipher data when this key has been lost.

5.3   Virtual or Physical Firewalls

Obviously, there will be firewalls in a virtualized architecture, but we can use physical or virtual one. Physical firewalls are well known and described. Some of them are certified and we know a lot about their security. Some virtual firewall are now available, and it seem more elegant to use them in a virtualized architecture. On both type of firewall, an issue is raised about their management. Some new threats should be taken into account. A simple human error could brake the full isolation (this threat exists also in a standard architecture). In that case traceability of the administration activity should be available to be able to build organisation processes to avoid such errors. This traceability which could available to the Cloud service provider as to the user, could be a good way to inspire confidence in a Cloud Computing architecture.

5.4   Virtual Switches: VLAN in the Architecture

Virtual LAN Network (VLAN) technology is well use, accepted in the IT world and can be used in a virtualized architecture. As for firewall some virtual switches begin to be available in these architecture. These VLAN can be used to isolate networks, but again as for firewalls the administration issue has to be solve and traceability is a possible way to help to solve it.

5.5 Securing Migration of VEEs

The security of migration of VEE between different RESERVOIR sites that have different security policies must be addressed. One approach to securing migration is to use security profiles. The service provider that submits a service manifest to a primary RESERVOIR site also needs to provide a required security profile. Submission to the RESERVOIR site would only be authorised if the required security profile matches the infrastructure security profile of the primary RESERVOIR site. Migration of VEEs to a destination site would only be authorised if the required security profile matches the destination security profile.

A security profile is defined in terms of security features found at each site such as the use of HTTPS, a firewall, an encrypted file system, a VPN tunnel or a VLAN. Security profiles is ordered from less secure to more secure. This ordering between security profiles provides the basis for comparing and matching security profiles.

5.6 Mitigating Techniques through the OpenTC Solution

Considering the architecture presented previously, many threats may be derived by the compromising of *runtime isolation*. The risks are carried out by the fact that a malicious software (malware) can be execute at VEEH level. These *malwares* could be installed either inside the VEEs or in between of hypervisors and hardware. Latest type of threats are well recognised in [6]. The authors underline the possibility to install a malware able to change the boot sequence. In our cloud platform, we don't have to make an in-dept introspection of hypervisors' functionalities. But, the architecture needs to monitor the hypervisor's behaviour and verify its authenticity and integrity.

Therefore, our cloud implementation we are developing, has to guarantee isolation at VEEH level and it has to be able to avoid the probability that a malicious software gains the control of a site. In order to mitigate these threats, we identify a set of capabilities based on Trusted Computing (TC), and in particular through its open source implementation: OpenTC.

Trusted Computing is an effort to bring some of the properties of closed, proprietary systems to open, commodity systems. This is done using a combination of hardware and software components. Furthermore, these components allow to check and enforce the integrity of a system, and authenticate itself to remote systems. The hardware block that provides trustiness to whole system is called Trusted Platform Module (TPM), that is tamper-resistant and has an embedded private key. This component is able to assure the identification of all the hardware or software components of the architecture, but it has to be available on all the equipments which is not always the case. Although TC is controversial as the hardware is not only secured for its owner, but also secured against its owner as well, we think, its feature may really increase the trustiness in Cloud Computing.

6 Conclusions and Perspectives

We have presented a pragmatic analysis of a range of potential threats to the emerging large-scale cross border virtualization infrastructures. The focal point of this work was cloud computing architectures. In the detailed presentation of these threats and their impact on the overall functioning of clouds is elaborated. We have also explored various security solutions to effectively address the security requirements of virtualization infrastructures. It is important to remember that security is a process, the threat picture is always changing, and threat analysis needs to be continuously updated. In other words, virtualization infrastructure should be subject to constant review and upgrade, so that any security loophole can be plugged as soon as it is discovered.

We are working on a comprehensive security model for a reference architecture of Cloud deployment. We plan to use this threats analysis in defining various core functionalities of the eventual security solutions.

References

1. Amazon Web Services: Overview of Security Processes,
   http://s3.amazonaws.com/aws_blog/AWS_Security_Whitepaper_2008_09.pdf
2. Comprehensive review of security and vulnerability protections for Google Apps,
   http://www.google.com/a/help/intl/en/admins/pdf/
   ds_gsa_apps_whitepaper_0207.pdf
3. Juan Caceres, R.M., Rochwerger, B.: Reservoir: An architecture for services, the first issue of the reservoir architecture document (June 2008),
   http://www.reservoir-fp7.eu/twiki/pub/Reservoir/Year1Deliverables/
   080531-ReservoirArchitectureSpec-1.0.PDF
4. Dolev, D., Yao, A.C.: On the Security of Public Key Protocols. In: Proceedings of the IEEE 22nd Annual Symposium on Foundations of Computer Science, pp. 350–357 (1982)
5. Foster, I., Zhao, Y., Raicu, I., Lu, S.: Cloud Computing and Grid Computing 360-Degree Compared. In: Grid Computing Environments Workshop, GCE 2008, November 2008, pp. 1–10 (2008)
6. King, S.T., Chen, P.M., Wang, Y., Verbowski, C., Wang, H.J., Lorch, J.R.: Subvirt: Implementing malware with virtual machines. In: SP 2006: Proceedings of the 2006 IEEE Symposium on Security and Privacy, Washington, DC, USA, pp. 314–327. IEEE Computer Society, Los Alamitos (2006)

Activity Control in Application Landscapes

A Further Approach to Improving Maintainability of Distributed Application Landscapes

Oliver Daute and Stefan Conrad

SAP Deutschland AG & Co. KG, University of Düsseldorf, Germany
oliver.daute@sap.com, conrad@cs.uni-duesseldorf.de

Abstract. The system administration has been waiting for a long time for procedures and mechanism for more control over process activities within complex application landscapes. New challenges come up due to the use of linked up software applications to implement business scenarios. Numerous business processes exchange data across complex application landscapes, for that they use various applications, retrieve and store data. The underlying technology has to provide a stable environment maintaining diverse software, databases and operating system components. The challenge is to keep the distributed application environment under control at any given time. This paper describes a steering mechanism to control complex application landscapes, in order to support system administration in their daily business. *Process Activity Control*, PAC is an approach to get activities under central control. PAC is the next reasonable step to gaining more transparency and visibility to improving system maintenance of Cloud Computing environments.

Keywords: Cloud computing, complex application landscape, distributed infrastructure, process activity control, RT-BCDB, Code of business process.

1 Introduction

More transparency and control inside complex application landscapes is required [6] [9] since concepts like Cloud Computing [17], client-server architectures, service-oriented architecture [12], or IT service management [5] make it possible to build up giant networked applications environments. New mechanisms are required to ensure maintainability, evolution and data consistency in order to support the operation of the underlying distributed information technology. Cloud Computing infrastructures require control, virtualization, availability and recovery of their applications and data.

Process Activity Control (PAC) is the next step after the introduction of the *Real-Time Business Case Database* (RT-BCDB) [1]. The concept of PAC concentrates on the control of processes activities which are currently running within an application landscape. The goal is to avoid indeterminate processing states which can cause further incidents within a Cloud environment.

Most enterprise or service frameworks are focused on business requirements which have improved the design of enterprise solutions significantly but often with too little

D.R. Avresky et al. (Eds.): Cloudcomp 2009, LNICST 34, pp. 83–92, 2010.
© Institute for Computer Sciences, Social-Informatics and Telecommunications Engineering 2010

consideration for the underlying information technology. Operation interests are neglected and little information about how to run a designed enterprise solution can be found. A sequence of application processes (e.g. a business case) is able to trigger process activities across the whole landscape, uses different applications, servers and exchanges data. The challenge for the system administration is to manage these complex Cloud environments and to react as swiftly as possible to incidents [11].

The missing outer control mechanism is the fundamental idea for *Activity Control in application landscape*. Activity Control is an approach to having power over processes in order to reduce incidents, to gain more stability and to improve maintainability. PAC and RT-BCDB are able to improving the system administration in Cloud application environments significantly.

2   Terms and Areas of Discussion

The term *RT-BCDB* [1] stands for Real-Time Business Case Database and it is an approach to collecting and providing information about business process activities in heterogeneous application landscapes. In RT-BCDB information about run-states of active business processes are collected and stored synchronously. This information supports the system administration during maintenance activities of complex application environments and is an important source of information for the business designers as well. In detail, RT-BCDB stores information about business cases, business processes, process owner, history of previous processing, execution frequencies, runtime, dependencies and availabilities of processing units and applications. Knowledge about run-states of business processes is important for maintaining and controlling processes and applications [1].

A *Cloud computing environment* or *application landscape* or *application infrastructure* can consist of 'simple' applications, ERPs, legacy systems, data warehouses, as well as middleware for exchanging data and connecting software applications. Clouds are complex distributed application landscapes.

A *business case* combines *(cloud) applications* and describes a sequence of activities to fulfill specific tasks. Business cases make use of different applications and databases across a landscape with regard to the enterprise needs. A *business (application) process* consumes data or provides them and can trigger other processes or services. Processes which have a high importance, such as invoicing, are called *core business processes*. An *enterprise solution* is built up of several software components and information sources. It is designed by the business requirements. Business cases determine the tasks of the customer's enterprise solution.

3   The Idea

Process Activity Control is required because of the continuously increasing complexity of application landscapes driven by business requirements, modern tools and enterprise application frameworks which make it more comfortable to design enterprise application solutions [8]. The challenge for the IT administration is to manage these application environments in any situation. New mechanisms are required to assist the system administration in their work.

Frequently, incidents within application landscapes interrupt business processes while they are performing a task. The malfunction of a processing unit or of an application can cause business processes failure. Business processes need to be restarted or rolled back for completion to reach a consistent state within the business data logic. The increasing complexity of software solution is the number one cause of system failures [3].

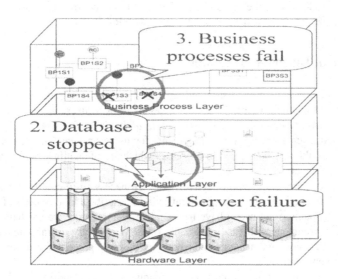

Fig. 1. Failure within the application environment

The idea of PAC is to minimize uncontrolled failure and reduce the amount of incidents. If problems within the application landscape are already known, for instance a database stopped processing then there is no reason for a business process to start with the risk of halting in a failure situation. PAC acts proactively and thus avoids disruptions when problems are known.

PAC also addresses another unsolved problem: the start and stop process of an application landscape or parts of it. It is still a challenge and complex matter to shutdown an application without the knowledge of dependent processes running within the environment. Business processes are triggered by different activators. At the moment, no outer control for business case in Cloud application environments is available.

The figure depicts a well-known situation in application environments without process control. When a server fails, all applications and database used to run on this processing unit will fail too. Business processes using these applications and databases will be impaired and must terminate immediately. In application environments without PAC this uncontrolled failure of business processes may result in unknown run-states or data inconsistencies.

From the perspective of a business case or an enterprise solution, a consistent state requires more than data integrity on database level. Also dependent interfaces or single process steps must be taken into considerations. Those can halt in an inconsistent state anywhere in an application environment. The challenge is to avoid these inconsistencies. The basis for this is the knowledge about business processes, dependencies, availabilities and run-states information. Our goal is to support the system administration in their work.

PAC works as an outer control mechanism for processes and is especially valuable in the control of core business processes. To interact with application processes, PAC makes use of RunControl commands. PAC is able to collect run-states and send them to RT-BCDB. PAC works best in collaboration with RT-BCDB.

4 Code of Business Processing

Various situations arise in distributed application landscapes because of missing form of identification. These are not easy to handle or to overcome in case of incidents. For activity control we propose a *Code of Business Processing*, CoBP. This code contains general rules and requirements for using an application environment. The code should only be applied to processes which are of significance for the enterprise solution itself.

Traffic laws are simple and effective. They are necessary to control and steer the traffic within a defined infrastructure. Traffic laws describe a kind of code of conduct which participants (road users) have to accept. It is an appropriate mechanism for a complex environment with easily learnable rules. We will try to translate some elements of traffic laws and network into a code for business processes used for complex application environments.

First CoBP: Each process must have a unique form of identification. This is required to identify a process and to steer the process while it is active. **Second**: Each process must have a given priority. The higher business processes must process first, unless PAC decides it differently. **Third**: Each business process must be documented. It must belong to a business case and visualization must exist. Procedures must be given for recovery purposes in case of a failure. **Fourth**: The higher a priority is the higher the charge for a business process. A process with a high priority does have a significant impact on all other processes that run within that environment.

Ideally, communication between processes should always take place on traceable ways. **Fifth CoBP**: Business Processes should use defined and traceable ways for processing. This forces the use of known interfaces, improves the traceability and supports the maintainability of Cloud application landscapes.

5 Basic Elements of PAC

Process Activity Control is an approach to controlling process activities in complex Cloud application environments. PAC is aware of the function states of processing units and applications. PAC will stop further processing in case problems occur within the application environment. This will prevent business processes running into undefined processing states.

PAC has to consider several issues in order to control process activities. A major task is, for instance, determining the function state of processes, applications and processing units. PAC can take advantage of the agents introduced with RT-BCDB.

The tasks of the agents are dependent on the kind of source of information. The agents inspect the given sources and try to identify run-state and availability information. On the hardware and application level, agents can search for a specific pattern in a log file to determine the function state. Application processes on operating system can be monitored as well to identify availability or throughput. A premature termination of an application process may point to a failure.

For smaller environments this mechanism provides information which is sufficient enough to control process activities. For large application landscapes PAC must also be informed of run-states of business processes. Therefore PAC will benefit when using the knowledge base of RT-BCDB.

The information is used to react to current circumstances within the application environment. PAC will try to avoid any starting of processes which will make use of a malfunctioning processing unit or impaired application or process or service.

Basic elements of PAC: a decision-control mechanism, a Custom Rule Set, the CoBP, an interface to RunControl, and a communication process to RT-BCDB.

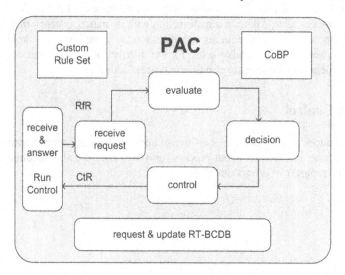

Fig. 2. Architecture of PAC

The decision-control mechanism is subdivided into four main activities: *receive request, evaluate, decision* and *control.* Each activity has one or more tasks.

Activity *'receive request'*, just receives the *Request for Run* (RfR) in sequence of income. Whenever an application process starts or stops or changes its run-state, then RunControl will send an RfR. The RfR contains the ID and the state of running.

Activity *'evaluate'*, evaluates the RunControl request against the information stored in RT-BCDB. The run-state table of RT-BCDB always reflects the status of process activities within the application environment. Any known problems with the availability of applications or processing units are taken into consideration.

The *'decision'* process is an activity based on CoBP, Custom Rule Set and the evaluation of the previous activity. A final decision will be prepared to return a *'Confirmation to Run* (CtR)' or to stop or to halt a business process or application.

The *'control'* activity is the steering part. It has two functions. The first function is to answer the RfR and to send a CtR. In case a business process must be paused, the *control* process waits to send the CtR until problems are solved. The second function is to stop business processes in case the application landscape has to be shut down. Vice versa *'control'* enables the start-up of business cases in a predefined sequence, for instance after system maintenance activities or after the elimination of incidents.

The *Custom Rule Set* contains customized rules given for a customer's application landscape. The rule set can contain an alteration of priorities or a list of business cases which have to run with a higher priority. Also preferred processing units can be part of the rule set.

Further basic elements are CoBP, described previously and the application interface which is used to communicate with RT-BCDB.

PAC as a control instance must monitor its own availability. Therefore at least two instances of PAC must run within the application environment. This is necessary to prevent that PAC is becoming a *single-point of failure* for the application infrastructure. One instance of PAC is the master instance and the second is functioning as the backup instance. If PAC detects a malfunction with its master instance then it passes control to the second instance. In normal operation the second instance should also be used to answer RfR. This makes sense for the distribution of workload of PAC and will avoid delays in the steering of business process activities.

6 Run-Control

PAC introduces an extension to *RunControl* commands. RunControl commands are used to receive information about process run-state. They are also required for controlling the progress of process activities.

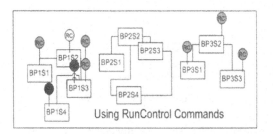

Fig. 3. Collecting Run-State

Whenever a process starts, stops or waits, the RunControl command will send a message with the process ID and the run-state. RunControl statements were first introduced with the architecture of RT-BCDB. There, RunControl statements are used to collect run-states and to store them immediately in the run-state table of RT-BCDB. Due to this an overview of current process activities is available at any time.

Several options are given to implement RunControl statements. One option is inserting RunControl statements into the source code. This makes sense especially for newly designed applications [2] [16] [14]. For existing applications adaptations are possible for instance during migration projects [13]. For sure, reverse engineering should be the preferred discipline to enrich the resource code with RunControl statements.

PAC adapts the concept of RunControl statements to its needs. The first change is to the business information flow [2]. Instead of sending run-states information using the agents, the RunControl statements send this information to PAC. PAC forwards the information to RT-BCDB. The second change is the extension of functionality. Each RunControl statement sends, in addition to run-state information, a *'Request to Run'*. The RunControl function waits until it receives a *'Confirmation to Run'* from PAC.

To distinguish between the two versions of RunControl statements, we will use an extended version for PAC and call it **RunControlAC**. The RunControlAC commands send the business case ID, run-state and an RfR.

```
RunControlAC(process-ID,run-state)
```

Fig. 4. RunControl for Activity Control

Certainly, some effort is needed for implementation of the RunControlAC. But with the constantly increasing complexity of Cloud application landscapes, a mechanism as described is indispensable for keeping distributed infrastructures under control. Consequently for the future design of business solution, applications should be developed with regard to run-state information or RunControl statements.

7 Improving System Maintainability

The aim of the concept is to gain more control over Cloud applications, as well as the prevention of incidents.

An example depicts how PAC is able to avoid incidents due to known problems. A failure of a server (processing unit) occurs and therefore an installed database must stop its processing. PAC recognizes this problem and stops further processing of business processes using the failed unit. Two business cases requesting to run are stopped by PAC and avoid indeterminate processing states. The application processes have to wait until the problem is solved. If a shadow database is available, PAC can move business processing to it.

PAC will make use of RT-BCDB information to decide the confirmation of a 'Request for Run'. If incidents to applications, processing units or business cases are known, then PAC will determine if a 'Request for Run' will make use of them. The run-states and availability information, stored in RT-BCDB, provides this important knowledge, as well as dependencies within the application infrastructure.

How to measure improvements in terms of *Return of Investments*? Some benefits are already shown and we will try to answer this question with regard to time, quality or money. We will start with time.

Time: Each incident which was prevented saves time. An incident costs time to identify the cause and time to solve. Additional time is needed for reporting and documentation of the solution process progress, and several persons of different departments are involved. Users are hindered in their work and will lose time. We assume that each incident costs in sum an average of 6 hours.

Money: Costs arise due to incident handling, software for incident tracking and support staff. Downtimes can cause less productivity and can result in fewer sales. In the worst case, especially in the area of institutional banks, an unsolved incident can cause bankruptcy within a few days [3].

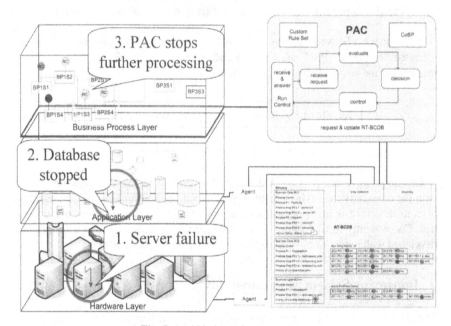

Fig. 5. Avoid indeterminate run-states

Quality is often not easy to measure. For Cloud application landscapes quality means availability, reliability, throughput and competitiveness. We assume that for large environments the investment in regard to the increase in quality will save money in the end. In smaller environments our concept will at least improve quality.

Maintenance tasks like updates or upgrades of the Cloud landscapes also require detailed information about the business processes possibly involved. PAC can prevent business process activities while parts of the application landscape are under construction. In case of performance bottlenecks, PAC is able to stop a business process in order to prevent that a problem from getting worse. Or PAC decides to shift an RfR to another Cloud application if possible. These are examples of how PAC is able to improving the maintainability of a Cloud application landscapes.

8 Extensions for Frameworks

Most enterprise or service frameworks are focused on the business requirements and neglect the operation interest. Concepts like SOA [12], IT Service Management [5] or

TOGAF [15] improve the design of application solutions but often with too little consideration for the underlying information technology. Business cases can be created easily by orchestrating services (composite application). But there is no information how to control them. No mechanisms are described how to react to problems within an application landscape. An active steering process is also not part of the frameworks. PAC is able to extend these frameworks and can reduce the TCO [4] significantly.

Virtualization, in the sense of representation, is one of the enablers of Cloud Computing infrastructures. Servers are pooled together acting like a large computing resource. Virtualization is the basis for new application platforms for managing distributed computing resources efficiently. Also process activities and their representation must be taken into consideration as presented in this paper. The goal is to gain more transparency and control over processes in order to reduce cost-intensive incidents and to avoid data inconsistencies on business process level.

Computing Clouds and the concepts, as mentioned above can benefit from the ideas of PAC & CoBP & RT-BCDB for gaining better maintainability and higher availability of an application landscape.

9 Conclusion

Maintenance and control of constantly increasing complexity of Cloud Computing environment are challenging tasks. New mechanisms as described are indispensable for keeping a distributed application infrastructure maintainable in the future.

PAC is a concept for gaining control, higher availability and better visibility of activities within Cloud application environments. Application processes will run into fewer incidents. The system administration can react more purposefully due to better transparency.

PAC is a further step to getting distributed application infrastructures landscapes under control. The concept works best in collaboration with the RT-BCDB [1]. Our ideas should encourage future research to invest more on these topics [7].

References

1. Daute, O.: Introducing Real-Time Business CASE Database, Approach to improving system maintenance of complex application landscapes. In: ICEIS 11th Conference on Enterprise Information Systems (2009)
2. Daute, O.: Representation of Business Information Flow with an Extension for UML. In: ICEIS 6th Conference on Enterprise Information Systems (2004)
3. Economist Intelligence Unit: Coming to grips with IT risk, A report from the Economist Intelligence Unit, White Paper (2007)
4. Gartner Research Group: TCO, Total Cost of Ownership, Information Technology Research (1987), http://www.gartner.com
5. ITIL, IT Infrastructure Library, ITSMF, Information Technology Service Management Forum, http://www.itsmf.net
6. Kobbacy, Khairy, A.H., Murthy, Prabhakar, D.N.: Complex System Maintenance Handbook. Springer Series in Reliability Engineering (2008)

7. Mei, L.: More Tales of Clouds: Software Engineering Research Issues from the Cloud Application Perspective. In: 33rd Annual IEEE International Computer Software and Applications Conference (2009)

8. Papazoglou, M., Heuvel, J.: Service oriented architectures: approaches, technologies and research issues, Paper. International Journal on Very Large Data Bases (VLDB) 16, 389–415 (2007)

9. Rosemann, M.: Process-oriented Administration of Enterprise Systems, ARC SPIRT project, Queensland University of Technology (2003)

10. Sarkar, S., Kak, A.C., Nagaraja, N.S.: Metrics for Analyzing Module Interactions in Large Software Systems. In: The 12th Asia-Pacific Software Engineering Conference, APSEC 2005 (2005)

11. Schelp, J.: Winter, Robert: Business Application Design and Enterprise Service Design: A Comparison. Int. J. Service Sciences 3/4 (2008)

12. SOA: Reference Model for Service Oriented Architecture Committee Specification (2006), http://www.oasis-open.org

13. Stamati, T.: Investigating The Life Cycle Of Legacy Systems Migration. In: European and Mediterranean Conference on Information Systems (EMCIS), Alicante Spain (2006)

14. Svatoš, O.: Conceptual Process Modeling Language: Regulative Approach, Department of Information Technologies, University of Economics, Czech Republic (2007)

15. TOGAF, 9.0: The Open Group Architecture Framework, Vendor- and technology-neutral consortium, The Open GROUP (2009), http://www.togaf.org

16. UML: Unified Modeling Language, Not-for-profit computer industry consortium, Object Management Group, http://www.omg.org

17. Vouk, M.: Cloud Computing – Issues, Research and Implementations. In: Proceedings of the 30th International Conference on Information Technology Interfaces (ITI 2008), pp. 31–40 (2008)

PerfCloud: Performance-Oriented Integration of Cloud and GRID

Valentina Casola[1], Massimiliano Rak[2], and Umberto Villano[3]

[1] Dipartimento di Informatica e Sistemistica,
Università degli studi di Napoli Federico II
casolav@unina.it
[2] Dipartimento di Ingegneria dell'Informazione,
Seconda Università di Napoli
massimiliano.rak@unina2.it
[3] Dipartimento di Ingegneria,
Università del Sannio
villano@unisannio.it

Abstract. Cloud Computing and GRID computing are two different but similar paradigms for managing large sets of distributed computing resources, and there have been many efforts that aim at integrating them. The *cloud on GRID* approach should provide to final users a simple way to manage their resources and to interact with the offered services. This paper proposes the *PerfCloud* architecture, which offers a set of services able not only to create Virtual Clusters (VCs) that become part of the GRID, but also to predict by simulation the performance of user applications. It also presents the `PerfCloudClient`, a user-friendly client with graphical interface to the *PerfCloud* services.

Keywords: Cloud Computing, GRID, Performance.

1 Introduction

Cloud computing, widely known after the success of the EC2 Amazon project [1], is an emerging paradigm, which is steadily spreading in the e-business world. In essence, cloud computing is based on the use of distributed computing resources that are easily allocated, de-allocated, migrated and possibly re-allocated on user request. As such, it relies heavily on the use of virtualization technologies (e.g., [2,3]), able to offer an almost unlimited amount of computing resources. Thanks to virtualization, which controls the access to physical resources in a transparent way, it is possible to offer computational resources that final users can configure as administrators, without any restriction.

On the other hand, GRID computing is basically a paradigm that aims at enabling access to high performance distributed resources using a service-oriented standardized approach. As such, it is widely diffused in the e-science world. In practice, GRID is born with the Globus project, and currently the Globus toolkit [4] and gLite [5] are the most relevant implementations available. In

D.R. Avresky et al. (Eds.): Cloudcomp 2009, LNICST 34, pp. 93–102, 2010.
© Institute for Computer Sciences, Social-Informatics and Telecommunications Engineering 2010

GRIDs, users can compose complex stateful services in order to build up complex and typically computation-intensive tasks. This is obtained by means of a middleware paradigm: every host has a GRID interface, and developers adopt middleware-dependent APIs for building up their applications.

In fact, cloud and GRID computing paradigms have many points in common: both adopt large datacenters , both offer resources to users, both aim at providing a common environment for distributed resources. The integration of the two environment is a debated issue [6]. At the state of the art, there are two main approaches for their integration:

- **GRID on Cloud:** a cloud IaaS (Infrastructure as a Service) approach is adopted in order to build up and to manage a flexible GRID system [7]. As in this context the GRID middleware runs on a virtual machine, the main drawback of this approach is performance. Virtualization inevitably entails performance losses as compared to the direct use of physical resources.
- **Cloud on GRID:** the stable GRID infrastructure is exploited to build up a cloud environment. This solution is usually preferred [8], because the cloud approach mitigates the complexity of the GRID. In this case, a set of GRID services is offered in order to manage (create, migrate ...) virtual machines. The use of *Globus workspaces* [8], with a set of GRID services for the Globus Toolkit 4 is the prominent solution, as in the Nimbus project [9].

Both approaches have positive aspects but also serious problems for overall system management, as the environments are very complex and managed through thin command-line based clients. In this paper, we essentially propose to use a Cloud on GRID approach, adopting the Virtual Workspaces GRID services to build up a Cluster on Demand (CoD) system. In other words, our system can create Virtual Clusters (VCs) on user request. These VCs are natively provided with support for high performance application development (HPC compilers, MPI, OpenMP, . . .). The newly created VCs are directly accessible through the Globus middleware (they contain a preconfigured Globus container) and so they contribute resources to the GRID environment.

PerfCloud, the architecture we are developing [10] and that is the object of this paper, offers a set of services able not only to create VCs on user request, but also to predict by simulation how fast the target application will run on the newly created system. This is an original approach, that can help the user to re-modulate the resources requested for his VC in order to meet his performance expectations. Alternatively, the performance predictions obtained through *PerfCloud* can be used for optimizing the application to be executed in the VC. For simulation purposes, target applications are described in a high-level description language (MetaPL); the performance predictions are obtained by a simulation environment named HeSSE [11].

From the user point of view, the use of *PerfCloud* is very simple. By invoking the GRID service VCService, it is possible to create the Virtual Cluster, to obtain an IP address to access it, and to build automatically a configuration file that will be successively used for simulation. An additional service (BenchService) runs a set of predefined benchmarks to characterize the performance of the new VC and measures the timing parameters needed by the simulator. Finally, the SimulationService accepts the high-level description of the application, runs the simulations, and returns the predicted response time of the given application on the previously created VC.

When a cloud is created on the top of a GRID, user access to services exploits underlying GRID access services. Moreover, all the security features of the cloud environment are implemented through the GRID infrastructure. Most state-of-the-art GRIDs, being oriented to HPC, offer only simple command line-based interfaces, and are not particularly user-friendly. We have implemented a client for *PerfCloud* that offers a simple interface to the virtualized resources. We will also present here the PerfCloudClient, an extensible metaclient component that makes it possible to invoke generic GRID services, together with specific performance-oriented *PerfCloud* services. PerfCloudClient is provided with graphical interface and is accessible through a tray icon on the host desktop. A small framework for writing new services makes it possible to define their graphical interfaces and to include them into the metaclient.

The remainder of this paper is structured as follows. In Section 2 we will illustrate the *PerfCloud* architecture. Sections 3 and 4 describe the main components of the architecture that enable the integration of the cloud and GRID environments, whereas Section 5 introduces the client that offers services to manage the infrastructure and provides graphical utilities for end-users. In Section 6 related work is briefly reported. Finally, the conclusions are drawn and our future work is sketched.

2   The PerfCloud Architecture

PerfCloud is a framework that provides performance prediction services in an e-science cloud. The design relies on the adoption of a set of grid services able to create a Virtual Cluster (VC) and to predict the performance of a given target application on that particular VC.

As mentioned in the introduction, *PerfCloud* builds a IaaS (Infrastructure as a Service) cloud environment upon a GRID infrastructure. The *PerfCloud* model of the infrastructure is a collection of clusters, each of which is composed of a front-end node (FE) and a set of computing nodes in a private network. Both the nodes and the network can be physical or virtual.

The clusters managed by *PerfCloud* participate in the underlying GRID and offer their computational resources to the GRID infrastructure. Their FEs host a Globus container and are certified within the GRID Virtual organization. The FEs also host job schedulers (such as PBS or Condor) to distribute the workload on their computing nodes.

Figure 1 describes the overall architecture of *PerfCloud*. The *PerfCloud* application client resides on a user machine (which has access to the GRID environment) and interacts with the *PerfCloud* system through invocation of GRID services. Furthermore, it manages GRID connections, also providing utilities for end-users as, for example, performance analysis services. The architecture provides different GRID services that enable the user to build up a new cluster as a GRID Virtual Workspace [8] with full access rights. The GRID services of *PerfCloud* also offer other performance evaluation services (simulation, tuning and benchmarking) that can be invoked to simulate and to predict the performance of the environment just built. In order to help user interaction with the clusters, *PerfCloud* offers a tunneling grid service that lets the users execute commands on the target clusters. Moreover, *PerfCloud* offers a set of virtual machine pre-configured images which can be adopted to set-up virtual clusters. The images are ready-to-use cluster configuration enriched with all the software needed to execute HPC applications (compilers, MPI and OpenMP platforms, Globus containers, job schedulers, ...).

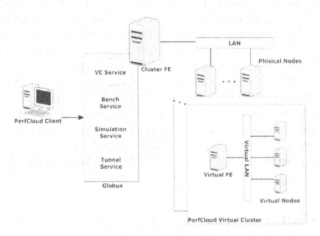

Fig. 1. The *PerfCloud* architecture

In light of the above, the *PerfCloud* architecture can be subdivided into three main components, as is shown in Fig. 1:

Services, which offer the *PerfCloud* functionalities to the GRID environment. The component implementation relies on a minimal set of four GRID services, named `VCService`, `BenchService`, `SimulationService` and `TunnelService`;

Images, which are the Virtual Cluster Node images, containing all the software needed to integrate the VC into the GRID environment (a GT container) and to offer services to the final user (a set of GS deployed on the VC container), along with other software needed for application development and execution (compilers, messaging libraries and run-time support, ...)

Client, which allows the final user to interact with the Cloud environment.

These components will be orderly dealt with in the next sections.

3 PerfCloud Services

The Services component is the core of the *PerfCloud* framework. It offers a minimal set of services, which add (virtual) cluster management capabilities to the GRID environment. The main service (VCService), which incorporates all the functionalities needed to manage the virtual clusters, has specific requirements (essentially, the Xen hypervisor) for the physical environment hosting the service. In the following, we will present a brief description of the service functionalities. The details about their implementation can be found in [10].

The VCService makes it possible to *design* a VC with the characteristics required by the user (number of virtual nodes, number of virtual CPUs for virtual node, network configuration, ...). It is important to point out that the physical system (usually a cluster) hosting this service has to be able to manage virtual machines, and so, in addition to the Globus workspaces, it requires the presence of the Xen hypervisor. The VCService service generates a file description that is used both for cluster creation and, possibly, for its successive simulation. It *creates* a VC, i.e., starts up on the cloud a set of virtual machine images, and allows to perform a performance evaluation of the newly created VC. This entails executing a set of benchmarks and storing their outputs, which are successively used for tuning the simulation model, evaluating the timing parameters typical of the VC created by the user. Since the information needed for building up the virtual cluster and the simulator configuration are similar, we defined an XML cluster description (see [10]). As shown in Figure 1, the VCs that are created and simulated in *PerfCloud* have the same organization of common physical clusters, i.e., they are composed of a Virtual Front-End (FE),which is the only node with a public IP address, and a set of nodes (slave machines) connected to the FE through a network (a private network built by means of Xen bridges).

The BenchService runs benchmarks on the virtual clusters and collects the results. The *PerfCloud* system provides a dedicated virtual image, which resides on one of the available physical machines (typically, on a machine not used for VCs). When this service is invoked, it starts up a wrapper Java runtime on the target virtual cluster, which launches the benchmarks. The results are collected on the Virtual FE of the virtual cluster, and successively returned to the service caller which stores the performance figures obtained for future use.

The SimulationService offers to the user a simple interface for predicting the performance of his application in a virtualized environment. The simulation package provides two main services: (a) HeSSEService, which accepts as input an application to be evaluated and returns the predicted response time; (b) TuningService, which tunes the simulator configuration to the target virtual cluster; it retrieves the simulator configuration from the VC resource, queries the DB for the benchmarking results and starts up the automatic tuning procedure to update the simulator configurations.

The TunnelService lets the user execute a given command on the target cluster resource, returning the standard output as result. Note that only a GRID-enabled user, i.e., a user owning a valid certificate, is able to execute the command. This service can be used as a base class for building up services from existing commands.

4 PerfCloud Virtual Clusters

The GRID services provided by *PerfCloud* rely on the availability of a virtualization layer on the physical clusters. In our development environment, all the physical clusters making up the GRID are configured using Rocks, a widely-used cluster distribution based on Red Hat Linux.The latest version of *PerfCloud* was tested on Rocks 5.1 with the Xen roll. The GRID middleware adopted is the Globus Toolkit 4, with the customizations offered by the Rocks GRID roll and a dedicated OpenCA certification authority. To exploit the GRID environment as basis for the cloud system, we adopted the GRID Virtual Workspaces version Tp2.2.

In order to let the above described architecture create virtual clusters, we built a set of scripts able to manage (create, destroy, pause, ...) a set of virtual machine images, pre-configured in order to define a cluster environment. The previously described **VCService** accepts an XML description of the clusters and invokes the scripts in order to setup the Virtual Cluster. The description lets the user choose the virtual cluster configuration and the distribution of virtual nodes on the physical cluster nodes.

The virtual nodes images reside on a cluster FE repository. When an user asks for a new virtual cluster, the images are duplicated and assigned to him. From that moment on, he can fully manage the virtual cluster through the GRID Services and the **PerfCloudClient**.

The virtual clusters created by *PerfCloud* are Red Hat Linux systems, configured with a large set of common HPC tools (gnu compilers, MPI, OpenMP, PBS and Globus). The virtual clusters are configured in order to communicate with each other through a private (virtual) network based on xenbridge. Only the virtual cluster FE has a public IP. The virtual clusters are preconfigured with a Globus container, with a certificate valid for the *PerfCloud* Virtual Organization, and host the **TunnelService**.

5 The PerfCloudClient

The cloud approach aims at offering the services of the GRID infrastructure to a large number of users, not only to the specialized ones, as highlighted by Shantenu Jha et al [6]. These consideration led us to develop a simple graphical interface that makes the interaction with *PerfCloud* very user-friendly.

Nevertheless, the main requirement for such an interface is to be easily extensible, in order to manage the continuous growth of new services, which will be made available to end users. The **PerfCloudClient** is a simple metaclient, presented as a tray icon. It is written in Java and so it is highly portable. The **PerfCloudClient** offers many functionalities to access the GRID infrastructure in a secure way (through the generation of a proxy certificate), to manage the connection, as well as further utilities.

According to the above notes, the scenarios are divided into three main use cases: Management of GRID Access and Connections, Management of *PerfCloud* Services and User Utilities.

5.1   Management of GRID Access and Connections

As we build up the Cloud environment on the top of GRID systems, we need to access to the GRID environment; the authentication procedure was developed by adopting the CoG Kit [12] and allows to generate a proxy certificate, as shown in Figure 2(a).

The access to a GRID environment is possible if the the environment has already been initialized and configured. As illustrated in Figure 2, the PerfCloudClient offers a setup procedure that enables the user to choose between the different GRID environments (the virtual organizations, top of the screenshot in Figure 2(b)), and possibly to launch the wizard for configuring the credentials (the SetupCertificate button and the wizard in Figure 2(c)). When a GRID environment is available, it is possible to choose the cluster to be accessed and to invoke the services.

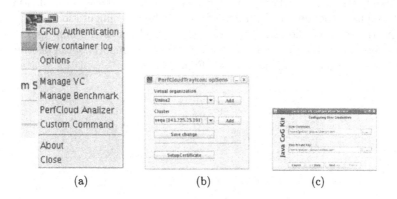

Fig. 2. Virtual Organization Setup procedure

It is important to point out that the PerfCloudClient is able to manage connections to multiple GRID environments (that offer *PerfCloud* services), and it is able to create virtual clusters on all of them. Moreover, once a VC is created, it appears in the list of the available clusters for the virtual organization in which it has been created.

5.2   Management of PerfCloud Services

The graphical interfaces that manage services are based on a simple template. This is composed of a set of buttons on the top of the window to invoke the services methods, and of a text box which reports the services output.

(a)   (b)

Fig. 3. Management of *PerfCloud* Services

As an example, let us consider the `TunnelService`, which allows a final user to execute a command on the selected cluster resource. Figure 3(a) shows the execution of the `ls -al` command on the target resource. Figure 3(b) shows the results of a `Log Viewer` command that invokes a customized version of the tunnel services and visualizes the log file of the Globus container.

5.3   User Utilities

Finally, the `PerfCloudClient` offers some user utilities that can be executed offline. Useful tools can be the graphical analyzer for performance evaluation, or the graphical tool for the definition of virtual cluster configurations.

At the state of the art, the Performance Analyzer is the only user utility available. It lets the user to build easily up graphical reports of the benchmarks performed on the virtual clusters (see Figure 4).

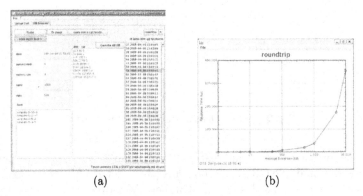

(a)   (b)

Fig. 4.   Analyzer User utility

6   Related Work - Cloud Technologies

The cloud paradigm appeared on the computing scene in 2005 with the Amazon Elastic Compute Cloud (EC2) [1]. Then a large set of related technologies has been developed. In commercial contexts, it is worth mentioning the IBMs Blue Cloud, the Sun Microsystems Network.com, the Microsoft Azure Services Platform, the Google App Engine and the Dell Cloud computing solutions. Most of these commercial systems adopt proprietary solutions (such as the virtualization engine by VMWare), and relatively few details are available on the adopted architectures. In the academic world, and especially in the HPC area, cloud computing is in "competition" with the GRID model, as outlined in [6].

The idea of GRID-Cloud integration and the adoption of virtualization techniques in GRID infrastructure was explored in research projects as Reservoir [13], and in technologies as openNebula [14] and virtual workspaces [8,15], with the derived cloud toolkit Nimbus[9].

At the state of the art, examples of e-science clouds are beginning to emerge [16,9,17,18]. They are based on the above-mentioned technologies and have architectures similar to the one presented in this paper, even if, at the best of the authors' knowledge, none of them provides performance evaluation and prediction tools as services integrated in the architecture.

As regards the user interfaces, both Nimbus [9] and openNebula [14], the prominent solutions for building e-science clouds, offer powerful clients. However, these clients are command line-based and do not provide any graphical interface.

7   Conclusions and Future Work

In this paper we have presented the architecture of *PerfCloud*, which offers cloud-on-GRID functionalities integrated with a simulation environment able to predict user application performance on the newly instantiated Virtual Clusters. The architecture of *PerfCloud* makes use of existing GRID and virtualization technologies to manage at low-level the virtual clusters, and integrates them in the existing GRID, also providing a dedicated set of services able to offer performance prediction functionalities. A client with graphical interface presented as a tray icon on the desktop makes interactions with users more straightforward and user-friendly than in any other existing cloud-GRID integration environment.

The main contribution of our work is undoubtedly the possibility to evaluate on-the-fly the performance of a given application on the particular VC received from the cloud. This is of great importance in the HPC world, where there is skepticism about the adoption of virtualization techniques because of the introduced overheads. Our research aims at making the resulting performance loss *predictable*. However, we think that the use of simple mechanisms to interact with the GRID/cloud is also an added value, as it may contribute to a wider diffusion of clouds in scientific and production environments.

As regards the evolution of our work, we will design services able to build up VCs tailored to the user performance requirements. In other words, the user will provide the application and the requested response time, and the system automatically will build up a suitable cluster. This will make it possible for the cloud to offer guarantees about the quality of service and to negotiate SLAs.

Acknowledgement. We wish to thank Raffaele Lettiero and Angelo Santillo for the technical efforts. This work has been supported by *LC3 -Lab. Pubblico-Privato di ricerca sul tema della comunicazione delle conoscenze culturali-* Nat. Project of MIUR DM1791 and by *Magda una piattaforma ad agenti mobili per il Grid Computing,* L.R. Campania n. 05 28/03/2002.

References

1. Amazon Inc.: Elastic compute cloud (2008), http://aws.amazon.com/ec2
2. Barham, P., et al.: Xen and the art of virtualization. SIGOPS Oper. Syst. Rev. 37, 164–177 (2003)
3. WMWare Staff: Virtualization overview (White Paper), http://www.vmware.com
4. Foster, I.T.: Globus toolkit version 4: Software for service-oriented systems. J. Comput. Sci. Technol. 21, 513–520 (2006)
5. Laure, E., et al.: Programming the Grid with gLite. Technical Report EGEE-TR-2006-001, CERN, Geneva (2006)
6. Jha, S., Merzky, A., Fox, G.: Using clouds to provide grids with higher-levels of abstraction and explicit support for usage modes. Concurr. Comput.: Pract. Exper. 21, 1087–1108 (2009)
7. Cherkasova, L., Gupta, D., Vahdat, A.: Optimizing grid site manager performance with virtual machines. In: Proc. of the 3rd USENIX Workshop on Real Large Distributed Systems, WORLDS 2006 (2006)
8. Keahey, K., Foster, I.T., Freeman, T., Zhang, X.: Virtual workspaces: Achieving quality of service and quality of life in the grid. Scientific Progr 13, 265–275 (2005)
9. University of Chicago: Nimbus project (2009),
   http://workspace.globus.org/clouds/nimbus.html
10. Mancini, E.P., Rak, M., Villano, U.: PerfCloud: GRID Services for Performance-Oriented Development of Cloud Computing Applications. In: Proc. of WETICE 2009, pp. 201–206. IEEE, Groninger (2009)
11. Mancini, E., Mazzocca, N., Rak, M., Villano, U.: Integrated tools for performance-oriented distributed software development. In: Proc. SERP 2003 Conf., USA, vol. 1, pp. 88–94 (2003)
12. von Laszewski, G., Foster, I.T., Gawor, J., Lane, P.: A java commodity grid kit. Concurrency and Computation: Practice and Experience 13, 645–662 (2001)
13. Reservoir Consortium: Reservoir project (2009),
    http://www03.ibm.com/press/us/en/pressrelease/23448.wss
14. Distributed Systems Architecture Research Group: Opennebula project. Technical report, Universidad Complutense de Madrid (2009), http://www.opennebula.org
15. Keahey, K., Foster, I.T., Freeman, T., Zhang, X., Galron, D.: Virtual workspaces in the grid. In: Cunha, J.C., Medeiros, P.D. (eds.) Euro-Par 2005. LNCS, vol. 3648, pp. 421–431. Springer, Heidelberg (2005)
16. Purdue University: Wispy project (2009),
    http://www.rcac.purdue.edu/teragrid/resources/#wispy
17. Masaryk University: Kupa project (2009),
    http://meta.cesnet.cz/cms/opencms/en/docs/clouds
18. Wang, L., Tao, J., Kunze, M., Castellanos, A.C., Kramer, D., Karl, W.: Scientific cloud computing: Early definition and experience (2008)

Combining Cloud and Grid with a User Interface

Jiaqi Zhao[1], Jie Tao[2], Mathias Stuempert[2], and Moritz Post[3]

[1] School of Basic Science, Changchun University of Technology, P.R. China
[2] Steinbuch Center for Computing, Karlsruhe Institute of Technology, Germany
jie.tao@iwr.fzk.de
[3] Innoopract Informationssysteme GmbH, Karlsruhe, Germany

Abstract. Increasing computing clouds are delivered to customers. Each cloud, however, provides an individual, non-standard user interface. The difference in cloud interfaces must burden the users when they work with several clouds for acquiring the services with expected price. This paper introduces an integrated framework that can be used by cloud users to access the underlying services in a uniform, cloud-independent manner. The framework is an extention of a graphical grid user interface developed within the g-Eclipse project. The goal of building a cloud user interface on top of a grid interface is to combine clouds and grids into a single realm, allowing an easy interoperation between the two infrastructures.

1 Introduction

Since Amazon announced its computing cloud EC2 [1] and storage cloud S3 [2], cloud computing becomes a hot topic. As a consequence, a number of cloud infrastructures have been established, both for commercial and research purpose. Examples are Google App Engine [13], Microsoft Live Mesh [15], Nymbus[8], Cumlus [16], Eucalyptus [5], and OpenNybula [4]. Currently, most of the cloud projects focus on Infrastructure as a Service and Software as a Service, but we are sure that other topics, such as Software as Platform as a Service and HPC as a Service, will be addressed in the near future.

Actually, cloud computing is not a completely new concept. It has similar features with grid computing. A detailed comparison between these two paradigms can be found in [11]. Grid computing has been investigated for thirty years. Many grid infrastructures, especially those at the international level, were well established. Hence, cloud computing will not replace grid computing; rather it provides the user community with additional computing platforms.

Grid computing has ever faced a problem: different middlewares have own requirement for accessing the infrastructure. This problem was solved by building an abstract layer to hide the middleware-specific implementation [7,14]. Cloud computing has the same problems. Currently, each cloud offers a different user interface, mostly command-line, requiring the user to install their client software and learn how to use the commands to request the services.

Our solution is an integrated, intuitive platform that can be used as a generic, standard interface to access any cloud. Users see an identical view, no matter which cloud is accessed. Furthermore, the interface uses graphical presentation, which is easier to operate than command-line options. Besides serving as a cloud interface, the platform

D.R. Avresky et al. (Eds.): Cloudcomp 2009, LNICST 34, pp. 103–111, 2010.
© Institute for Computer Sciences, Social-Informatics and Telecommunications Engineering 2010

is also a bridge to connect the cloud with the grid. In this case, we build the cloud user interface on top of an existing grid framework that was developed within the g-Eclipse project.

g-Eclipse [7,10] aims at providing a generic framework that allows users to access the power of the existing grid infrastructures via a standardized, customizable, and intuitive interface. This framework is designed for all grid users, operators, and application developers. Grid users can interact with grid resources in a simple, graphical way without having to know the technical details. For example, files can be transferred across grid sites by drag&drop; job submission needs only a mouse click. Resource providers can use the intuitive tools to operate and maintain the grid sites, manage the virtual organizations, and perform benchmarking. Application developers reduce the development cycle with the g-Eclipse support of remote building and deployment tools.

g-Eclipse is designed to support users of various virtual organizations. It uses a layered infrastructure with middleware-independent interfaces and middleware specific functionalities. Currently, standard middleware functionalities are provided.

This work extends g-eclipse with a cloud-independent infrastructure, including editors and views for service presentation and templates for supporting cloud programming models. Based on this infrastructure, various cloud platforms can be connected to the g-Eclipse framework with an individual implementation for accessing the specific cloud. This paper describes the design of the cloud infrastructure and the connection to the Amazon EC2 as an example.

The remainder of the paper is organized as following. Section 1 first gives an introduction to the g-Eclipse framework. This is followed by the concept and design of an integrated cloud user interface in Section 3. Section 4 describes our initial implementation of the proposed concept with EC2 and demonstrates how to access this cloud via the extended g-Eclipse framework. The paper concludes in Section 5 with a brief summary and several future directions.

2   g-Eclipse: Building a Framework to Access the Power of the Grid

The g-Eclipse framework was originally designed to provide a high-level abstraction for accessing grid infrastructures based on traditional grid middleware systems such as gLite [6] or GRIA [9]. It is build on top of the well-known Eclipse framework [12] and makes extensive use of its design-patterns. The abstraction layer – called the Grid Model – unifies the structure and functionality of grids in a set of well defined Java interfaces. Basic implementations of these interfaces for generic functionalities, as well as a UI layer, are provided to present and access underlying infrastructures in a standardized way. On top of these core parts, middleware specific implementations of the Grid Model can be plugged-in. This so called implementation layer enables the access to infrastructures based on the corresponding middlewares.

So far the g-Eclipse project has integrated two different middlewares, i. e. gLite which focuses on the scientific user and GRIA which targets industry and commerce. The current gLite implementation covers all use-cases foreseen in the Grid Model. Therefore, this part may be seen as finalized. The GRIA implementation is in an early

Fig. 1. Screenshot of the g-Eclipse user interface

state and mainly covers the grid user's use cases. Further development, e.g. for Globus Toolkit 4, is currently ongoing.

Fig. 1 shows a screenshot of the g-Eclipse framework for grid users. The left column of the platform is a Grid Project view where all projects created by the user are depicted. Project is a fundamental concept in g-Eclipse. It is the interface for any grid operations. Hence, a project has to be created before any action can be invoked.

The concrete view in Fig. 1 contains four projects where the last one, with the name of g-Eclipse, was expended. Each project consists of several folders for storing temporal files and for presenting information. For example, all established grid connections can be found in the folder "Connection". The lower window on the right side of Fig. 1 depicts the contents of this folder. The three connections are built for different machines to transfer data. Files can be moved from one machine to another by drag&drop. The folder "Job Description" holds all job descriptions that define computing tasks. A job description file can be simply created using a multi-editor shown on the upper side of the right column of Fig. 1. Users need only specify the executables and parameters, a job description with the grid standard is created automatically. The jobs can be submitted with a mouse click and the results are demonstrated in the folder "Jobs". The last folder is a specific one showing the VO related information, including the deployed applications, the computing and storage resources, as well as the available services.

Overall, g-Eclipse built a platform allowing an easy access to grid infrastructures. It also integrated tools for support application development. More importantly, it enables an interoperation between different grids. Therefore, we select this platform as the base for an intuitive, unified cloud user interface.

3   A Cloud Framework Based on g-Eclipse

We intend to develop a cloud user interface like g-Eclipse for the grid. The interface provides basiç functionalities for accessing a scientific cloud. This includes facilities for authority and authentication, for data management, for service deployment, and for accesses to the computing resources and services. It also contains tools for debugging and visualizing applications, for benchmarking, and for resource management.

Following the g-Eclipse architecture, the cloud interface contains a core and a cloud-specific implementation, where the core plug-ins provide the basic functionality to access a cloud platform. For this, an extension of the g-Eclipse core is essential to define interfaces for cloud specific functionality, e.g. cloud services.

In a cloud world, everything is observed as a service: hardware is a service, software is a service, and infrastructure is a service. Therefore, a cloud access interface must support the presentation, request, and deployment of services. The following components are required:

- A multi-layer editor for users to specify service request.
  A cloud service is combined with various parameters. Different services have also individual formation of the parameters. For example, CPU frequency and memory size are typical specifications for a hardware service, while version number and file size are parameters to describe a software package. The multi-layer editor allows the user to describe the requested services in detail.
- A view for showing the available services.
  The service view will be designed and implemented for presenting the services which are available in a cloud or requested by the users.
- An editor for service deployment and publication.
  Cloud developers or resource providers need an interface to describe new services and then publish them. Again, service related metrics and SLA values are necessary parameters. An editor will be provided for this task.

In addition, cloud computing has its own programming languages and models. Currently, MapReduce [3] is regarded as an adequate paradigm for writing cloud applications. It can be expected that more models will be designed in the future. We intend to develop templates to support application developers, with an initial implementation for MapReduce.

The functionalities listed above are common for all clouds. They form the base for accessing any cloud with g-Eclipse. Additionally, a specific implementation is required for each different cloud to cover its individual feature, in the same way that g-Eclipse handles different grid middlewares. The development work is currently on-going.

4   An Initial Implementation: Access the Amazon Web Service

For verifying our concept of building a cloud framework using g-Eclipse, we first extended this grid user interface with several cloud related components with respect to the Amazon Web Services. We then implemented additional plug-ins for accessing EC2. Theses plug-ins are responsible for handling AWS specific issues, such as accounting, running machine image, and logging in a machine.

Fig. 2. Screenshot of the VO wizard for creating an AWS VO

In the grid world, any user must be a member of a virtual organization (VO). To access a grid infrastructure with g-Eclipse, a VO has to be created or imported. Cloud computing does not apply the VO concept. However, we make use of this concept in the AWS implementation in order to specify the endpoints for accessing an underlying cloud infrastructure. A screenshot of the wizard for creating an AWS VO is shown in Fig. 2.

As shown in the figure, the VO wizard allows users to define a VO which can be later used to create a project. The user has to specify the name of the VO, the AWS access identifier, and the access points to the underlying clouds. This wizard is implemented for AWS, but can be directly applied for accessing other similar clouds, for example, Eucalyptus.

To use the Amazon cloud services, a user has to provide a secrete ID. This issue is solved in g-Eclipse by reusing its Authentication Token that is actually designed for grid authentication.

Fig. 3 shows the wizard for creating such a token. As can be seen, users can give their AWS credentials using this wizard. g-Eclipse then uses these credentials to create tokens and relies on the tokens to interact with the cloud for authentication.

Fig. 3. Screenshot of the wizard for creating an authentication token

As mentioned in Section 1, g-Eclipse uses the project concept for grid actions. This concept is reused for cloud operations. By creating a project bound to a cloud VO a user is able to query and access his personalized resources that are available from the specified cloud services.

Fig. 4 is a screenshot of an AWS project on g-Eclipse, where the VO folder is expanded. It can be seen that the cloud resources, like the Amazon machine images (AMI), are presented in the service subtree of the project's VO. These AMIs are listed in separate folders for distinguishing those owned by the user and those accessible to the user. Furthermore, the user's security groups can be managed within this tree.

From context menu actions a user is able to start instances of these AMIs by creating an Eclipse launch configuration. Fig. 5 shows the corresponding launch dialog that allows the user to specify various parameters such as the type and the number of instances to be launched. In addition, from this dialog it is possible to specify a payload file that is uploaded and made accessible to the running instances. This file is usually used to parameterize these instances. Once one or more instances have been launched they appear in the VO tree as computing nodes. These nodes may be accessed by using the integrated SSH console that is part of g-Eclipse.

After an instance is launched g-Eclipse offers the possibility to access this machine via a SSH shell. In order to use this connection method, the security group used to launch the AMI has to open the port 22 (ssh default port). Because the ssh connection method uses the Eclipse connection infrastructure, the ssh private key has to be inserted into the list of available keys. The running instances can be connected using an action in the context menu. This action opens the SSH login data dialog with the correct external DNS name inserted. The only parameter to be provided is the login name which is "root". There is no need for a password, since it is contained within the ssh private key. Fig. 6 shows a sample dialog.

Fig. 4. Screenshot of a project view with EC2

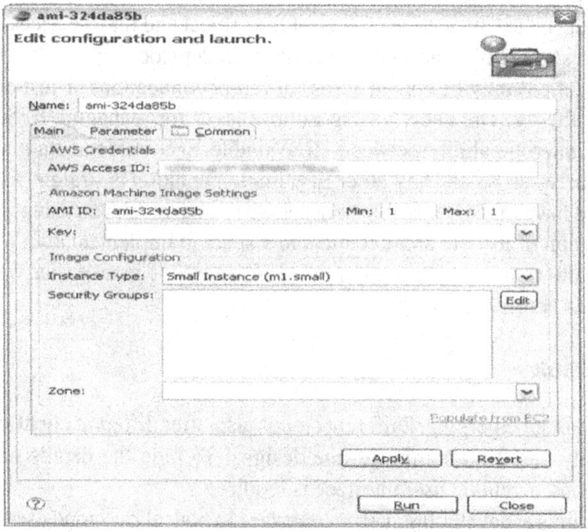

Fig. 5. Screenshot of the launch configuration dialog for launching an AWS machine image

Fig. 6. Screenshot of the SSH login wizard

The Amazon S3 service is integrated as an Eclipse File System implementation. The VO subtree of an AWS project lists the corresponding buckets as storage. From these storage items a user is able to mount these buckets as connections. Such connections appear afterwards in the Connections folder of the project and may be accessed within the project, in the same way of accessing any other folder (local or remote). Files located in these connections may be copied across different connections or just opened, edited and saved on the fly. The underlying g-Eclipse layer for managing EFS implementations ensures interoperability between all available EFS implementations. Therefore, file transfers between S3 and any other EFS implementation is straight-forward.

Overall, we have made it possible to access the Amazon clouds using g-Eclipse with a slight extension of its core architecture and a specific implementation for AWS. This achievement allows the user not only to access the clouds in an easier way but also to move their data across grids and clouds.

5   Conclusion

Cloud platforms are emerging. Different clouds also offer different client side interfaces that are mainly based on command-line designs. To hide the details of cloud client implementations, a generic user interface is required.

This work aims at developing such an interface to both allow cloud users to access the underlying infrastructures in a unified, graphical way and build a bridge between grid and cloud. The interface is an extension of an existing grid framework developed within the g-Eclipse project. To verify our concept, an initial implementation with respect to the Amazon Web Services has been completed. Currently, the entire cloud infrastructure is under development. Furthermore, implementations for connecting other cloud are also planned.

References

1. Amazon Web Services. Amazon Elastic Compute Cloud (Amazon EC2),
   `http://aws.amazon.com/ec2/`
2. Amazon Web Services. Amazon Simple Storage Service (Amazon S3),
   `http://aws.amazon.com/s3/`
3. Dean, J., Ghemawat, S.: MapReduce: Simplified Data Processing on Large Clusters. Communications of the ACM 51(1), 107–113 (2008)
4. Sotomayor, B., et al.: Capacity Leasing in Cloud Systems using the OpenNebula Engine. In: Proceedings of CCA 2008 (2008)
5. Nurmi, D., et al.: The Eucalyptus Open-source Cloud Computing System. In: Proceedings of CCA 2008 (2008)
6. Laure, E., et al.: Programming the Grid with gLite. Computational Methods in Science and Technology 12(1), 33–45 (2006)
7. Kornmayer, H., et al.: gEclipse- An Integrated, Grid Enabled Workbench Tool for Grid Application Users, Grid Developers and Grid Operators based on the Eclipse Platform. In: Proceedings of the 2nd Austrian Grid Symposium, Innsbruck, Austria (September 2006), `http://www.geclipse.eu/`
8. Keahey, K., et al.: Science Clouds: Early Experiences in Cloud Computing for Scientific Applications. In: Proceedings of CCA 2008 (2008)
9. Surridge, M., et al.: Experiences with GRIA - Industrial applications on a Web Services Grid. In: E-SCIENCE 2005: Proceedings of the First International Conference on e-Science and Grid Computing, pp. 98–105 (2005)
10. Wolniewicz, P., et al.: Accessing Grid computing resources with g-Eclipse platform. Computational Methods in Science and Technologie 13(2), 131–141 (2007)
11. Foster, I.T., Zhao, Y., Raicu, I., Lu, S.: Cloud Computing and Grid Computing 360-Degree Compared. In: Grid Computing Environments Workshop, pp. 1–10 (2008)
12. Gamma, E., Beck, K.: Contributing To Eclipse: Principles, Patterns, And Plug-Ins. Addison-Wesley Professional, Reading (2003)
13. Google. Google App Engine,
    `http://code.google.com/intl/de-DE/appengine/`
14. Malawski, M., Bartyński, T., Bubak, M.: A Tool for Building Collaborative Applications by Invocation of Grid Operations. In: Bubak, M., van Albada, G.D., Dongarra, J., Sloot, P.M.A. (eds.) ICCS 2008, Part III. LNCS, vol. 5103, pp. 243–252. Springer, Heidelberg (2008)
15. Microsoft. Live Mesh, `https://www.mesh.com/welcome/default.aspx`
16. Wang, L., Tao, J., Kunze, M.: Scientific Cloud Computing: Early Definition and Experience. In: Proceedings of the 2008 International Conference on High Performance Computing and Communications (HPCC 2008), pp. 825–830 (2008)

Cloud Computing Infrastructure

Track Session 3

A Performance Analysis of EC2 Cloud Computing Services for Scientific Computing

Simon Ostermann[1], Alexandru Iosup[2], Nezih Yigitbasi[2], Radu Prodan[1], Thomas Fahringer[1], and Dick Epema[2]

[1] University of Innsbruck, Austria
simon@dps.uibk.ac.at, radu@dps.uibk.ac.at, tf@dps.uibk.ac.at
[2] Delft University of Technology, The Netherlands
A.Iosup@tudelft.nl, M.N.Yigitbasi@tudelft.nl, D.H.J.Epema@tudelft.nl

Abstract. Cloud Computing is emerging today as a commercial infrastructure that eliminates the need for maintaining expensive computing hardware. Through the use of virtualization, clouds promise to address with the same shared set of physical resources a large user base with different needs. Thus, clouds promise to be for scientists an alternative to clusters, grids, and supercomputers. However, virtualization may induce significant performance penalties for the demanding scientific computing workloads. In this work we present an evaluation of the usefulness of the current cloud computing services for scientific computing. We analyze the performance of the Amazon EC2 platform using micro-benchmarks and kernels.While clouds are still changing, our results indicate that the current cloud services need an order of magnitude in performance improvement to be useful to the scientific community.

1 Introduction

Scientific computing requires an ever-increasing number of resources to deliver results for growing problem sizes in a reasonable time frame. In the last decade, while the largest research projects were able to afford expensive supercomputers, other projects were forced to opt for cheaper resources such as commodity clusters and grids. Cloud computing proposes an alternative in which resources are no longer hosted by the researcher's computational facilities, but leased from big data centers only when needed. Despite the existence of several cloud computing vendors, such as Amazon [4] and GoGrid [13], the potential of clouds remains largely unexplored. To address this issue, in this paper we present a performance analysis of cloud computing services for scientific computing.

The cloud computing paradigm holds good promise for the performance-hungry scientific community. Clouds promise to be a cheap alternative to supercomputers and specialized clusters, a much more reliable platform than grids, and a much more scalable platform than the largest of commodity clusters or resource pools. Clouds also promise to "scale by credit card," that is, scale up immediately and temporarily with the only limits imposed by financial reasons,

D.R. Avresky et al. (Eds.): Cloudcomp 2009, LNICST 34, pp. 115–131, 2010.
© Institute for Computer Sciences, Social-Informatics and Telecommunications Engineering 2010

Table 1. A selection of cloud service providers. VM stands for virtual machine, S for storage.

Service type	Examples
VM,S	*Amazon (EC2 and S3)*, Mosso (+CloudFS), ...
VM	GoGrid, Joyent, infrastructures based on Condor Glide-in [28]/Globus VWS [12]/Eucalyptus [21], ...
S	Nirvanix, Akamai, Mozy, ...
non-IaaS	3Tera, Google AppEngine, Sun Network, ...

as opposed to the physical limits of adding nodes to clusters or even supercomputers or to the financial burden of over-provisioning resources. However, clouds also raise important challenges in many areas connected to scientific computing, including performance, which is the focus of this work.

An important research question arises: *Is the performance of clouds sufficient for scientific computing?* Though early attempts to characterize clouds and other virtualized services exist [33,10,23,29], this question remains largely unexplored. Our main contribution towards answering it is:

1. We evaluate the performance of the Amazon Elastic Compute Cloud (EC2), the largest commercial computing cloud in production (Section 3);
2. We assess avenues for improving the current clouds for scientific computing; this allows us to propose two cloud-related research topics for the high performance distributed computing community (Section 4).

2   Amazon EC2

We identify three categories of cloud computing services: Infrastructure-as-a-Service (IaaS), that is, raw infrastructure and associated middleware, Platform-as-a-Service (PaaS), that is, APIs for developing applications on an abstract platform, and Software-as-a-Service (SaaS), that is, support for running software services remotely. The scientific community has not yet started to adopt PaaS or SaaS solutions, mainly to avoid porting legacy applications and for lack of the needed scientific computing services, respectively. Thus, in this study we are focusing on IaaS providers.

Unlike traditional data centers, which lease physical resources, most clouds lease virtualized resources which are mapped and run transparently to the user by the cloud's virtualization middleware on the cloud's physical resources. For example, Amazon EC2 runs instances on its physical infrastructure using the open-source virtualization middleware Xen [7]. By using virtualized resources a cloud can serve with the same set of physical resources a much broader user base; configuration reuse is another reason for the use of virtualization. Scientific software, compared to commercial mainstream products, is often hard to install and use [8]. Pre- and incrementally-built virtual machine (VM) images can be run on physical machines to greatly reduce deployment time for software [20].

Table 2. The Amazon EC2 instance types. The ECU is the CPU performance unit defined by Amazon.

Name	ECUs (Cores)	RAM [GB]	Archi [bit]	I/O Perf.	Disk [GB]	Cost [$/h]	Reserve [$/y], [$/3y]	Reserved Cost [$/h]
m1.small	1 (1)	1.7	32	Med	160	0.1	325, 500	0.03
m1.large	4 (2)	7.5	64	High	850	0.4	1300, 2000	0.12
m1.xlarge	8 (4)	15.0	64	High	1690	0.8	2600, 4000	0.24
c1.medium	5 (2)	1.7	32	Med	350	0.2	650, 1000	0.06
c1.xlarge	20 (8)	7.0	64	High	1690	0.8	2600, 4000	0.24

Many clouds already exist, but not all provide virtualization, or even computing services. Table 1 summarizes the characteristics of several clouds currently in production; of these, Amazon is the only commercial IaaS provider with an infrastructure size that can accommodate entire grids and parallel production infrastructures (PPI) workloads.

EC2 is an IaaS cloud computing service that opens Amazon's large computing infrastructure to its users. The service is elastic in the sense that it enables the user to extend or shrink his infrastructure by launching or terminating new virtual machines (*instances*). The user can use any of the five *instance types* currently available on offer, the characteristics of which are summarized in Table 2. An ECU is the equivalent CPU power of a 1.0-1.2 GHz 2007 Opteron or Xeon processor. The theoretical peak performance can be computed for different instances from the ECU definition: a 1.1 GHz 2007 Opteron can perform 4 flops per cycle at full pipeline, which means at peak performance one ECU equals 4.4 gigaflops per second (GFLOPS). Instances can be reserved in advanced for one or three years per location which results in a lower hourly cost letting user with long usage periods benefit in a subscription way.

To create an infrastructure from EC2 resources, the user first requires the launch of one or several instances, for which he specifies the instance type and the VM image; the user can specify any VM image previously registered with Amazon, including Amazon's or the user's own. Once the VM image has been transparently deployed on a physical machine (the resource status is *running*), the instance is booted; at the end of the boot process the resource status becomes *installed*. The installed resource can be used as a regular computing node immediately after the booting process has finished, via an ssh connection. A maximum of 20 instances can be used concurrently by regular users; an application can be made to increase this limit. The Amazon EC2 does not provide job execution or resource management services; a cloud resource management system can act as middleware between the user and Amazon EC2 to reduce resource complexity. Amazon EC2 abides by a Service Level Agreement in which the user is compensated if the resources are not available for acquisition at least 99.95% of the time, 365 days/year. The security of the Amazon services has been investigated elsewhere [23].

Table 3. The benchmarks used for cloud performance evaluation. B, FLOP, U, MS, and PS stand for bytes, floating point operations, updates, makespan, and per second, respectively. The other acronyms are described in the text.

Type	Suite/Benchmark	Resource	Unit
SJSI	lmbench/all	Many	Many
SJSI	Bonnie/all	Disk	MBps
SJSI	CacheBench/all	Memory	MBps
SJMI	HPCC/HPL	CPU, float	GFLOPS
SJMI	HPCC/DGEMM	CPU, double	GFLOPS
SJMI	HPCC/STREAM	Memory	GBps
SJMI	HPCC/RandomAccess	Network	MUPS
SJMI	HPCC/b_{eff}	Memory	μs, GBps

3   Cloud Performance Evaluation

In this section we present a performance evaluation of cloud computing services for scientific computing.

3.1   Method

We design a performance evaluation method, that allows an assessment of clouds. To this end, we divide the evaluation procedure into two parts, the first cloud-specific, the second infrastructure-agnostic.

Cloud-specific evaluation. An attractive promise of clouds is that there are always unused resources, so that they can be obtained at any time without additional waiting time. However, the load of other large-scale systems (grids) varies over time due to submission patterns; we want to investigate if large clouds can indeed bypass this problem. Thus, we test the duration of resource acquisition and release over short and long periods of time. For the short-time periods one or more instances of the same instance type are repeatedly acquired and released during a few minutes; the resource acquisition requests follow a Poisson process with arrival rate $\lambda = 1s$. For the long periods an instance is acquired then released every 2 min over a period of one week, then hourly averages are aggregated from the 2-minutes samples taken over a period of one month.

Infrastructure-agnostic evaluation. There currently is no single accepted benchmark for scientific computing at large-scale. In particular, there is no such benchmark for the common scientific computing scenario in which an infrastructure is shared by several independent jobs, despite the large performance losses that such a scenario can incur [5]. To address this issue, our method both uses traditional benchmarks comprising suites of jobs to be run in isolation and replays workload traces taken from real scientific computing environments. We design two types of test workloads: SJSI/MJSI–run one or more single-process jobs on a single instance (possibly with multiple cores) and SJMI–run a

Table 4. The EC2 VM images. FC6 stands for Fedore Core 6 OS (Linux 2.6 kernel).

EC2 VM image	Software	Archi	Benchmarks
ami-2bb65342	FC6	32bit	Bonnie & LMbench
ami-36ff1a5f	FC6	64bit	Bonnie & LMbench
ami-3e836657	FC6 & MPI	32bit	HPCC
ami-e813f681	FC6 & MPI	64bit	HPCC

single multi-process jobs on multiple instances. The SJSI, MJSI, and SJMI workloads all involve executing one or more from a list of four open-source benchmarks: *LMbench* [17], *Bonnie* [9], *CacheBench* [18], and the HPC Challenge Benchmark (HPCC) [15]. The characteristics of the used benchmarks and the mapping to the test workloads are summarized in Table 3.

Performance metrics. We use the performance metrics defined by the benchmarks used in this work. We also define and use the *HPL efficiency* for a real virtual cluster based on instance type T as the ratio between the HPL benchmark performance of the cluster and the performance of a real environment formed with only one instance of same type, expressed as a percentage.

3.2   Experimental Setup

We now describe the experimental setup in which we use the performance evaluation method presented earlier.

Environment. We perform all our measurements on the EC2 environment. However, this does not limit our results, as there are sufficient reports of performance values for all the Single-Job benchmarks, and in particular for the HPCC [2] to compare our results with. For our experiments we build homogeneous environments with 1 to 128 cores based on the five EC2 instance types.

   Amazon EC2 offers a wide range of ready-made machine images. In our experiments, we used the images listed in Table 4 for the 32 and 64 bit instances; all VM images are based on a Fedora Core 6 OS with Linux 2.6 kernel. The VM images used for the HPCC benchmarks also have a working pre-configured MPI based on the `mpich2-1.0.5` [31] implementation.

Optimizations, tuning. The benchmarks were compiled using GNU C/C++ 4.1 with the `-O3 -funroll-loops` command-line arguments. We did not use any additional architecture- or instance-dependent optimizations. For the HPL benchmark, the performance results depend on two main factors: the Basic Linear Algebra Subprogram (BLAS) [11] library, and the problem size. We used in our experiments the GotoBLAS [30] library, which is one of the best portable solutions freely available to scientists. Searching for the problem size that can deliver peak performance is extensive (and costly); instead, we used a free mathematical problem size analyzer [3] to find the problem sizes that can deliver results close to the peak performance: five problem sizes ranging from 13,000 to 55,000.

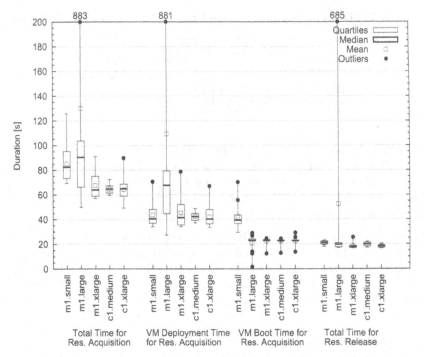

Fig. 1. Resource acquisition and release overheads for acquiring single instances

3.3   Experimental Results

The experimental results of the Amazon EC2 performance evaluation are presented in the following.

Resource Acquisition and Release. We study three resource acquisition and release scenarios: for single instances over a short period, for multiple instances over a short period, and for single instances over a long period of time.

Single instances. We first repeat 20 times for each of the five instance types a resource acquisition followed by a release as soon as the resource status becomes installed (see Section 2). Figure 1 shows the overheads associated with resource acquisition and release in EC2. The total resource acquisition time (*Total*) is the sum of the *Install* and *Boot* times. The *Release* time is the time taken to release the resource back to EC2; after it is released the resource stops being charged by Amazon. The c1.* instances are surprisingly easy to obtain; in contrast, the m1.* instances have for the resource acquisition time higher expectation (63-90s compared to around 63s) and variability (much larger boxes). With the exception of the occasional outlier, both the VM *Boot* and *Release* times are stable and represent about a quarter of *Total* each.

Multiple instances. We investigate next the performance of requesting the acquisition of multiple resources (2,4,8,16, and 20) *at the same time*; this

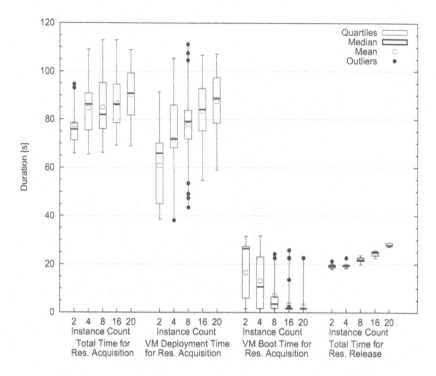

Fig. 2. Instance resource acquisition and release overheads when acquiring multiple c1.xlarge instances at the same time

corresponds to the real-life scenario where a user would create a homogeneous cluster from Amazon EC2 resources. When resources are requested in bulk, we record acquisition and release times for each resource in the request, separately. Figure 2 shows the basic statistical properties of the times recorded for c1.xlarge instances. The expectation and the variability are both higher for multiple instances than for a single instance.

Long-term investigation. Last, we discuss the *Install* time measurements published online by the independent CloudStatus team [1]. We have written web crawlers and parsing tools and taken samples every two minutes between Aug 2008 and Nov 2008 (two months). We find that the time values fluctuate within the expected range (expected value plus or minus the expected variability). We conclude that in Amazon EC2 resources can indeed be provisioned without additional waiting time due to system overload.

Performance of SJSI Workloads. In this set of experiments we measure the raw performance of the CPU, I/O, and memory hierarchy using the Single-Instance benchmarks listed in Section 3.1.

Compute performance. We assess the computational performance of each instance type using the entire LMbench suite. The performance of int and int64

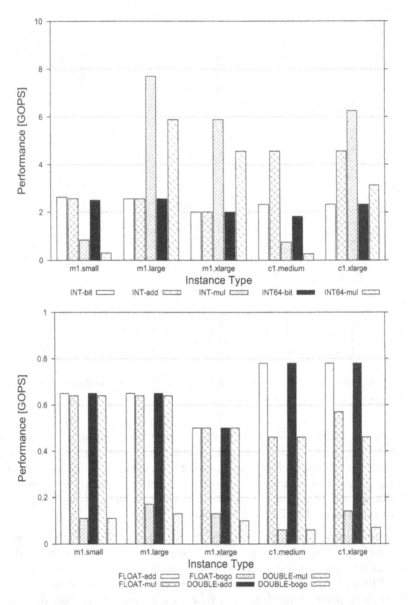

Fig. 3. LMbench results. The Performance of 32- and 64-bit integer operations in giga-operations per second (GOPS) (*top*), and of floating operations with single and double precision (*bottom*)

operations, and of the float and double float operations is depicted in Figure 3 top and bottom, respectively. *The GOPS recorded for the floating point and double operations is* $6 - 8\times$ *lower than the theoretical maximum of ECU (4.4 GOPS).* Also, the double float performance of the `c1.*` instances, arguably the most

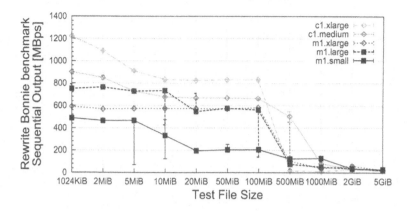

Fig. 4. The results of the Bonnie Rewrite benchmark. The performance drop indicates the capacity of the memory-based disk cache.

Table 5. The I/O performance of the Amazon EC2 instance types and of 2002 [14] and 2007 [6] systems

Instance Type	Seq. Output			Seq. Input		Rand. Input
	Char [MB/s]	Block [MB/s]	Rewrite [MB/s]	Char [MB/s]	Block [MB/s]	[Seek/s]
m1.small	22.37	60.18	33.27	25.94	73.46	74.4
m1.large	50.88	64.28	24.40	35.92	63.20	124.3
m1.xlarge	56.98	87.84	33.35	41.18	74.51	387.9
c1.medium	49.15	58.67	32.80	47.43	74.95	72.4
c1.xlarge	64.85	87.82	29.96	44.98	74.46	373.9
'02 Ext3	12.24	38.75	25.66	12.67	173.68	-
'02 RAID5	14.45	14.32	12.19	13.50	73.03	-
'07 RAID5	30.88	40.63	29.03	41.91	112.69	192.9

important for scientific computing, is mixed: excellent addition but poor multiplication capabilities. Thus, as many scientific computing applications use heavily both of these operations, the user is faced with the difficult problem of selecting between two choices where none is optimal. Finally, several floating and double point operations take longer on c1.medium than on m1.small.

I/O performance. We assess the I/O performance of each instance type with the Bonnie benchmarks, in two steps. The first step is to determine the smallest file size that invalidates the memory-based I/O cache, by running the Bonnie suite for thirteen file sizes in the range 1024 Kilo-binary byte (KiB) to 40 GiB. Figure 4 depicts the results of the rewrite with sequential output benchmark, which involves sequences of read-seek-write operations of data blocks that are dirtied before writing. For all instance types, a performance drop begins with the 100MiB test file and ends at 2GiB, indicating a capacity of the memory-based disk cache of 4-5GiB (twice 2GiB). Thus, the results obtained for the file sizes

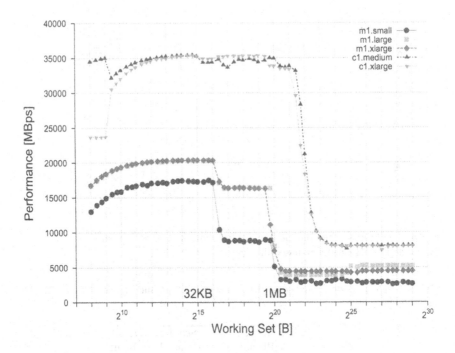

Fig. 5. CacheBench Rd-Mod-Wr benchmark results, one benchmark process per instance

above 5GiB correspond to the real I/O performance of the system; lower file sizes would be served by the system with a combination of memory and disk operations. We analyze the I/O performance obtained for files sizes above 5GiB in the second step; Table 5 summarizes the results. We find that the I/O performance indicated by EC2 (see Table 2) corresponds to the achieved performance for random I/O operations (column 'Rand. Input' in Table 5). The *.xlarge instance types have the best I/O performance from all instance types. *For the sequential operations more typical to scientific computing all EC2 instance types have in general better performance when compared with similar modern commodity systems*, such as the systems described in the last three rows in Table 5.

Memory hierarchy performance. We test the performance of the memory hierarchy using CacheBench on each instance type. Figure 5 depicts the performance of the memory hierarchy when performing the Rd-Mod-Wr benchmark with 1 benchmark process per instance. The c1.* instances perform very similar, almost twice as good as the next performance group formed by m1.xlarge and m1.large; the m1.small instance is last with a big performance gap for working sets of 2^{17}–2^{19}B. We find the memory hierarchy sizes by extracting the major performance drop-offs. The visible L1/L2 memory sizes are 64KB/1MB for the m1.* instances; the c1.* instances have only one performance drop point around 2MB (L2). Looking at the other results (not shown), we find that L1 c1.* is only 32KB. For the Rd and Wr unoptimized benchmarks we have obtained similar

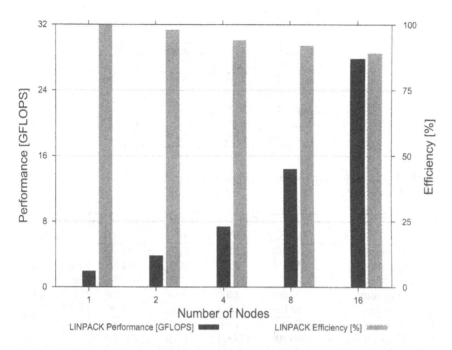

Fig. 6. The HPL (LINPACK) performance of `m1.small`-based virtual clusters

results up to the L2 cache boundary, after which the performance of `m1.xlarge` drops rapidly and the system performs worse than `m1.large`. We speculate on the existence of a throttling mechanism installed by Amazon to limit resource consumption. If this is true, the performance of computing applications would be severely limited when the working set is near or past the L2 boundary.

Reliability. We have encountered several system problems during the SJSI experiments. When running the LMbench benchmark on a `c1.medium` instance using the default VM image provided by Amazon for this architecture, the test did not complete and the instance became partially responsive; the problem was reproducible on another instance of the same type. For one whole day we were no longer able to start instances–any attempt to acquire resources was terminated instantly without a reason. Via the Amazon forums we have found a solution to the second problem (the user has to perform manually several account/setup actions); we assume it will be fixed by Amazon in the near future.

Performance of SJMI Workloads. In this set of experiments we measure the performance delivered by homogeneous clusters formed with EC2 instances when running the Single-Job-Multi-Machine (in our case Instance) benchmarks. For these tests we execute the HPCC benchmark on homogeneous clusters of size 1–16 instances.

HPL performance. The performance achieved for the HPL benchmark on various virtual clusters based on the `m1.small` instance is depicted in Figure 6.

Table 6. HPL performance and cost comparison for various EC2 instance types

Name	Peak Perf.	GFLOPS	GFLOPS /ECU	GFLOPS /$1
m1.small	4.4	1.96	1.96	19.6
m1.large	17.6	7.15	1.79	17.9
m1.xlarge	35.2	11.38	1.42	14.2
c1.medium	22.0	3.91	0.78	19.6
c1.xlarge	88.0	49.97	2.50	62.5

Table 7. The HPCC performance for various platforms. HPCC-x is the system with the HPCC ID x [2].

Provider, System	Peak Perf. [GFLOPS]	HPL [GFLOPS]	STREAM [GBps]	RandomAc. [MUPs]	Latency [μs]	Bandw. [GBps]
EC2, m1.small	4.40	1.96	3.49	11.60	-	-
EC2, m1.large	17.60	7.15	2.38	54.35	20.48	0.70
EC2, m1.xlarge	35.20	11.38	3.47	168.64	17.87	0.92
EC2, c1.medium	22.00	3.91	3.84	46.73	13.92	2.07
EC2, c1.xlarge	88.00	51.58	15.65	249.66	14.19	1.49
EC2, 16 x m1.small	70.40	27.80	11.95	77.83	68.24	0.10
EC2, 16 x c1.xlarge	1408.00	425.82	16.38	207.06	45.20	0.75
HPCC-228, 8 cores	51.20	27.78	2.95	10.29	5.81	0.66
HPCC-227, 16 cores	102.40	55.23	2.95	10.25	6.81	0.66
HPCC-224, 128 cores	819.20	442.04	2.95	10.25	8.25	0.68

The cluster with one node was able to achieve a performance of 1.96 GFLOPS, which is 44.54% from the peak performance advertised by Amazon. For 16 instances we have obtained 27.8 GFLOPS, or 39.4% from the theoretical peak and 89% efficiency. We further investigate the performance of the HPL benchmark for different instance types; Table 6 summarizes the results. The c1.xlarge instance achieves good performance (51.58 out of a theoretical performance of 88 GFLOPS, or 58.6%), but the other instance types do not reach even 50% of their theoretical peak performance. The low performance of c1.medium is due to the reliability problems discussed later in this section. Cost-wise, the c1.xlarge instance can achieve up to 64.5 GFLOPS/$ (assuming an already installed instance is present), which is the best measured value in our test. This instance type also has in our tests the best ratio between its Amazon ECU rating (column "ECUs" in Table 2) and achieved performance (2.58 GFLOPS/ECU).

HPCC performance. To obtain the performance of virtual EC2 clusters we run the HPCC benchmarks on *unit clusters* comprising one instance, and on *16-core clusters* comprising at least two instances. Table 7 summarizes the obtained results and, for comparison, results published by HPCC for four modern and similarly-sized HPC clusters [2]. For HPL, only the performance of the c1.xlarge is comparable to that of an HPC system. However, for DGEMM, STREAM, and RandomAccess the performance of the EC2 clusters is similar or

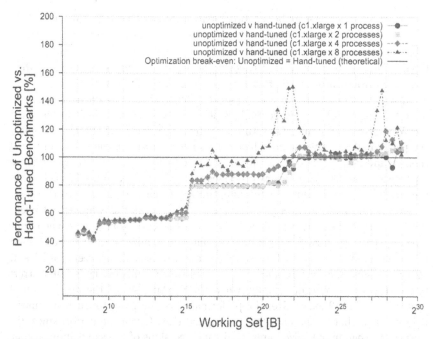

Fig. 7. CacheBench Wr hand-tuned benchmark results on the `c1.xlarge` instance type with 1–8 processes per instance

better than the performance of the HPC clusters. We attribute this mixed behavior to the network characteristics: the EC2 platform has much higher latency, which has an important negative impact on the performance of the HPL benchmark. In particular, this relatively low network performance means that the ratio between the theoretical peak performance and achieved HPL performance increases with the number of instances, making the virtual EC2 clusters poorly scalable. Thus, for scientific computing applications similar to HPL the virtual EC2 clusters can lead to an order of magnitude lower performance for large system sizes (1024 cores and higher), while for other types of scientific computing the virtual EC2 clusters are already suitable execution environments.

Reliability. We have encountered several reliability problems during these experiments; the two most important were related to HPL and are reproducible. First, the `m1.large` instances hang for an HPL problem size of 27,776 (one process blocks). Second, on the `c1.medium` instance HPL cannot complete problem sizes above 12,288 even if these should still fit in the available memory; as a result, the achieved performance on `c1.medium` was much lower than expected.

4   How to Improve Clouds for Scientific Computing?

Tuning applications for virtualized resources: We have shown throughout Section 3.3 that there is no "best"-performing instance type in clouds–each instance type has preferred instruction mixes and types of applications for which it behaves better than the others. Moreover, a real scientific application may exhibit unstable behavior when run on virtualized resources. Thus, the user is faced with the complex task of choosing a virtualized infrastructure and then tuning the application for it. But *is it worth tuning an application for a cloud?* To answer this question, we use from CacheBench the hand-tuned benchmarks to test the effect of simple, portable code optimizations such as loop unrolling etc. We use the experimental setup described in Section 3.2. Figure 7 depicts the performance of the memory hierarchy when performing the Wr hand-tuned then compiler-optimized benchmark of CacheBench on the `c1.xlarge` instance types, with 1 up to 8 benchmark processes per instance. Up to the L1 cache size, the compiler optimizations to the unoptimized CacheBench benchmarks leads to less than 60% of the peak performance achieved when the compiler optimizes the hand-tuned benchmarks. This indicates a big performance loss when running applications on EC2, unless time is spent to optimize the applications (high roll-in costs). When the working set of the application falls between the L1 and L2 cache sizes, the performance of the hand-tuned benchmarks is still better, but with a lower margin. Finally, when the working set of the application is bigger than the L2 cache size, the performance of the hand-tuned benchmarks is lower than that of the unoptimized applications. Given the performance difference between unoptimized and hand tuned versions of the same applications, and that tuning for a virtual environment holds promise for stable performance across many physical systems, *we raise as a future research problem the tuning of applications for cloud platforms.*

New providers seem to address most of the bottlenecks we identified in this work by providing cloud instances with high speed interconnections like penguin computing [24] with their Penguin on Demand™ (POD™) and HPC as a Service™ offers. HPC as a Service extends the cloud model by making concentrated, non-virtualized high-performance computing resources available in the cloud.

5   Related Work

There has been a spur of research activity in assessing the performance of virtualized resources, in cloud computing environments and in general [33, 10, 23, 29, 21, 19, 32, 26, 27]. In contrast to these studies, ours targets computational cloud resources for scientific computing, and is much broader in size and scope: it performs much more in-depth measurements, compares clouds with other off the shelf clusters.

Close to our work is the study of performance and cost of executing the Montage workflow on clouds [10]. The applications used in our study are closer to the mainstream HPC scientific community. Also close to our work is the seminal study of Amazon S3 [23], which also includes an evaluation of file transfer between Amazon EC2 and S3. Our work complements this study by analyzing the performance of Amazon EC2, the other major Amazon cloud service. Several small-scale performance studies of Amazon EC2 have been recently conducted: the study of Amazon EC2 performance using the NPB benchmark suite [29], the early comparative study of Eucalyptus and EC2 performance [21], etc. Our performance evaluation results extend and complement these previous findings, and give more insights into the loss of performance exhibited by EC2 resources.

On the other hand scientists begin to adapt the cloud infrastructure for their scientific computing. They run their calculations in the cloud [16], extend clusters on demand with IaaS resources [10] and execute big workflows on a resource mix from traditional grids and clouds [22]. This shows the growing importance of IaaS cloud providers for scientific computing and the need to have performance estimates for the different offered types beyond the marketing information offered by the providers.

6   Conclusions and Future Work

With the emergence of cloud computing as the paradigm in which scientific computing is done exclusively on resources leased only when needed from big data centers, e-scientists are faced with a new platform option. However, the initial target of the cloud computing paradigm does not match the characteristics of the scientific computing workloads. Thus, in this paper we seek to answer an important research question: *Is the performance of clouds sufficient for scientific computing?* To this end, we perform a comprehensive performance evaluation of a large computing cloud that is already in production. Our main finding is that the performance and the reliability of the tested cloud are low. Thus, this cloud is insufficient for scientific computing at large, though it still appeals to the scientists that need resources immediately and temporarily. Motivated by this finding, we have analyzed how to improve the current clouds for scientific computing, and identified two research directions which hold each good potential for improving the performance of today's clouds to the level required by scientific computing. New provider [24] seem to address this directions and we plan to test their services to see if they can hold their claims.

We will extend this work with additional analysis of the other services offered by Amazon: Storage (S3), database (SimpleDB), queue service (SQS), Private Cloud, and their inter-connection. We will also extend the performance evaluation results by running similar experiments on other IaaS providers [25] and clouds also on other real large-scale platforms, such as grids and commodity clusters. In the long term, we intend to explore the two new research topics that we have raised in our assessment of needed cloud improvements.

Acknowledgment

This work is partially funded by the European Union through the IST-034601 edutain@grid project and the Austrian Federal Ministry for Education, Science and Culture through the GZ BMWF-10.220/0002-II/10/2007 Austrian Grid project.

References

1. The Cloud Status Team. JSON report crawl (January 2009),
   http://www.cloudstatus.com/
2. The HPCC Team. HPCChallenge results (Sept. 2009),
   http://icl.cs.utk.edu/hpcc/hpcc_results.cgi
3. Advanced Clustering Tech. Linpack problem size analyzer (December 2008),
   http://www.advancedclustering.com/
4. Amazon Inc. Amazon Elastic Compute Cloud (Amazon EC2) (September 2009),
   http://aws.amazon.com/ec2/
5. Arpaci-Dusseau, R.H., Arpaci-Dusseau, A.C., Vahdat, A., Liu, L.T., Anderson,
   T.E., Patterson, D.A.: The interaction of parallel and sequential workloads on a
   network of workstations. In: SIGMETRICS, pp. 267–278 (1995)
6. Babcock, M.: XEN benchmarks. Tech. Rep. (August 2007),
   http://mikebabcock.ca/linux/xen/
7. Barham, P., Dragovic, B., Fraser, K., Hand, S., Harris, T.L., Ho, A., Pratt, I.,
   Warfield, A.: Xen and the art of virtualization. In: SOSP. ACM, New York (2003)
8. Bradshaw, R., Desai, N., Freeman, T., Keahey, K.: A scalable approach to deploying
   and managing appliances. In: TeraGrid Conference 2007 (June 2007)
9. Bray, T.: Bonnie, 1996 (December 2008), http://www.textuality.com/bonnie/
10. Deelman, E., Singh, G., Livny, M., Berriman, J.B., Good, J.: The cost of doing
    science on the cloud: the Montage example. In: SC, p. 50. IEEE/ACM (2008)
11. Dongarra, J., et al.: Basic linear algebra subprograms technical forum standard.
    Int'l. J. of High Perf. App. and Supercomputing 16(1), 1–111 (2002)
12. Foster, I.T., Freeman, T., Keahey, K., Scheftner, D., Sotomayor, B., Zhang, X.: Vir-
    tual clusters for grid communities. In: CCGrid, pp. 513–520. IEEE, Los Alamitos
    (2006)
13. GoGrid. GoGrid cloud-server hosting (September 2009), http://www.gogrid.com
14. Kowalski, A.: Bonnie - file system benchmarks. Tech. Rep., Jefferson Lab (October
    2002), http://cc.jlab.org/docs/scicomp/benchmark/bonnie.html
15. Luszczek, P., Bailey, D.H., Dongarra, J., Kepner, J., Lucas, R.F., Rabenseifner,
    R., Takahashi, D.: S12 - The HPC Challenge (HPCC) benchmark suite. In: SC, p.
    213. ACM, New York (2006)
16. Assuncao, A.C.M., Buyya, R.: Evaluating the cost-benefit of using cloud computing
    to extend the capacity of clusters. In: Kranzlmüller, D., Bode, A., Hegering, H.-G.,
    Casanova, H., Gerndt, M. (eds.) 11th IEEE International Conference on High Per-
    formance Computing and Communications, HPCC 2009. ACM, New York (2009)
17. McVoy, L., Staelin, C.: LMbench - tools for performance analysis (December 2008),
    http://www.bitmover.com/lmbench/
18. Mucci, P.J., London, K.S.: Low level architectural characterization benchmarks for
    parallel computers. Technical Report UT-CS-98-394, U. Tennessee (1998)
19. Nagarajan, A.B., Mueller, F., Engelmann, C., Scott, S.L.: Proactive fault tolerance
    for HPC with Xen virtualization. In: ICS, pp. 23–32. ACM, New York (2007)
20. Nishimura, H., Maruyama, N., Matsuoka, S.: Virtual clusters on the fly - fast,
    scalable, and flexible installation. In: CCGrid, pp. 549–556. IEEE, Los Alamitos
    (2007)
21. Nurmi, D., Wolski, R., Grzegorczyk, C., Obertelli, G., Soman, S., Youseff, L.,
    Zagorodnov, D.: The Eucalyptus open-source cloud-computing system. UCSD
    Tech. Rep. 2008-10 (2008), http://eucalyptus.cs.ucsb.edu/

22. Ostermann, S., Prodan, R., Fahringer, T.: Extended grids with cloud resource management for scientific computing. In: Grid 2009: IEEE/ACM International Conference on Grid Computing (October 2009)
23. Palankar, M.R., Iamnitchi, A., Ripeanu, M., Garfinkel, S.: Amazon S3 for science grids: a viable solution? In: DADC 2008: Proceedings of the 2008 international workshop on Data-aware distributed computing, pp. 55–64. ACM, New York (2008)
24. Penguin Computing. Reliable hpc linux systems (September 2009), http://www.penguincomputing.com/
25. Prodan, R., Ostermann, S.: A survey and taxonomy of infrastructure as a service and web hosting cloud providers. In: Grid 2009: IEEE/ACM International Conference on Grid Computing (October 2009)
26. Quétier, B., Néri, V., Cappello, F.: Scalability comparison of four host virtualization tools. J. Grid Comput. 5(1), 83–98 (2007)
27. Sotomayor, N., Keahey, K., Foster, I.: Overhead matters: A model for virtual resource management. In: VTDC, pp. 4–11. IEEE, Los Alamitos (2006)
28. Thain, D., Tannenbaum, T., Livny, M.: Distributed computing in practice: the Condor experience. Conc. & Comp.: Pract. & Exp. 17(2-4), 323–356 (2005)
29. Walker, E.: Benchmarking Amazon EC2 for HP Scientific Computing. Login 33(5), 18–23 (2008)
30. Wang, P., Turner, G.W., Lauer, D.A., Allen, M., Simms, S., Hart, D., Papakhian, M., Stewart, C.A.: Linpack performance on a geographically distributed linux cluster. In: IPDPS. IEEE, Los Alamitos (2004)
31. Worringen, J., Scholtyssik, K.: MP-MPICH: User documentation & technical notes (June 2002)
32. Youseff, L., Seymour, K., You, H., Dongarra, J., Wolski, R.: The impact of paravirtualized memory hierarchy on linear algebra computational kernels and software. In: HPDC, pp. 141–152. ACM, New York (2008)
33. Youseff, L., Wolski, R., Gorda, B.C., Krintz, C.: Paravirtualization for HPC systems. In: Min, G., Di Martino, B., Yang, L.T., Guo, M., Rünger, G. (eds.) ISPA Workshops 2006. LNCS, vol. 4331, pp. 474–486. Springer, Heidelberg (2006)

Cyberaide Virtual Applicance: On-Demand Deploying Middleware for Cyberinfrastructure

Tobias Kurze[1], Lizhe Wang[3], Gregor von Laszewski[2], Jie Tao[1], Marcel Kunze[1], Fugang Wang[3], David Kramer[4], Wolfgang Karl[4], and Jaliya Ekanayake[2]

[1] Steinbuch Center for Computing, Karlsruhe Institute of Technology,
Karlsruhe 76344, Germany
[2] Pervasive Technology Institute, Indiana University at Bloomington,
Bloomington, IN 47408
[3] Service Oriented Cyberinfrastructure Laboratory,
Rochester Institute of Technology, Rochester, NY 14623
[4] Department of Computer Science,
Karlsruhe Institute of Technology, Karlsruhe 76131, Germany

Abstract. Cyberinfrastructure offers a vision of advanced knowledge infrastructure for research and education. It integrates diverse resources across geographically distributed resources and human communities. Cyberaide is a service oriented architecture and abstraction framework that integrates a large number of available commodity libraries and allows users to access cyberinfrastructure through Web 2.0 technologies. This paper describes the Cyberaide virtual appliance, a solution of on-demand deployment of cyberinfrastructure middleware, i.e. Cyberaide. The proposed solution is based on an open and free technology and software – Cyberaide JavaScript, a service oriented architecture (SOA) and grid abstraction framework that allows users to access the grid infrastructures through JavaScript. The Cyberaide virtual appliance is built by installing and configuring Cyberaide JavaScript in a virtual machine. Established Cyberaide virtual appliances can then be used via a Web browser, allowing users to create, distribute and maintain cyberinfrastructure related software more easily even without the need to do the "tricky" installation process on their own. We argue that our solution of providing Cyberaide virtual appliance can make users easy to access cyberinfrastructure, manage their work and build user organizations.

Keywords: JavaScript, Cyberinfrastructure, Virtual Appliance.

1 Introduction

Research topics of modern cyberinfrastructure cover the development of a wide range of computing and information processing infrastructures and services, for example, advanced data acquisition/storage/processing/visualization, high performance computing environments for advanced scientic & engineering applications, and other networked services. There are a lot of scenarios where an advanced cyberinfrastructure is needed. Especially in the scientific domain such

D.R. Avresky et al. (Eds.): Cloudcomp 2009, LNICST 34, pp. 132–144, 2010.
© Institute for Computer Sciences, Social-Informatics and Telecommunications Engineering 2010

infrastructures are of great use. Nevertheless, users who wants to use an advanced cyberinfrastructure may find it hard to use or are just unable to use it due to the complexity involved. This is where the Cyberaide toolkit becomes handy. Cyberaide is a lightweight middleware for users to access advanced modern cyberinfrastructure. It provides various user interfaces and toolkits for users to access resources, submit jobs and manage user organizations. However it takes some time and effort to set it up. For users of Cyberaide it would be much easier and more convenient to have a tool that installs and deploys Cyberaide automatically. As the services provided by Cyberaide can be accessed through a web interface it is an obvious choice to deploy Cyberaide as a virtual appliance.

A virtual appliance provides a lot of benefits compared to "traditional software": simple installation and setup; very easy deployment process; helping augment the efficient utilization of underlying hardware [1]. The appliance can be tested to ensure that all the software is working correctly on the hardware described by the virtual appliance itself. Additionally a virtual appliance is maintained by the creators of the appliance and not by the users, allowing to create correct updates with higher confidence [2].

We propose to use virtual appliances to simplify users' work in accessing cyberinfrastructures. The solution is to create a Cyberaide Virtual Appliance on the fly, then to deploy and configure it, and finally to expose its services to the users. With the cyberaide virtual appliance, users can on-demand build middleware to access production cyberinfrastructure, like TeraGrid, and organize their work on the cyberinfrastructure.

The rest of the paper is organized as follows. Section 2 introduces related work and provides background information. This is followed by an overview of the Cyberaide Toolkit in Section 3. Section 4 illuminates the proposed Cyberaide Virtual Appliance solution, follwed by some test results in Section 5. Section 6 concludes with a short summary and an outlook about future work.

2   Background and Related Work

Advanced cyberinfrastructure facilitates the development of new applications, allows applications to interoperate across institutions and disciplines, insures that data and software acquired at great expense are preserved and easily available and empowers enhanced collaboration over distance, time and disciplines. Cyberaide is a service oriented architecture that enables users to access and manipulate cyberinfrastructure resources. The Cyberaide toolkit originate from grid portal framework and Globus Toolkit project. The development of grid portals has started some time ago and one of the first usable libraries supporting grid portal development was the Java CoG Kit [3]. Another important resource is the TeraGrid portal [4] that is used to obtain access to grid resources. TeraGrid itself uses the Globus Toolkit [5] to manage resources. Unfortunately this solution doesn't integrate JavaScript. To tackle this issue Cyberaide Javascript [6] has been developed. It is a grid abstraction framework that enables the easy access to grids through JavaScript.

Another important technology base for building the Cyberaide Virtual Appliance is virtualization. One of the earliest VM solutions has been provided by IBM in 1972 [7]. Nowadays different solutions are available that can be classified into several categories according to the virtualization technique used. One solution is XEN [8], which uses the paravirtualization [9] technique. Another virtualization technique is Full Virtualisation. VMware Server [10], KVM [11] and Microsoft Virtual PC [12] are representatives of this category.

To reduce the complexity of software development a relatively new approach is to use Virtual Appliances. Some software systems are difficult to compile, to link, and to install and have been well tested just on a specific version of tools and platforms. A software publisher can bundle the necessary tools in an appliance and distribute it to users [13].

The Grid Appliance is an example of a Virtual Appliance. It is a *virtual machine based system which enables an execution environment in which users are given the opportunity to voluntarily share resources and run unmodified x86/Linux applications* [14]. Another interesting appliance is Cern VM [15] which is built using rBuilder [16] and provides a minmal Linux base to run LCG (LHC Computing Grid [17]) applications. CernVM is available as a raw system image file or as a VMware image.

Some related work on cloud computing [18, 19] uses virtual machine and virtual appliance as basic building blocks. Eucalyptus [20] is a cloud computing system that implements what is commonly referred to as *Infrastructure as a Service (IaaS)* [21]. It provides the possibility to run and control virtual machine instances which are deployed across a variety of physical resources and offers an entry-point into a cloud for users and administrators. A computing cloud is a pool of network enabled virtualized resources and services that can be dynamically reconfigured to adjust to a variable load, providing scalable, QoS guaranteed computing platforms on demand. There are multiple definitions for the term 'cloud computing', please refer to [18, 19] for more details. OpenNEbula [22] decouples a server not only from the physical infrastructure but also from the physical location by enabling the dynamic deployment and re-placement of virtualized services within and across sites. It's a tool that can be used to manage clouds, even public clouds when combined with a cloud interface. The Xen Grid Engine [23, 24] is an extension of the Sun Grid Engine cluster management system based on the Xen Hypervisor. It supports for virtual machine management and offers increased usability and security features for cluster environments.

3   Cyberaide: A Light Weight Middleware for Production Grid

As introduced in the frist section, there are a lot of scenarios where an advanced cyberinfrastructure is needed, but it might be difficult to use one. A possible solution to this dilemma is provided by Cyberaide. Several tools have been developed under the Cyberaide logo; well-known examples are Cyberaide toolkit and Cyberaide Shell. Consecutively Cyberaide toolkit's architecture will be shortly introduced and explained.

Cyberaide enjoys the following essential features:

- *Ease of use*: make the JavaScript based API and interfaces useful for Grid and Web developers.
- *Low installation footprint*: support fast downloads as well as an easy maintenance through a small manageable code base.
- *Security*: gain access to Grid resources in order to avoid compromising the system. This is especially important due to known limitations of JavaScript.
- *Basic Grid functionality*: is provided for developers to create Grid-based client applications.
- *Advanced functionality*: is offered as many developers do not want to replicate functionality provided by other Grid middleware and upperware.

The framework is designed in layers and comprised of different components. (see also Fig. 1). A web client that provides access to Grid functionality and components that can be deployed in a web server are provided. A service called *"mediator service"* mediates tasks to the Grid and basically is a secure server that provides most of the functionalities in regard to the Grid.

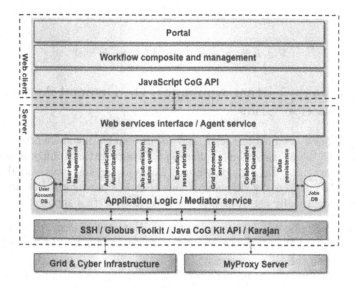

Fig. 1. System Architecture

- Web client: provides elementary functionality to access the Grid through a portal user interface.
- Server: contains two logical parts:
  - Agent service: is the intermediate service between Web client and mediator service; works as proxy for users to interact with the mediator service.

- Mediator Service: is the bridge between the Grid and the client library. The mediator service offers different functionalities and contains the application logic.

Because of the separation between the service and the client the development of Cyberaide shell was possible. this is a system shell that facilitates the use of cyberinfrastructures. It contains four high level design components: object management, cyberinfrastructure backends, command line interpreters, and services (see Fig. 2).

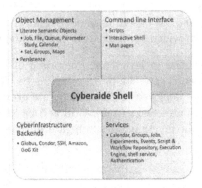

Fig. 2. High level design of Cyberaide Shell

4 Cyberaide Virtual Appliance: On Demand Accessing Production Grids

To help users focus on their work and to also enable unexperienced users to work with Cyberaide, a virtual appliance for Cyberaide that configures itself for the most part might be a good solution. There are several tools available that facilitate the creation of a virtual appliance. Below, some information about two different tools usually used to create the Cyberaide virtual appliance is listed.

- VMware Studio [25] is a tool provided by VMware and is an appliance itself. It provides a Web Interface through which an appliance can be configured easily with the following steps:
  - Configure a "virtual hardware", for example, memory, hard disk, network.
  - Choose an operating system (an ISO image has to be provided for the selected OS, by default only a few operating systems are supported)
  - Configure the software that should be installed on the virtual machine. Packages that are available on the installation medium (.iso) can be selected and will be installed automatically.
  - Set a target machine and directory. The appliance will then be copied to the specified location. VMware Studio is also able to automatically start the created appliance on a specified and correctly configured VMware

Server [10]. The created virtual machine consists of a vmx and a vmdk file that can be used with any hypervisor solution supporting these formats. (ESX, VMware Workstation, etc.)

- The second commonly used tool is *VMBuilder* [26]. VMbuilder basically is just a script that automates the process of creating a ready to use VM based on Ubuntu [27]. VMbuilder is part of JeOS 8.10 (Ubuntu: Intrepid Ibex). It offers the same abilities as VMware Studio does, except for the web interface used to configure the appliance. Nevertheless the configuration is still quite easy and done via some configuration files. In addition to that, there is no need for an ISO image on the local machine; VMbuilder automatically downloads all necessary files from the Internet. The operating system that will be installed (by default) is JeOS [28], a very efficient variant of the Ubuntu Server operating system, configured specifically for virtual appliances.

Since both tools show their own features, it is not easy to decide on one for building our Cyberaide virtual appliance. In order to make a decent choice we have evaluated and tested both tools. The following subsection outlines this evaluation process.

4.1 Evaluation of Tools

The two possible solutions to create the Virtual Appliance as presented above are free and offer all needed functionality. To finally make up a decision the pros and cons of each tool have been evaluated. A listing of some evaluation criteria and the corresponding results are given in Table 1.

Table 1. Evaluation of virtual appliance creation tools

Criteria	VMwareStudio	JeOSVMBuilder
ease of use	very good, web-based interface	less comfortable, only CLI
supported OSs	Ubuntu[1], SUSE, RedHat, CentOS	Ubuntu JeOS[2] only
supported hypervisors	VMware only	KVM, Xen and VMware
auto-start on hypervisor	supported	not supported
encountered problems	a lot[3]	no serious problems

[1] different distributions available.
[2] efficient variant of the Ubuntu Server operating system.
[3] see succeeding description.

Even though VMware Studio has some features ahead of JeOSVMBuilder there occured a lot of problems while using it. For example: In theory an automated transfer of the created appliance to a target host, which is running VMware Server, is supported, but didn't work properly. Another drawback of VMware's solution is the package management. To directly install a certain package into the appliance it's necessary to also add in all dependencies of this package. This results in a tricky and less comfortable configuration.

Despite JeOSVMBuilder only supporting Ubuntu as operating system, its support for a large range of hypervisors is much more important. In addition, the applied operating system (Ubuntu JeOS [28]) is light and allows a very small virtual image file size and a good performance of the virtual machine.

On the other hand, JeOSVMBuilder doesn't provide functions to copy the created image on a target machine nor does it allow to start the created appliance on a hypervisor. However, this missing functionality can be added easily with a small script.

Overall, JeOSVMBuilder is better for our use case. The details about how adaptable this tool is can be seen in the following subsection.

4.2 Solution Description

After having evaluated the different possibilities we selected JeOSVMBuilder to create the Cyberaide virtual appliance. This command line tool requires just two basic parameters[1] to create a trivial virtual appliance. In the presented solution VMware is used as hypervisor and Ubuntu JeOS as operating system. All available parameters may either be passed to JeOSVMBuilder on the command line directly or by using some configuration files. The proposed solution uses four configuration files that control and set up the building process of the virtual appliance:

- A basic configuration file that allows to define some basic parameters such as: platform type (i386), amount of memory of the virtual appliance, packages that should be directly installed, etc.
- A hard-disk configuration file that defines the size of each available (virtual) hard-disk and the number and size of all the partitions that will be created on these hard-disks.
- Boot.sh: Shell script that will be executed during the first boot of the new appliance.
- Login.sh: Shell script that will be executed after the first logon in the new appliance.

The essential part of the build process of the Cyberaide appliance is located in the two shell scripts. The boot.sh script sets some system environment parameters and installs and downloads required software. As some of the packages require user input (for example: user has to accept license of Sun's JDK) a completely unattended installation is not possible, hence those installations that require user input or rely on packages that need user input are started using the login.sh script.

Fig. 3 depicts the complete installation process:

- The user starts a script and passes some parameters such as proxy-host and proxy-port to it. This adapts the VMbuilder configuration files and starts the VMbuilderscript.

---

[1] 1.)target OS (always Ubuntu) and 2.)target hypervisor.

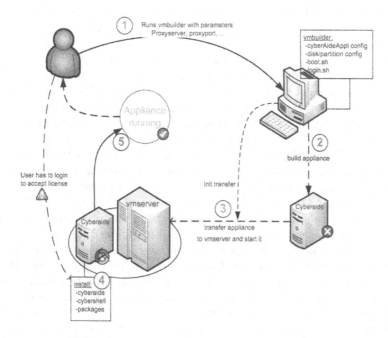

Fig. 3. Cyberaide Virtual Appliance: Build Process

- VMbuilder then creates a virtual machine and installs some basic packages in it.
- The virtual machine files are moved to the VMserver and the appliance is started for the first time.
- Boot and Login scripts are executed. Because of some licensing issues the user has to login into the new appliance and accept the Sun license. Then the rest of the installation is completed and the appliance is completely created.
- The appliance is running and the services are ready to be used.

Besides the Boot and Login scripts, another two scripts were written, one for adapting the VMbuilder configuration files and the other for transferring the appliance to the target host and starting it on the specified hypervisor. To ensure a secure communication between the host running VMbuilder and the target host (and the hypervisor (host) (if different)) ssh is used. As the connections between the hosts mentioned above have to be established in an automated manner it's preferable to use certificates instead of passwords for ssh.

4.3   Scenario

A possible scenario where an advanced cyberinfrastructure may be of use is a grid and additional tools simplifying the use of it. To set up and to configure a grid middleware is not an easy task, so additional tools that provide an abstraction layer may be introduced to make it possible to use the grid services through a web interface, for example. One tool that provides such functionality is Cyberaide.

As Cyberaide itself relies on some other tools its configuration is not an easy task either. A (scientific-)user may find it too complicated or may just not be able to install all necessary tools. This is where the auto-install and deployment process of Cyberaide, exactly what we do, comes into play.

This scenario assumes the existence of a grid (e.g. TeraGrid) and a user that wants to run some jobs on this grid. The user may be a physicist and not familiar with all details of the grid and how to configure his tools to use the grid. Because he prefers to focus on his work and not to loose a lot of time setting up his tools nor tinkering around with the grid, he decides to leave this time consuming step to someone else. The IT department informs him, that there is a toolkit available named Cyberaide and that it can be installed by just running a deployment and installation script available on a machine running in the computing center. The user, keen to try this tool (and leaving the work to it) starts the script from his local machine and continues working. In the meantime a virtual appliance is created and set up. After the process has been finished the user receives a message that contains a description how to use the Cyberaide appliance and how to configure it. This last configuration step is quite easy and should not take a lot of time. As illustrated in this scenario the use of Cyberaide toolkit and the automated installation and deployment process saves a lot of time and helps users focus on their actual work.

5   Performance Evaluation and Discussion

5.1   Test of Cyberaide Virtual Appliance

The motivation was to provide a solution that facilitates the creation and the deployment of the Cyberaide toolkit. The proposed solution provides a very simple interface (see Fig. 4) that allows the creation of the appliance in an easy way. It also includes an efficient way to transfer the appliance to a target system from where it can automatically be started on a hypervisor.

There still are some inconveniences such as the need to log in during the installation phase to accept the license or the small effort it takes to set up the secured communications between the hosts. But finally the installation and deployment of Cyberaide is really easy and comfortable for an user. Some facts about the creation process are given in table 2.

The time to generate the appliance as well as the time needed to transfer it to the computer where the hypervisor is running strongly depends the network (and/or Internet) speed of the concerned systems. The numbers related to the building time (as given in table 2) have been measured by using a system which has a very fast internet connection. They may be extremely different on other systems or in another network environment.

Once the basic appliance (OS & basic packages only) is generated and transfered to a hypervisor, the second part of the installation is performed by the appliance itself. It downloads and installs all necesarry packages which takes more time than the first part of the installation does.

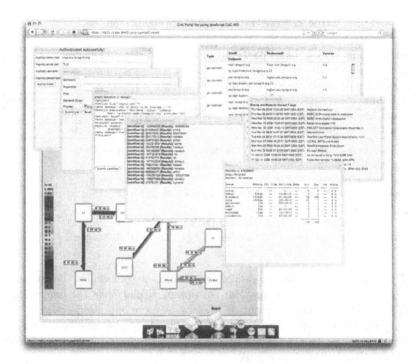

Fig. 4. Cyberaide Web Interface

The last installation steps are performed after the first login and basically install Cyberaide and all related components.

Finally the user has just to set up his certificates and keyfiles. The complete procedure takes in total about one hour (depending on the hardware) and needs just 2 user interactions (first login: accept license and set up certificates user login).

5.2 Test of Cyberaide Virtual Appliance on TeraGrid

To demonstrate that the appliance works, the LINPACK 1000x1000 benchmark program in single precision (1000s) and in double precision (1000d) have been tested on one node on TeraGrid. The benchmark is available at http://www.netlib.org/benchmark/.

Please note that this is just an exemplary program and the purpose of this test is not to measure the performance of the grid or any part of it.

The test has been performed using Cybershell which is included in the appliance. First step is to retrieve credentials. This can be done in Cybershell with the myproxylogon command: *security myproxylogon -u USERNAME*. Cybershell also provides an easy way to list available nodes *(execution listnodes)* and running jobs *(execution listjobs)*. To finally submit a job the following command can be used: *execution s -id 12 -cmd myscript.sh.*

Table 2. Some key numbers of the creation process

building time (OS & basic packages only)	ca. 10 minutes[1]
building time (until first login)	ca. 20 minutes[2]
installation & deployment time after first login	ca. 15 minutes[3]
total time	ca. 45 minutes to one hour
virtual image file size (OS & basic packages only)	ca. 400 MByte[4]
virtual image file size (total)	ca. 2,8 GByte

[1] includes download time of OS & packages (without local repository).
[2] installation continues after login for license reasons.
[3] remaining packages will be downloaded and deployed after login.
[4] less than 200 MByte (ca. 190 MByte) zipped size.

Technical Info:
Host machine: Core i7 3,2 GHz, 6 GByte DDR3, fast Internet (2MB/s)
VMbuilder: Ubuntu 8.10 on VMware Server 2 (1 Core, 384MB assigned)

The submitted job is then scheduled and run on one (or more) of the execution nodes for example the node tg-c254. On this particular node the unoptimized 1000d benchmark reported about 66 MFlops. A more optimized version (-O2) reports 133 MFlops. As mentioned above this should not be considered as a real performance measurement of the grid, but only demonstrates that principally Cyberaide Virtual Appliance works.

6   Conclusion and Future Work

The Cyberaide Virtual Appliance provides a lot of functionality and in the same time is quite easy to use even for inexperienced users. The web interface as well as the secure shell (ssh) access to the Virtual Appliance provide a comfortable way to interact with it.

Cyberaide Virtual Appliance improves the Cyberaide Toolkit with a simple user interface and is a step forward that provides a faster, more reliable and easier installation, setup and configuration phase which finally results in a more productive working environment.

However, there are still some problems with the prototypical implementation:

– Large amount of data has to be downloaded during the installation. This may cause high cost in data transfer and long creation time depending on the Internet access speed.
– Uncomfortable start of building process.
– DHCP server has to be available and leasing addresses to Virtual Appliances.

Future work on Cyberaide Virtual Appliance may attack these problems. Possible solutions might be:

– To reduce the amount of data that has to be downloaded a *local repository* for software packages and the JeOS image could be created. This will accelerate the creation process of the Virtual Appliance as well as reduce costs by avoiding transfers from the Internet. Another point may be that in the future some of the necessary packages are no longer available in the Internet repositories due to updates, etc... A local repository guarantees the presence of all necessary packages and versions.

- At the moment the installation process is started via the console on a local machine. It might be even more comfortable to have a web interface where a user can request the Cyberaide Virtual Appliance to be installed on a certain machine and to be started on a specified hypervisor. Once the machine is up and running all information the user may need to proceed (e.g. IP address of Virtual Appliance) could be displayed directly in the browser.
- By default, the Virtual Appliances tries to use the bridged networking interface of the hypervisor it's running on and expects to receive a DHCP lease while booting. Hence a DHCP server and a virtual bridged networking adapter has to be provided. In a future version NAT support might be included.

In summary, we use the virtual appliance approach to automate the process of installing the middleware for accessing cyberinfrastructures. The initial product is available for users. Problems mentioned above will be solved in the near future.

Acknowledgment

Work conducted by Gregor von Laszewski and Lizhe Wang is supported (in part) by NSF CMMI 0540076 and NSF SDCI NMI 0721656.

References

1. Herrod, S.A.: Future of virtualization technology
2. Sapuntzakis, C.P., Lam, M.S.: Virtual appliances in the collective: A road to hassle-free computing. In: Jones, M.B. (ed.) HotOS, pp. 55–60. USENIX (2003)
3. von Laszewski, G., Foster, I.T., Gawor, J., Lane, P.: A java commodity grid kit. Concurrency and Computation: Practice and Experience 13(8-9), 645–662 (2001)
4. Teragrid portal, http://www.teragrid.org/userinfo/portal.php
5. The globus toolkit, http://www.globus.org
6. von Laszewski, G., Wang, F., Younge, A., He, X., Guo, Z., Pierce, M.: Cyberaide javascript: A javascript commodity grid kit, pp. 1–10 (2008)
7. Vm history, http://www.vm.ibm.com/history/
8. Barham, P., Dragovic, B., Fraser, K., Hand, S., Harris, T.L., Ho, A., Neugebauer, R., Pratt, I., Warfield, A.: Xen and the art of virtualization. In: Scott, M.L., Peterson, L.L. (eds.) SOSP, pp. 164–177. ACM, New York (2003)
9. Whitaker, A., Shaw, M., Gribble, S.D.: Denali: Lightweight virtual machines for distributed and networked applications. In: Proceedings of the USENIX Annual Technical Conference (2002)
10. Vmware server, http://www.vmware.com/products/server/
11. Kvm - kernel based virtual machine, http://www.linux-kvm.org/page/Main_Page
12. Microsoft virtual pc, http://www.microsoft.com/windows/virtual-pc/default.aspx

13. Sapuntzakis, C.P., Brumley, D., Chandra, R., Zeldovich, N., Chow, J., Lam, M.S., Rosenblum, M.: Virtual appliances for deploying and maintaining software. In: LISA, pp. 181–194. USENIX (2003)
14. Wolinsky, D.I., Figueiredo, R.J.: Simplifying resource sharing in voluntary grid computing with the grid appliance. In: IPDPS, pp. 1–8. IEEE, Los Alamitos (2008)
15. Cernvm, http://cernvm.cern.ch/cernvm/
16. rbuilder, http://www.rpath.com/rbuilder/
17. Lcg, http://lcg.web.cern.ch/LCG/
18. Wang, L., Tao, J., Kunze, M., Castellanos, A.C., Kramer, D., Karl, W.: Scientific cloud computing: Early definition and experience. In: HPCC, pp. 825–830. IEEE, Los Alamitos (2008)
19. Vaquero, L.M., Rodero-Merino, L., Caceres, J., Lindner, M.: A break in the clouds: towards a cloud definition. SIGCOMM Comput. Commun. Rev. 39(1), 50–55 (2009)
20. Eucalyptus, http://www.eucalyptus.com/
21. Nurmi, D., Wolski, R., Grzegorczyk, C., Obertelli, G., Soman, S., Youseff, L., Zagorodnov, D.: The eucalyptus open-source cloud-computing system. In: Proceedings of Cloud Computing and Its Applications (October 2008)
22. Opennebula, http://www.opennebula.org/doku.php?id=start
23. Xge - xen grid engine, http://mage.uni-marburg.de/trac/xge
24. Fallenbeck, N., Picht, H.J., Smith, M., Freisleben, B.: Xen and the art of cluster scheduling. In: First International Workshop on Virtualization Technology in Distributed Computing, VTDC 2006, p. 4 (2006)
25. Vmware studio, http://www.vmware.com/support/developer/studio/index.html
26. Jeosvmbuilder, https://help.ubuntu.com/community/JeOSVMBuilder
27. Ubuntu, http://www.ubuntu.com/
28. Jeos, http://www.ubuntu.com/products/whatisubuntu/serveredition/jeos.
29. Kleinrock, L.: Ucla to be 1st station in nationwide computer network (July 1969), http://www.lk.cs.ucla.edu/LK/Bib/REPORT/press.html
30. von Laszewski, G., Younge, A., He, X., Wang, F.: Cyberaide shell: Interactive task management for grids and cyberinfrastructure, http://cyberaide.googlecode.com/svn/trunk/papers/08-gridshell/vonLaszewski-08-gridshell.pdf, mailto:laszewski@gmail.com
31. Foster, I.: What is the grid? a three point checklist (June 2002)
32. Oasis soa reference model, http://www.oasis-open.org/committees/tc_home.php?wg_abbrev=soa-rm

Cloud Computing Platforms

Track Session 2

Service Supervision Patterns: Reusable Adaption of Composite Services

Masahiro Tanaka[1], Toru Ishida[1,2], Yohei Murakami[1], and Donghui Lin[1]

[1] Language Grid Project,
National Institute of Information and Communications Technology (NICT)
3-5 Hikaridai, Seika-cho, Kyoto, Japan
{mtnk,yohei,lindh}@nict.go.jp
[2] Department of Social Informatics, Kyoto University
Yoshida-Honmachi, Sakyo-ku, Kyoto, 606-8501, Japan
ishida@i.kyoto-u.ac.jp

Abstract. A composite Web service provided as a "cloud" service should make its constituent Web services transparent to users. However, existing frameworks for composite Web services cannot realize such transparency because they lack capability of adapting changes of behaviors of constituents Web services and business rules of service providers. Service Supervision, proposed in the previous work, allows us to flexibly adapt a composite Web service by combining control execution functions which control behavior of running instances of composite Web services. However, much flexibility of the execution control functions sometimes makes it difficult to design adaptation processes due to absence of accumulated know-how such as guidelines. Moreover, it often costs a lot to port adaptation processes to the model of composite Web service to be adapted. To solve the problems, we first organized various adaptation processes based on some previous works. Then we proposed Service Supervision patterns, which consist of typical requirements for adaptation and WS-BPEL processes satisfying the requirements by using execution control functions. The patterns are easy for designers of composite Web services to understand and make it possible to reduce cost to port them to the model of a composite service.

1 Introduction

In Cloud Computing, servers which provide Web services are transparent to users and users do not need to care numbers or locations of the servers. As for a composite Web service, which combines multiple Web services, the constituent Web services of the composite Web service should also be transparent to users when it is provided as a "cloud service". However, it is often difficult to realize the transparency because the constituent Web services can be provided by various service providers and the behaviors of the services can unexpectedly change. Therefore a composite Web service has to be capable of adapting to the changes.

For example, there are still many services deployed outside cloud and throughput of the services may decline in an environment where too many requests can

D.R. Avresky et al. (Eds.): Cloudcomp 2009, LNICST 34, pp. 147–163, 2010.
© Institute for Computer Sciences, Social-Informatics and Telecommunications Engineering 2010

be given during a certain period. In that case, a composite Web service which combines such services needs to replace the constituent Web service with an alternative one in order to keep overall performance of the composite Web service. Another example is changes of business rules of service providers. If a service provider which provides one of the constituent Web services changes their business rules and becomes to require some preprocesses before execution of its service, the business logic of the composite Web service must be changed.

However, WS-BPEL[1], a standard language for a composite Web service, is not flexible enough to realize adaptation to frequent changes of the environment or business rules. In the existing framework for WS-BPEL, a model of a composite Web service (a definition of a WS-BPEL process) deployed on the execution engine cannot be modified. Therefore we need to modify the model first and then deploy it on the execution engine in order to adapt a composite Web service to an environment or business rules. This has often prevented flexible and rapid adaptation.

To make up the lack of flexibility, in [2], we proposed Service Supervision, which changes the behavior of a composite Web service without modifying its model using execution control functions such as step execution or changing an execution point. By providing the execution control functions as Web services, we make it possible to define a composite Web service which controls other composite Web service for adaptation. One of the major advantages of Service Supervision is reusability of the composite Web service which implements adaptation. Moreover, the execution control functions realizes more flexible control than that by some previous works on runtime adaptation([3,4,5,6]).

In the environment which frequently changes, however, we still have the following problems even if we introduce Service Supervision.

- **Difficulty in designing adaptation**
  Much flexibility of execution control functions sometimes makes it difficult to design adaptation processes due to the absence of accumulated know-how such as guidelines.
- **Cost of updating model**
  When permanent demand of an adaptation becomes apparent, it is better to update the model of the composite service. But it often costs a lot to port an adaptation process using execution control functions to the model of the composite Web service to be adapted.

Therefore we proposed Service Supervision Patterns, which guide designing adaptation processes for composite Web services. Software patterns including design patterns[7] have achieved a great success in design and analysis of software. Also in the area of workflows, workflow patterns[8] have been widely accepted.

In this paper, we organized various adaptations of composite Web services and extracted typical execution controls as Service Supervision patterns. The Service Supervision patterns consist of requirements for adaptation and WS-BPEL processes which implement the adaptation using execution control functions. Therefore it is easy for designers of composite Web services to reuse the patterns. The patterns also show how to port the WS-BPEL processes for adaptation to the model of Web service to be adapted.

The rest of this paper is organized as follows. In Section 2, first we describe Service Supervision used to realize adaptation of a composite Web service and explain the prototype we implemented. Next we organize typical adaptation processes of composite Web services and show how to realize the adaptation process using execution control functions in Section 3. Then we propose Service Supervision patterns by extracting processes frequently appear in the previous section. After introducing some related works in Section 5, we conclude this paper in Section 6.

2   Service Supervision

In [2], the authors proposed Service Supervision, which changes the behavior of a running instance of a composite Web service without changing the model of the composite Web service. We show the overview of Service Supervision and explain the prototype that we developed in this section.

Several researches have tried to change behaviors of a composite Web service without modifying the model of a composite Web service. For example, Language Grid[9] provides dynamic binding, which allows a user to specify endpoints (addresses for accessing Web services) when invoking the composite Web service. In this work, a composite Web service is designed based on only the interfaces of the constituent Web services. AO4BPEL[6] and Dynamo[5] allow a user to add processes at certain points in a composite Web service based on the concept of AOP (aspect-oriented programming). However, some functions for adaptation, such as changing an execution point, cannot be achieved by adding a process by AOP.

On the other hand, Service Supervision monitors and changes the state of running instances and controls execution of the instances. This makes it possible not only to add a process to an existing composite Web service, but also to control execution state, including changing an execution point. Using Service Supervision, we can adapt a composite Web service to changes of the environment and business rules without modifying the model and deploying it.

2.1   Execution Control Functions

We implemented execution control functions shown in Table 1 to realize Service Supervision. The functions get/set the state of a running instance of composite Web service or control execution of a composite Web service itself.

The functions are provided as Web services. Therefore we can define a composite Web service which controls the behavior of an instance of other composite Web service by combining the execution control functions.

Although the execution control functions do not change the model of the composite Web service, they realize various processes required for adaptation.

Take an example to clarify the necessity of the execution control functions. In an environment where many Web services are published by various providers,

Table 1. Execution control functions

API	Effect
step	Execute the next activity in a composite Web service.
suspend, resume	Suspend/Resume execution of a composite Web service.
getVariable, setVariable	Get/Set variable defined in a composite Web service.
getState, setState	Get/Set states of activities, such as ready, running, finished and suspended.
setAddress	Set an endpoint address of an invocation in a composite Web service.
setEP	Set the activities which is executed next.
setBP	Set a breakpoint at an activity in a composite Web service and a callback Web service invoked when the the execution stops at the breakpoint.

such as the Language Grid[9], a Web service can be shared by some composite Web services in an unexpected way. For example, execution of the composite Web service in Fig. 1(a) may fail in such an environment. This composite Web service translates a long document. It first splits the given document into sentences (**split**) and then translates the sentences by the machine translation service (**translate**) in the loop. Next, it merges the results of translation (**merge**).

Assume that the provider of the machine translation service newly introduced a limit on number of invocations of its service because too many requests were given during a certain period. In such case, execution by a user may unexpectedly cause a failure of exectuion by another user. Thus, when the number of invocations approaches the limit, we need to switch the service to different one by other provider. To implement this solution, we need to modify the document translation service as shown in Fig. 1(b). Before invoking the machine translation service, the composite Web service invokes the external service to increment the recorded number of invocations (**count**).

However, the change of the model is not efficient when many service providers are involved and policies of the service providers frequently change.

Our solution based on Service Supervision is to introduce a composite Web service shown in the upper part of Fig. 2. This composite Web service counts

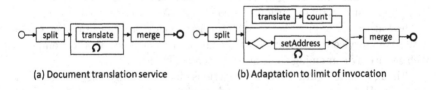

(a) Document translation service   (b) Adaptation to limit of invocation

Fig. 1. Modification of a composite Web service for adaptation

the number of invocations of the machine translation service and changes the endpoint address to that of another machine translation service when needed.

The composite Web service first sets a breakpoint (setBP) before the invocation of the machine translation service **translate** in the document translation service. It also sets invocation of **count** as the callback Web service for the breakpoint. When **count** is invoked, it increments the recorded number of invocations of the machine translation service (**increment**). If the number of invocations of the machine translation service exceeds the limit, the endpoint address of the machine translation service is changed (**setAddress**).

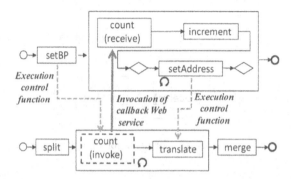

Fig. 2. Composite Web service which controls other composite Web service

One of the major advantages of our solution is reusability of the composite Web service for the adaptation. The composite service in the upper part of Fig. 2 can be applied to various composite Web services in which the number of invocation of a constituent Web service is limited just by setting the breakpoint.

2.2 Prototype

We developed a prototype of Service Supervision by extending an existing WS-BPEL engine, ActiveBPEL[1] as shown in Fig. 3.

The architecture consists of two parts: Composite Web service execution engine and interaction control engine. On the Composite Web service execution engine, both a composite Web service to be controlled and a composite Web service which controls it using execution control functions are executed.

The interaction control engine is responsible for coordination among more than one instances of composite Web services based on a given choreography because some adaptation processes require the instances to be synchronized. Assume that two instances of the document translation service try to invoke **count** (**invoke**) in Fig. 2 at almost the same time. The composite Web service in the upper part of Fig. 2 receives the request for **count** (**receive**) that arrives first and starts to increment the number of invocations. If the composite Web service

---

[1] http://www.activevos.com/community-open-source.php

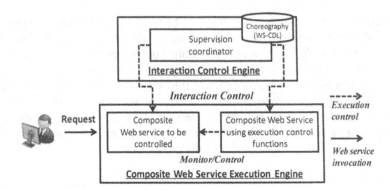

Fig. 3. The implemented prototype

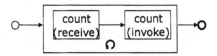

Fig. 4. Choreography for definition of control protocol

receives the request from another instance of the document translation service while incrementing the number of invocations, count (invoke) fails because it is not waiting for the request at count (receive).

To solve this problem, we introduce choreography, which defines the protocol of interactions between a composite Web service which controls other composite services and the composite Web service being controlled. We adopt WS-CDL (Web Service Choreography Description Language)[10], a standard language for choreography of Web services. We show an example of choreography in Fig. 4, which defines protocol of interactions between the two composite Web services shown in Fig. 2.

In Figure 4, a rectancle which has a word inside represents an interaction between the two composite Web services. This protocol ensures that the execution of count (receive) in the composite Web service which controls the document translation composite Web service and count (invoke) in the document translation composite Web service are processed in this order.

3   Adaptation of Composite Service Using Execution Control

In this section, we organize various adaptation of composite Web service explained in some previous works[11,12,13,14]. The aim is to extract reusable processes for various adaptation like the composite Web service shown in the upper part of Fig. 2.

Some adaptation processes described in this section can be realized by the existing framework, such as WS-BPEL. But it is not flexible enough to adapt WS-BPEL process to frequent change of environment or business rule by changing the model of a composite Web service. Therefore we assume that an adaptation process is temporarily realized by Service Supervision, and that it is ported to the model when the adaptation process is permanently required.

3.1 Exception Handling

WS-BPEL provides exception handling mechanism. In a dynamic or open environment, however, the exception handling of WS-BPEL is not flexible enough.

Using execution control functions, we can realize more flexible adaptations as follows:

- **Recovery**
  Exceptions which are unexpected at the design time can be recovered by dynamically adding processes for montoring and recovering.
- **Alert**
  Continuous check of consistency of data enables us to detect symptoms of exceptions and to show an alert.
- **Avoid exception**
  We can often avoid exceptions by adding a preprocess of an input to a service or replacing a task which may cause an exception with a human task,
- **Enforcement by humans**
  In case that execution of a composite Web service cannot recover from an exception by an existing recovering process, humans often need to set states of tasks manually.

3.2 Dynamic Change

We show major adaptation processes which cover the change of requirements of users or state of services below.

- **Dynamic binding**
  In dynamic environment, we often need to select services at runtime. This is achieved by getting a list of available services and setting an endpoint address.
- **On-the-fly composition**
  According to the operator's request, the system is often required to generate a new process and temporarily add it into the composite Web service.

3.3 Human Involvement

BPEL4People[15] is an extension of WS-BPEL and realizes combination of human tasks and Web services. Using the extension, we can define an invocation of a human task in the manner similar to that of a Web service. When a human task is invoked, the task is sent to a person who is responsible for the task. The human task is finished when the person inputs the result of the task.

However, human tasks often cause an unexpected problem due to the much flexibility of human behavior. We show adaptation processes required to handle the problems with human tasks below.

- **Negotiation**
  When the result of a human task is not good enough, the task needs to be executed again. This process often includes negotiation between the person who performs the task and the evaluator because the evaluation can be subjective and the evaluator must give a concrete instruction for re-execution.
- **Flexibility control**
  When the granularity of a human task is coarse, a person who is responsible for the task can efficiently perform his task. But deviation from the requirements of the task is prone to occur due to the flexibility. On the other hand, we can reduce deviation by defining fine tasks. In that case, the efficiency often declines. Therefore we need to control flexibility by configuring granularity of tasks.
- **Guideline**
  When the detail of the procedure of a task is not defined, showing guidelines can be a help for reducing deviation from the implicit requirements.
- **Clarify responsibility**
  More than one person or organization often involve in a task. If the task sometimes causes an exception, it is required to decompose the task in order to clarify the responsibility of people or organizations involved.
- **Reassignment** Based on the performance record of a person who is responsible for a task or changes of business rules, we often need to change the assignment of people to tasks. Therefore the operator needs to dynamically configure the assingment or invoke a composite Web service which decides the assignment.

3.4   Monitoring

An operator often needs to obtain and aggregate information of instances of a composite Web service. However, the existing standard framework, such as WS-BPEL, does not provide enough functions for monitoring. Therefore Service Supervision can help the operator monitor execution states from the following aspects:

- **Aggregate state information**
  By aggregating information of states of tasks (e.g. assigned, running, suspended, etc.) over multiple running instances, operators can know load on each Web service or a person who is responsible for the tasks.
- **Macro** An operator often needs to perform a complex procedure which collects and aggregate information of running instances. Therefore we need allow the operator to define his/her own procedure.

3.5 Migration

Migrating to a new SOA system often confuses users because procedures and operations for the users sometimes completely change. The load on the users can be reduced by incremental migration as shown below:

- **Plug-in**
  When a user interface for humans which is used before the migration, plugging it into a composite Web service which are newly introduced allows people work in a practiced manner.
- **Partial reuse**
  People who work following a business process can be confused if the whole business process is update at once. Therefore, we sometimes need to begin with replacing a part of the current business process with that of new one.
- **Transfer**
  When the model of a composite Web service is updated, a running instance which is created from the old model is sometimes required to migrate to the new model. Therefore we have to be able to create a new instance from the new model and migrate the execution state of the instance of the old model to new one keeping consistency.

4 Service Supervision Patterns

The adaptation processes described in the previous section can be realized by combining execution control functions shown in Section 2. However, the much flexibility of the execution control functions sometimes makes it difficult to implement the adaptation processes because a designer usually does not have experience on design using execution control functions. Therefore we propose Service Supervision patterns, which consists of typical requirements and WS-BPEL processes using execution control functions as solutions.

Software patterns, including design patterns, have achieved a great success in design and analysis of software. Also in the area of workflow, workflow patterns

Table 2. Comparison among software patterns, workflow patterns, and Service Sueprvision patterns

	Software patterns	Workflow patterns	Service Supervision patterns
Problem	Requirements for analysis, development and optimization of software	Requirements for construction of business flow	Requirements for adaptation
Solution	Direction of design and development	Activity diagram	Composite service using execution control functions
Focus	Abstraction of system architecture and design	Analysis of business	Operation and lifecycle of composite services

have been proposed and they show the design of workflows which satisfy various requirements[8]. On the other hand, Service Supervision patterns give requirements for adaptation process as problems and composite Web services which satisfy the requirements by combining execution control functions as solutions. For example, the composite Web service which is shown in Fig. 2 and controls the document translation service can be seen as a pattern which monitors the execution and adds some processes by generalizing "count" and "setAddress".

Table 2 shows the comparison among software patterns, workflow patterns, and Service Sueprvision patterns we propose in this paper.

Service Supervision patterns are easy for designers of composite Web services to understand because the solutions are described in WS-BPEL processes. Moreover, we need little change to port them to the model of a composite Web service to be adapted.

A composite Web service defined in a Service Supervision pattern consists of the following elements:

- Control constructs and activities of WS-BPEL
- Execution control functions
- Template task

A composite Web service provided as a solution of Service Supervision patterns runs on the same execution engine as composite Web services to be adapted. The execution control functions are ones that introduced in Section 2. A template task is defined according to the required adaptation processes.

We describe each Service Supervision pattern below. Tasks labeled as T represent template tasks. We omit activities which define dataflow for the simplicity.

4.1 Trigger Patterns

Runtime adaptations of a composite Web service are triggered when some changes or events which require adaptation are detected. Such detection is performed (a) at a certain point in a composite Web service, (b) continuously, (c) on operator's request, or (d) when time-out of a task happens. The following patterns realize the triggers for adaptations.

Pattern 1: Synchronous Watch

- **Description.** The task set to the template task is executed at a certain point of the composite Web service to be adapted.
- **Implementation.** Set a breakpoint at the point to which some processes should be added and set the composite Web service of this pattern as a callback Web service.
- **Example.** Adding a process for validation of the result of a constituent service and an exception handling process.
- **Porting to model.** Insert tasks set to the template task into the point where the breakpoint is set.

Pattern 2: Continuous Watch

- **Description.** The task set to the template task is continuously executed during the execution of composite Web service to be adapted.
- **Implementation.** Execute all tasks of composite Web service to be adapted by *step* execution and execute the template task after each *step*.
- **Example.** Checking consistency of data handled by the composite Web services.
- **Porting to model.** To add a monitoring process to many points in a composite Web service seriously declines the performance. Therefore this pattern should be used to find the point where some monitoring is required before the model is changed.

Pattern 3: Asynchronous Watch

- **Description.** The task set to the template task is executed on request.
- **Implementation.** Start execution of the template task after receiving a request.
- **Example.** Reporting execution state of a composite Web service on the request by operator's request.
- **Porting to model.** Add an asynchronous *Receive*, the task set to the template task and *Reply*.

Pattern 4: Timeout

- **Description.** The task set to the template task is executed when a task does not finish in a certain period of time.
- **Implementation.** Execute the target task by *step* and finish the instance of this pattern by *terminate*, which is a WS-BPEL activity. If the specified period of time elapses before the target task finishes, *suspend* execution of the composite Web service and recover the target task by the task set to the template task.
- **Example.** When a service is temporarily available or a human task is taking too long, this pattern makes it possible to dynamically change services or assignment of people.
- **Porting to model.** Replace *step* with the target task as asynchronous invocation and put the composite Web service of this pattern instead of the target task.

4.2   Evaluation and Retry Patterns

When the result of a task is invalid or the quality of the result is not good enough, we need to retry the task until an appropriate result is obtained. We show the two following patterns for the validation/evaluation of the result and retry.

Pattern 5: Automatic Retry

- **Description.** This pattern assumes that validation and retry are automatically performed. After validating the result of a task, this pattern retries the task if needed. The composite Web service which changes the conditions of execution of the task is set to template task.

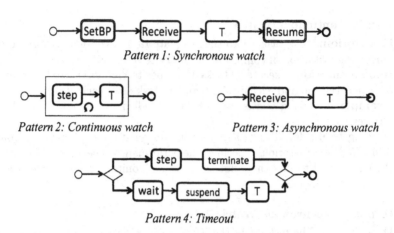

Fig. 5. Trigger patterns

- **Implementation.** Set execution point by *setEP*, retry the task by *step*, and change of the condition of execution at the template task in loop. To restore the execution state before retry, we introduced *getState* and *setState*.
- **Example.** This pattern enables us to switch a service to an alternative when execution of the service fails. This pattern also realizes the cycle of evaluation and change of parameters, which is shown as Program Supervision[16].
- **Porting to model.** Put the task to be retried and template task in loop and add activities which set states before retry.

Pattern 6: Human Evaluation

- **Description.** This pattern retries a task when the quality of the result of the task is not good enough. This pattern assumes that both the target task and the evaluation are performed by humans. Therefore this pattern allows people who are responsible for the tasks to communicate with each other by introducing a task for evaluation as a template task.
- **Implementation.** Instead of the task for changing conditions of execution in Automatic Retry pattern, put the task for evaluation and communication after *step* of the target task.
- **Example.** This pattern allows an evaluator to show the guideline for the task to a person who is responsible for the task even if the guideline was not defined when the model of composite Web service is designed.
- **Porting to model.** Put the task to be retried and the task set to template task in loop.

4.3   Patch Patterns

The following patterns are used to make up small defect keeping the most of initial behaviors.

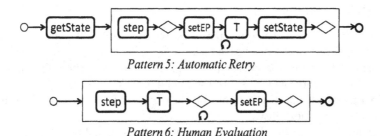

Pattern 5: Automatic Retry

Pattern 6: Human Evaluation

Fig. 6. Evaluation and retry patterns

Pattern 7: Add Alternative

- **Description.** This pattern adds a task which is an alternative of a task in a composite Web service when a given condition is satisfied.
- **Implementation.** Put the template task and the target task in conditional branches.
- **Example.** When a Web service often causes an exception under a certain condition, this pattern can be applied to temporarily delegate the task to humans.
- **Porting to model.** Replace the target task with the conditional branches defined in this pattern.

Pattern 8: Partial Execution

- **Description.** This pattern executes a part of an existing composite Web service.
- **Implementation.** *step* the tasks to be executed and *skip* other tasks.
- **Example.** This pattern realizes an incremental migration to a new composite Web service.
- **Porting to model.** Remove the tasks which are skipped by this pattern from the model of composite Web service.

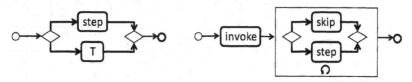

Pattern 7: Add Alternative   *Pattern 8: Partial Execution*

Fig. 7. Patch patterns

4.4 Granularity Control Patterns

The following patterns compose or decompose tasks to control flexibility of human tasks.

Pattern 9: Compose

- **Description.** This pattern replaces consecutive tasks with one task which is equivalent to the consecutive tasks.
- **Implementation.** *skip* tasks defined in the model of a composite Web service and execute the task set to the template task.
- **Example.** This pattern is applied if the efficiency for a human task declines due to lack of flexibility.
- **Porting to model.** Replace consecutive tasks with the task set to the template task.

Pattern 10: Decompose

- **Description.** This pattern decomposes a task into some subtasks.
- **Implementation.** Execute the predefined subtasks and *skip* the task to be decomposed.
- **Example.** When a task is virtually executed by some people, this pattern is applied to clarify the responsibility of each person.
- **Porting to model.** Replace the target task with the subtasks set to the template tasks.

Pattern 9: Compose   *Pattern 10: Decompose*

Fig. 8. Granularity control patterns

Table 3. Possible adaptations by Service Supervision patterns

Patterns / Adaptation	Synchronous watch	Continuous watch	Asynchronous watch	Time out	Auto retry	Human evaluation	Add alternative	Partial execution	compose	decompose
Exception handling										
Recovery	●	●		●	●					
Alert	●	●	●	●						
Avoid	●	●					●	●		●
Enforcement			●	●		●				
Dynamic Change										
Dynamic binding			●	●	●					
On-the-fly composition			●			●	●			
Human Involvement										
Negotiation	●		●			●				
Control flexibility			●	●		●			●	●
Guideline	●		●			●				
Clarify responsibility			●	●		●				●
Reassignment					●	●				
Monitoring										
Aggregate state info	●	●	●							
Macro	●	●	●							
Migration										
Plug-in	●						●	●	●	
Reuse	●						●	●		
Transfer			●					●		

Table 3 shows adaptations described in Section 3 and Service Supervision patterns which can be used for each adaptation.

All adaptations are triggered by one of Trigger patterns. Using Trigger patterns, the operator can easily start or stop the adaptation processes. However, the adaptation processes have to be defined before they are applied. This is the reason the patterns do not work well for adaptations which require us to define an extreamly wide range of processes, such as on-the-fly composition and transfer, although the patterns can be frequently reused for rather simple adaptations such as exception handling.

5 Related Works

Software patterns, which describe typical problems and solutions in software development, have been expanded against the background of complexity of recent software development. The most well-known software patterns are design patterns[7] and they show means for system design based on object-oriented programming. On the other hand, van der Aalst et al. proposed workflow patterns[8], which show requirements for constructing business flows and activity diagrams as the solutions. The workflow patterns focus on analysis of business, excluding perspective of system implementation.

Similarly, Service Supervision patterns proposed in this paper also aims at reusing know-how about design. But Service Supervision patterns focus on adaptation processes which can be realized by execution control functions and there is no previous work on reuse related to composite Web service for adaptation as far as we know.

Several previous works have tried to change behaviors of a composite Web service without modifying the composite Web service. Most of them have adopted the concept of AOP (Aspect-oriented Programming).

Some works monitor the messages exchanged between services and modify them[3,4,5]. However, the works depend on their own descriptions. This leads to the cost of design when adaptation is ported to the model of the composite Web service.

AO4BPEL[6] enables us to insert processes described in BPEL into before or after an activity in an existing composite Web service as a pointcut. Therefore the processes defined for adaptation using AO4BPEL can easily be inserted into the model of a composite Web service. But some adaptation processes cannot be realized by the method because it does not provide execution control functions such as setting execution point. The authors also introduced some applications, but they are not comprehensively organized.

6 Conclusion

Service Supervision, which controls the behavior of running instances of composite Web services using execution control functions, allows us to flexibly adapt composite Web service to changes of the environment or business rules. This makes constituent Web services of a composite Web services transparent to users and allows us to provide the composite Web services as a "cloud" service. However, the much flexibility of Service Supervision sometimes makes it difficult for the designer of composite Web services to design adaptation processes due to the absence of accumulated know-how. Moreover, it often costs to port the adaptation processes to the model of composite Web service to be adapted.

Therefore we proposed Service Supervision patterns, which provide typical requirements for adaptation and reusable WS-BPEL processes which implements the adaptation. The contributions of this work are as follows:

- We organized various adaptation processes based on some previous works and explained how they can be implemented using control execution functions.
- We extracted typical execution controls for adaptation processes and showed how to port them to the model of a composite Web service.

The Service Supervision patterns can reduce the load on the designer who implements adaptation processes or ports them to the model.

In future work, it is required to investigate the effect on the performance of each pattern. We expect that the temporary adaptation is achieved by Service Supervision, and then it is ported to the model when the permanent demand of the adaptation becomes apparent. Therefore the investigation on the performance helps the operator decide when and how the adaptation should be ported to the model.

Acknowledgment

This work was supported by Strategic Information and Communications R&D Promotion Programme (SCOPE) of the Ministry of Internal Affairs and Communications of Japan.

References

1. Business process execution language for web services (BPEL), version 1.1 (2003), http://www.ibm.com/developerworks/library/ws-bpel/
2. Tanaka, M., Ishida, T., Murakami, Y., Morimoto, S.: Service supervision: Coordinating web services in open environment. In: IEEE International Conference on Web Services, ICWS 2009 (2009)
3. Moser, O., Rosenberg, F., Dustdar, S.: Non-intrusive monitoring and service adaptation for ws-bpel. In: 17th International World Wide Web Conference (WWW 2008), pp. 815–824 (2008)
4. Mosincat, A., Binder, W.: Transparent runtime adaptability for BPEL processes. In: Bouguettaya, A., Krueger, I., Margaria, T. (eds.) ICSOC 2008. LNCS, vol. 5364, pp. 241–255. Springer, Heidelberg (2008)
5. Baresi, L., Guinea, S., Plebani, P.: Policies and aspects for the supervision of BPEL processes. In: Krogstie, J., Opdahl, A.L., Sindre, G. (eds.) CAiSE 2007 and WES 2007. LNCS, vol. 4495, pp. 340–354. Springer, Heidelberg (2007)

6. Charfi, A., Mezini, M.: AO4BPEL: An aspect-oriented extension to BPEL. World Wide Web 10(3), 309–344 (2007)
7. Gamma, E., Helm, R., Johnson, R., Vlissides, J.: Design patterns: elements of reusable object-oriented software. Addison-Wesley, Reading (1995)
8. van der Aalst, W.M.P., Hofstede, A.t., Kiepuszewski, B., Barros, A.: Workflow patterns. Distributed and Parallel Databases 14(3), 5–51 (2003)
9. Ishida, T.: Language Grid: An infrastructure for intercultural collaboration. In: IEEE/IPSJ Symposium on Applications and the Internet (SAINT 2006), pp. 96–100 (2006)
10. Web services choreography description language version 1.0 (2005), http://www.w3.org/TR/ws-cdl-10/
11. Kammer, P.J., Bolcer, G.A., Taylor, R.N., Hitomi, A.S., Bergman, M.: Techniques for supporting dynamic and adaptive workflow. Computer Supported Cooperative Work (CSCW) 9(3), 269–292 (2000)
12. Müller, R., Greiner, U., Rahm, E.: Agentwork: a workflow system supporting rule-based workflow adaptation. Data and Knowledge Engineering 51(2), 223–256 (2004)
13. van der Aalst, W.M.P., Basten, T., Verbeek, H.M.W., Verkoulen, P.A.C., Voorhoeve, M.: Adaptive workflow. on the interplay between flexibility and support. In: Proceedings of the first International Conference on Enterprise Information Systems, pp. 353–360 (1999)
14. Han, Y., Sheth, A., Bussler, C.: A taxonomy of adaptive workflow management. In: ACM Conference on Computer Supported Cooperative Work, CSCW 1998 (1998)
15. WS-BPEL extension for people (bpel4people), version 1.0 (2007), http://www.ibm.com/developerworks/webservices/library/specification/ws-bpel4people/
16. Thonnat, M., Clement, V., Elst, J.v.d.: Supervision of perception tasks for autonomous systems: The OCAPI approach. In: 3rd Annual Conference of AI, Simulation, and Planning in High Autonomy Systems, pp. 210–217 (1992)

Cloud Computing Platforms

Track Session 3

Self-managed Microkernels:
From Clouds towards Resource Fabrics

Lutz Schubert[1], Stefan Wesner[1], Alexander Kipp[1], and Alvaro Arenas[2]

[1] HLRS – Höchstleistungsrechenzentrum Universität Stuttgart,
Nobelstr. 19, 70569 Stuttgart, Germany
{schubert,wesner,kipp}@hlrs.de
[2] STFC Rutherford Appleton Laboratory, e-Science Centre,
Didcot, OX11 0QX, UK
alvaro.arenas@stfc.ac.uk

Abstract. Cloud Computing provides a solution for remote hosting of applications and processes in a scalable and managed environment. With the increasing number of cores in a single processor and better network performance, provisioning on platform level becomes less of an issue for future machines and thus for future business environments. Instead, it will become a major issue to manage the vast amount of computational resources within the direct environment of each process – across the web or locally. Future resource management will have to investigate in particular into dynamic & intelligent processes (re)distribution according to resource availability and demand. This paper elaborates the specific issues faced in future "cloud environments" and proposes a microkernel architecture designed to compensate these deficits.

Keywords: distributed operating systems, SOA, multi-core systems, large-scale HPC, heterogeneous systems.

1 Misconceiving the Cloud?

Cloud Computing is often considered the future of computing platform provisioning: reliable application hosting over the web allows easy accessibility from everywhere to everything. Notably, however, this is a slight misconception of the actual working focus of "cloud computing", which focuses primarily on the manageability and scalability aspects of hosting. Remote hosting as such (i.e. reliable server farms) is not in itself a novelty and has been supported by multiple providers for a long time now – with remote access such as enabled by VMWare[1] or Remote Desktop[2], and replicated virtual machines, this already provided most of the capabilities associated today with Clouds. Only increased network and computational performance, as well as the advent of simple web "APIs" have allowed the sudden success of this approach.

Virtualisation, enhanced routing, on-the-fly replication, reconfigurable resources etc. are the core features of modern clouds and thus lead to other, more commercially

---

[1] http://www.vmware.com/

[2] http://www.microsoft.com/windows/windows-vista/features/remote-desktop-connection.aspx

D.R. Avresky et al. (Eds.): Cloudcomp 2009, LNICST 34, pp. 167–185, 2010.
© Institute for Computer Sciences, Social-Informatics and Telecommunications Engineering 2010

oriented use cases which make use of the more innovative features of cloud computing. This includes aspects such as hosting of web "services" (e-Commerce) with demand-specific scalability and thus availability, as well as improved reliability – in other words, the application and data is highly available, independent of problems with the resources and amount of concurrent invocations. This becomes particularly interesting for e-Commerce environments with a high amount of customers, such as Amazon or eBay, which notably belong to the first entities actually making use of cloud-like environments internally.

Many users mistake cloud computing with high performance computing and whilst the same principles can principally be applied in the HPC environment, machine restrictions and requirements of the respective applications only allow for a certain degree of scalability and manageability, as replication is not easily achieved with the amount of resources in use, and scalability in the context of HPC is dependent on the algorithm, not the amount of requests.

Considering the current development in processor architectures and in network performance, future systems will effectively incorporate a cloud *environment* within a single machine. Due to their nature, these machines effectively allow for both: distributed / parallelised process execution (current HPC), as well as scalable and reliable application hosting. It should be noted in this context that "cloud computing" is not a technology as such, but rather a concept, respectively a paradigm. This paper will therefore examine the specific requirements put forward towards hosting applications in future environments, and elaborate an approach to address these requirements using approaches from Cloud Computing, Grid and SOA.

2   From Historical to Future Systems

The current development in computing system clearly indicates that the amount of cores being integrated into a single processor / machine will steadily increase in future years, whilst the speed of individual cores will increase only minimally. Implicitly, the system will not become more efficient regarding individual (single-thread) applications, but will provide an improved *overall* performance by allowing for parallel execution of multiple processes or threads concurrently.

Such systems are effectively identical to what was considered computer farms a few years back, where multiple computers are hosted within the same environment and can communicate with each other in order to coordinate and distribute processes. The Grid and P2P computing emerged from such environments, in order to maximize usage of otherwise unused resources (machines), e.g. during lunch-break or when no applications are running on the respective machines. Whilst the Grid has moved towards a different scope of distributed computing, one can still clearly see the relationship to Grid, SOA and in particular clouds: managing applications in a distributed environment so as to ensure reliability and higher performance. In particular in the P2P environment, one particular task consisted in replicating the same application with different configuration settings so as to produce a set of "integratable" results in the end: this only worked for "embarrassingly parallel" tasks, but still allowed for a definite increase in overall execution performance.

The tasks of such systems are similar to what modern operating systems (OS) have to face in multi-core environments: distribution of processes, according to individual schedules, as well as integration of results and management of cross-machine calls. As opposed to P2P systems with typically little to no requirements towards synchronization of the tasks, Grid systems investigated into coordinated execution of processes in distributed environments, whilst finally clouds are little concerned with distributed execution, but with distribution and scheduling of individual processes.

An efficient multi-core operating system should obviously not be restricted to parallel execution of standalone processes (thus reducing the scheduling problem), but should particularly support parallelized and highly scalable (multi-thread) processes. Accordingly, such a system needs to draw from all of the paradigms and concepts above in order to provide the necessary scalability, reliability and manageability of distributed processes in distributed environments.

2.1 Classical Approaches

In order to identify the specific capabilities to be fulfilled by future systems, it is recommendable to examine the classical concepts towards managing distributed environments in more detail so as to make best use of the multi-core capabilities:

Grid Systems. The modern grid integrates different resource types on a *service* level, i.e. principally follows the concepts of Virtual Organisations [1, 2], where the combination of individual services leads to enhanced capabilities. However, the Grid does provide means for common interfaces that allow the coordinated integration of heterogeneous resources for higher, abstract processes and applications.

Distributed Applications. Some computational algorithms can execute logical parts in parallel, so as to improve the overall process through multiple instantiation of the same functional block. One may distinguish between optimal parallel code (no data exchange between the blocks) and distributed applications that share some kind of data. Of particular interest thereby is the capability to control communication and to deal with the scheduling issues involved in multiple resource exploitation.

Cloud Environments. In a world of high connectivity, not only scalability of individual (distributed) applications is relevant, but also scalability in the sense of accessibility to a specific service / resource, i.e. replication of individual processes according to demand. This requires enhanced control over the resources and maintenance of multiple, potentially coupled instances of processes and data.

2.2 Scoping Future Multi-core Systems

As described above, the current cloud approach is insufficient to address the requirements of future multi-core systems, respectively might become obsolete with the capacities of such systems. However, in order to exploit the capabilities of multi-core systems, and in order to address the respective requirements towards future applications, clouds and related approaches provide a strong conceptual basis to realize such future support.

In light of the development of middleware and hardware, multi-core systems *should* be able to support the following capabilities:

Concurrency. The most obvious capability (to be) fulfilled by multi-core systems consists in the "real" concurrent execution of processes and applications, i.e. running (at least) one process per core so that they can be executed in real parallel instead of constant switching – however, each core may host multiple processes which are executed in a multitasking manner. The scheduling mechanism will thereby decide how to distribute processes across cores so that e.g. higher priority jobs compete with fewer processes on the same core, or get more time assigned than other jobs.

This feature is a simple extension to classical multitasking operating systems that assign jobs with different time slots in the overall execution schedule according to their respective priority. All current main stream operating systems choose this approach to exploit the multi-core feature for performance improvement, yet this approach only improves the net performance of the whole system, not of single processes.

Parallelism. More importantly than distributing individual processes to single cores, an application or job may be separated into *parallel* threads which can be executed concurrently at the same time. As opposed to concurrent individual processes, parallel processes share communication and information directly with each other – depending on the actual use cases either at nominated integration points, "offline" (i.e. via a common stack) or at even based, at random, unpredicted points in time. This poses additional constraints on timing and distribution of job instances / threads in the environment in order to ensure communication, respectively to reduce latency. Individual infrastructures thereby have a direct impact on this issue.

Typically, it is up to the developer to respect all this aspects when coding distributed applications. However, the requirements put forward to the developer will increase in future systems due to multiple reasons: *heterogeneous* resources will require dedicated code; *concurrent* processes will put additional strain on communication management (see above); processes and applications will *compete* with each other over resources; *latencies* will differ between setup and may thus lead to different communication strategies to be employed.

As the computing system grows and the complexity increases, the developer needs a simpler way to exploit the infrastructure with his / her code. Implicitly the infrastructure needs to provide stronger means and support the parallelization work.

Scalability. Parallel processes require that part of the code / a thread will be executed multiple times concurrently – in some cases the number is directly defined by the infrastructure (number of computing cores available) and not (only) by the application. In addition to this, in particular in the server domain, the same process may have to be instantiated and executed multiple times concurrently, e.g. when multiple invocations are executed at the same time.

Multi-core processors allow real parallel execution of one instance per core. Obviously, the system is restricted by the number of cores and the processing speed, with any number of instances higher than the number of cores impacting more and more on the reaction. With additionally concurrent jobs competing for the computational resources, managing scalability becomes a complicated aspect of both cloud and server provisioning, but also for specific common user cases, in particular where the processes have high computational requirements.

This aspect also strongly relates to data management issues involved in parallelism (cf. above), as some instances will have to share data between them, whilst others will host their own data environment (often also referred to as "stateless" vs. "stateful").

Reliability. Server architectures often use mechanisms of data and process replication in order to increase the respective reliability. Additional approaches include dedicated checkpointing and rollback. Whilst in classical "common" usage scenarios the cost for reliability was too high for the benefit gained from it, in particular cloud, server and HPC environments strongly require reliability features.

Depending on the relevance of the application and data, multi-core platforms should hence be able to support reliability.

Dynamicity. With multiple processes competing over the same resources (instead of, as in most cloud, server and HPC use cases typically only hosting one dedicated job), different resources will become available and unavailable over time, to which the distribution of processes must adapt. This ranges from simple (re)distribution of processes across the infrastructure to up- and downscaling of specific instances (see parallelism and scalability).

Notably, the degree of necessity per requirement and the degree of support by the system itself depends on the actual usage scenario. Nonetheless, in order in particular to ensure *portability* of applications across platforms and systems, i.e. in order to allow developers to provide their code equally as service, process or web application, it is mandatory that the essential basis of the system is identical.

3 The Monolithic Mistake

The current approach to dealing with multiple computational resources in a *tightly coupled* system consists in one central instance controlling all processes across these resources, i.e. all scheduling and communication is essentially centralised. It is notable that *loosely coupled* systems typically host communication support and essential system control features per node (as opposed to core), whilst only overall scheduling is centralised in the cluster. This decision is basing primarily on communication latency which will seriously impact on the performance of HPC systems and even though latency is much diminished in tightly coupled systems, the central instance will act as a bottleneck that potentially can lead to clashes, unnecessarily stalling the individual processes:

Monolithic kernels are often said to scale well with the amount of processes on many processors (see e.g. [16]). It should be noted though that this is not identical to scaling well with the amount of processors. Most tests are executed on a limited number of cores where the increment in the number of processes effectively shows similar behaviour in single-core machines, i.e. scalability is primarily restricted by memory and processor-speed, not by the operating system itself, as the degree of concurrency and hence the additional strain on process management is comparatively low.

The main reason for this consists in the fact that the OS primarily deals with system requests, context switches and device access, not with the process itself. In other words, as long as the processes do not require something from the OS and whilst the scheduler does not demand a context switch between processes, the OS' tasks are not affected by the amount of processes. Obviously with an increase in the number of jobs, the amount of requests increase – notably, in a single core system the average amount of context switches does not increase as they are defined by the scheduling algorithm and only indirectly by the amount of processes (depending on the scheduling strategy).

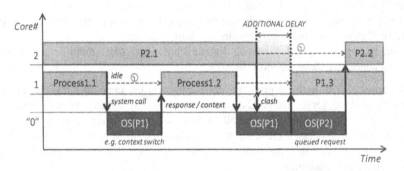

Fig. 1. System requests of concurrent cores may clash if they occur within the same timeframe (time-relationships exaggerated)

With the increasing amount of cores the operating system in particular has to deal with more system requests – however, this alone would not impact drastically on the performance, as system requests are comparatively few and quick as opposed to process execution. Hence, scalability would only be affected if more system requests need to be handled than a single core can execute. More drastic, however, is the impact of system request clashes which arises from the concurrent nature of process execution: as depicted in Fig. 1, a second core may request an operation from the operating system whilst the latter is still dealing with a request from the first core.

Under normal conditions these clashes hardly affect the overall performance, as they occur rarely and as the delay caused by it is comparatively short. However, with the number of cores rising to a few thousands, clashes become more regular, thus leading to a significant overall delay in processing and hence decreasing the effective performance per core.

Fig. 2 depicts this issue in an exaggerated fashion for the sake of visibility[3]: most monolithic kernels (and in particular most developers) assume that processes are executed in a fashion similar to Fig. 2 above, i.e. with short gaps between processes caused by context switches, respectively by other system requests. In reality, however, these requests overlap and causing the OS to queue the messages and execute them in sequential fashion, thus delaying process execution even further. Fig. 2 below indicates how these overlaps summarise during a given timeframe, whereas dark blocks depict the delay caused in addition to the (expected) system request execution time and the arrows reflect the accumulated delay per core within the timeframe. Note that we assume in both cases that a full core ("0") is dedicated to OS execution for the sake of simplicity.

---

[3] Actual figures will be published in a separate paper – please contact the authors for more information.

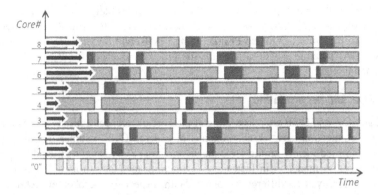

Fig. 2. Multiple processes executed in real parallel lead to significant process delays due to overlaps in system requests – the dark blocks denote *additional* delays, the arrows reflect the full delay in the timeframe. This figure assumes that one core ("0") is designated completely to the operating system.

Obviously, this impact depends directly on the amount of cores and the number of processes running per core. With an expected number of thousands of cores in the near future, the monolithic kernel will become a bottleneck for concurrent processes.

In order to overcome this effect, each core must hence maintain enough information to allow execution of main and repeating system requests. This puts additional constraints on the scheduling and the memory management system – in particular since the actual memory per core is still comparatively small in common multicore systems. With the current communication structure in multicore processors, it is also impossible for individual cores to access the memory extension (L2 cache) without going via the main controller, and thus automatically blocking access for other processes, so that the same clash situation arises again (see e.g. [3]). Even though parallel memory access is being researched, a good strategy for exploiting the level 1 cache is still required in order to maintain a low latency.

Of course, there are further issues that impact on the performance of monolithic systems – particularly worth mentioning are distributed scheduling in centralised systems and the tight hardware binding: in heterogeneous, large-scale systems, additional overhead has to be put on the main instance, in order to maintain processes and resources. In [7] we discuss the concepts of application execution across distributed resource fabrics (similar to clouds), with a particular focus on aspects related to scheduling and dynamic infrastructures (as opposed to the kernel structure).

4 Moving on to Micro-kernels

It has often been claimed that the messaging overhead caused by the component-based segmentation of the micro-kernel approach impacts stronger on performance than the centralistic approach pursued by monolithic systems [4]. This is generally true, if one takes an essential centralistic approach with the microkernel architecture too. In essence, such an approach is identical to a monolithic system with all communication having to be routed via a central instance – with the additional overhead of complicated messaging protocols. However, this is essentially a specific use case of the microkernel architecture where the monolithic kernel is basically structured according to the Object-Oriented Programming (OOP) and Service Oriented Architectures (SOA) paradigm. It does not take the full consequences from the microkernel approach though:

4.1 SOA and Segmentation

Though SOA and OOP are related, one of the core differences consists in the communication connection between components: in general, OOP assumes that all components are hosted locally on the same machine, whilst SOA is not restricted to specific communication models – in fact, there is a certain tendency to assume that components are deployed on different resource. With respect to microkernel architectures, this implies in particular that functionalities can be separated not only "methodologically" but also with respect to their distribution across resources. Or more specifically: each core can host part of the operating system.

Typically, in modern processor architectures, one must distinguish between hierarchical internal memory (L1 & L2 cache) and external memory. Even though external memory is fast, its latency is too high for efficient computation (the processor being faster than the memory) and it brings in yet another bottleneck factor, as the cores cannot directly access the memory individually, but have to be routed via a processor-central controller (cf. Fig. 3). Future systems will allow for more flexibility with this respect, i.e. by granting parallel access to the external memory [5] – however, the main issue, latency, will still apply.

To reduce latency and thus improve performance of the system, the full execution environment should be available in level 1 cache, so that calls and jumps can be processed locally without requiring access to external memory. This is the ideal approach for single core systems, where changes in the memory structure do not affect other processes (on other cores). However, the main problem is not posed by the synchronisation between individual memory views, but in particular by the restriction in size per L1 cache – in particular with the growing amount of cores, cache memory impacts heavily on the price of the processor. In order to host the *full* execution context, however, the cache would have to cater for a) the full process code, b) the application data and c) the operating system or at least all exposed functions and methods. Together, this exceeds the limits of the cache size in almost all cases.

This is a well-known problem in High Performance Computing, where a particular challenge consists in identifying the best way(s) to distribute and access application specific data. As the cache in supercomputing nodes is way larger than the one in common multi-core systems, the thread or code part is typically fully hosted in the cache, without having to think about further split-ups. As opposed to this, however, system calls will all be routed to the main node, as this is the classical monolithic OS approach (cf. above).

The main idea of Service Oriented Architectures, similar to OOP, consists in splitting up the main process into individual methods, functionalities and sub-processes that can principally be hosted in different locations. The main challenge thereby consists in finding a sensible block size that is not too small so as to create messaging overhead and not too big so as to impact on flexibility again – typically a logical

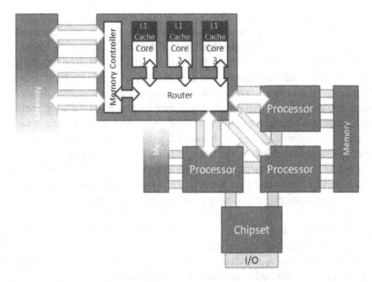

Fig. 3. The architecture of a multi-core & -processor system (adapted from [3])

segmentation provides the best results in this context. The same principle can be applied to data segmentation and is principally applied in distributed data management, though typically the segmentation criterion is comparatively arbitrary and not related to data analysis.

By applying SOA paradigms to both code *and* data, the core cache can be filled with smaller parts rather than with the full execution environment, which would exceed the available space. Obviously, this is not a general solution though, as it immediately poses the following problems:

1. Dynamicity: during normal execution, the process will jump between methods of which only parts are loaded in memory, so that constant loading and unloading has to take place.
2. Dependencies: code and data stand in a direct relationship, i.e. data access has to be considered when separating code and data blocks.
3. Integrity: with multiple code segments accessing the same data blocks and potential replications of the same data, updates need to be communicated in order to ensure integrity of the process' behaviour
4. Distribution: segmented code is not necessarily executed and loaded in a strict sequential fashion anymore – accordingly, multiple cores may host parts of the code, replicate data etc. In order to ensure integrity, dependencies and so as to actually improve performance, this distribution needs to respect the process' restrictions, requirements and capabilities.

4.2 SOA and Operating Systems

As noted, micro-kernel operating systems principally follow an object (or service) oriented approach where functionalities are segmented into libraries with flexible communication interfaces. This allows on-demand loading of libraries according to need, as well as distribution across multiple cores for more efficient execution. In other words, each core's cache may host part of the OS' functionality according to the respective processes' needs. This effectively distributes the load of the operating systems on cache and core across the system and, at the same time, increases the availability of system functionalities for the executed processes, thus improving performance and reducing the risk of clashes caused by procedure calls (cf. section 3).

Since segments can be replicated, essential, recurring functionalities (such as virtual memory management) can be hosted on each core at the same time so that no bottleneck issue arises directly. However, any access to remote resources and in this case including "external" memory (cf. section 4.1), will be subject to the same message queuing problems (and thus bottlenecks) as calls to a centralized operating system. Regarding actual physical devices (such as printers, hard drive, network etc.), the according latency is typically so high that delays are expected anyway. As for resources with "lower" latencies (such as external memory in this case), replication and background updating strategies reduce the risk of bottlenecks and improve access. By estimating *future* data access, data can be loaded in the background thus further reducing the delay caused by loading and unloading memory.

Fig. 4 illustrates the assignment of logical process *blocks* and data *segments* to the cache of individual computing units of a multi-core processor (cf. Fig. 3). Note that a full distribution is not necessarily the most efficient way to handle a single, non-parallel process: as all code blocks are executed in a sequential fashion, cores would either idle whilst they wait for the respective block to get invoked, or switch between different assigned and scheduled process blocks of the respective core.

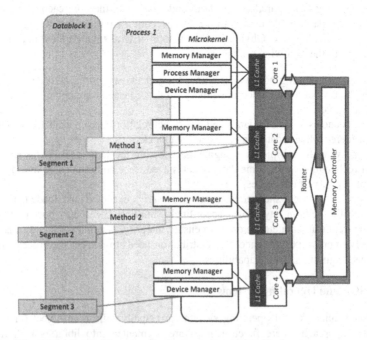

Fig. 4. Distributing Operating System, process and data block across cores

Hence, it is most crucial to find the best distribution of a) a single process' code and data blocks with respect to their interaction with one another, their invocation frequency and their respective resource requirements (see below), b) operating system unit with respect to their relationship to the code blocks, i.e. which functionalities are required by the respective process part(s) and finally c) overall processes and operating system capabilities to make the most of common requirements (e.g. towards capabilities) and adhere to the overall scheduling and prioritization criteria.

5 Principles of the Service-Oriented Operating System

Though we focus particularly on the multi-core, i.e. tightly coupled use case here in this paper, the principle communication modes between the distributed components actually depends on the setup, where obviously higher latency communication impacts on the distribution of blocks across the infrastructure (in order to meet the interaction requirements).

In this section, we will discuss the principle behaviour of SOA based microkernels, with a specific focus on the segmentation of code and data according to relationship information, requirements and restrictions.

5.1 Microkernel Base Structure

As noted, the microkernel structure is component-based, i.e. segmented into logical functional units where each "component" fulfils essential capabilities for specific tasks. For example, virtual memory management, device management, execution management etc. all build units of their own, that may even be further sub-segmented, respectively that can be adapted according to specific parameters – likewise, e.g. a local virtual memory manager instance only needs to maintain information relevant for hosted process parts and the device manager only needs to provide interfaces to devices actually required by the local processes etc.

At process load time, the requirements of the respective process are retrieved respectively analysis is initiated (cf. below) and the according operative components will be shifted to the core along with initial data and assigned code block. Note that if microkernel components are already assigned to the respective core, that adaptations may be needed to reflect the new requirements. In principle, each context switch could rearrange the local microkernel component arrangement – obviously, this would cause unnecessary load and the main task in identifying potential segmentations consists in reducing such overhead.

The space in this document is insufficient to represent the full architecture of a SOA based microkernel operating system (short S(o)OS: Service-oriented Operating System) – for more details please refer to [7, 9]. Instead, we will focus on one of the core components only, namely the virtual memory manager:

The virtual memory manager is hosted on almost all cores – it is responsible for virtualising the infrastructure per process (execution environment) and for analyzing the code behavior. In essence, it is a dynamic routing mechanism which forwards requests to and from the code to the respective location in the external memory.

Distributed process manager maintains a high level overview over the processes and control distributed execution (i.e. passing the execution points between cores whilst maintaining the execution context).

Micro schedulers replace the centralized scheduler and are responsible for scheduling the processes *per* resource, rather than for the full system. Micro schedulers are aligned to the overall priority and scheduling assignment.

Virtual device controller provides a virtual interface to resources of any kinds to allow the process to access resources without having to implement the protocol details – this is similar to e.g. the Hardware Abstraction Layer of Microsoft systems, but acts on top of the I/O manager to allow remote integration independent of the underlying communication protocol.

I/O manager, like in any other operating system, provides the communication interface between resources. It incorporates different communication layers, thus integrating tightly e.g. into the distributed virtual memory (see above).

5.2 Relationship Analysis and Distribution

The main important feature to enable service oriented microkernels as described above consists in the capability to split code and data into meaningful blocks that can be hosted by individual cores, respectively fit into their cache. As this segmentation must be dynamic, to meet the (changing) requirements and constraints of the execution system, the according distribution depends only secondarily on the information provided by the developer, even though programming models such as MPI [6] foresee that individual methods can be distributed and that specific communication modes exist with and between these segments. In order to increase performance and capability of such distributed models, new programming paradigms will be needed – as this is of secondary relevance for this paper, the according findings will be published in a separate document (see also [7]). We therefore assume in the following that no additional information has been provided by the developer, even though the model described below principally allows for extended programming annotations.

Code and data segmentation follows the principle of graph partitioning whereas nodes represent code / data blocks and edges their relationship with one another. As the code has already been compiled, i.e. since the source code is not available for structural analysis, segmentation must base on "behavioral" blocks rather than methods and class structure. At the same time, this provides better relationship information than pure code analysis, as frequency of invocation is often determined by environmental conditions, events, parameters etc. In order to analyze and obtain this kind of information, all code is enacted within a virtual memory environment, where access to data and other code areas is routed via extended paging information. This is principally identical to the way any modern operating system treats memory.

By applying a divide and conquer approach, the virtual memory is divided into logical blocks that represent the code's "typical" execution path and its relationship to data, system calls and other processes (cf. Figure 5, left). Such information is gained by following the calls and read / write access via the virtual memory. This relationship information can be represented as a directed graph (cf. Figure 5, right), whereas an edge between code nodes implies invocations, respectively jumps, whilst an edge to a data node represents a write action, respectively an edge from such a node represents read access. By analyzing access, invocation and access frequency, the graph can furthermore be annotated with a weight (w) representing the likelihood of one node calling / accessing another, as well as a frequency (f) that designates how often the respective code is accessed during a given timeframe at all (note that this information can principally be derived from a full invocation graph and the according weights of the nodes).

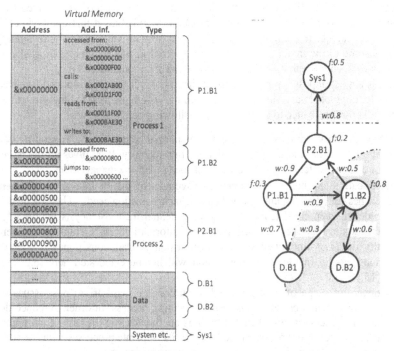

Fig. 5. Annotated memory and relationship analysis. f stands for the "frequency" of execution in a given timeframe and w for the likelihood that the caller invokes the respective node.

Implicitly, the information exactness increases over the amount of executions and during the time actually using the respective processes or applications. It is therefore recommended to expect a minimal number of invocations or wait until a certain stability of the graph is reached before actually applying the segmentation and distribution – even if this means that the infrastructure cannot be optimally exploited in the beginning. Otherwise, there is a high risk that additional code movements will produce more overhead than gain.

Principally, such annotation data could be provided by the developer (cf. comments above), but this would exceed the scope of this paper.

5.3 Code and Data Segmentation

As stated, code and data needs to be segmented in a fashion that meets multiple requirements and constraints, such as cache size, relationship with data and other code (including system calls) etc. so that the unnecessary overhead on the core is reduced. Such overhead is caused in particular by loading and unloading context information, processing message queues due to centralisation and so on. Ideally, all processes, all their contexts and all according system data fit into the cache of the respective core – this, however, is most unlikely. Therefore, the segmentation must find a distribution, where common requirements of concurrent processes are exploited and where relationships between codes and data are maintained to a maximum.

Figure 5, right side designates such a potential segmentation given the relationship as stated in the table (Figure 5., left) and the temporal information represented by f (frequency of execution in a given timeframe) and w (likelihood that one code calls another code block, respectively accesses a specific data area). The figure already indicates some of the major concerns to be respected in this context, such as shared data segments, concurrent invocations, cross-segment communication etc.

As it is almost impossible for the core cache to hold all the code blocks, all related data (including global variables) and the according system processes at the same time, the micro kernel has hence to account for the following potential issues:

- Dynamic (un)loading of process blocks is normal behavior for all operating systems executing more processes than fit into memory. It involves all the issues of context switching plus overhead for load / memory management.
- Replication and hence consistency management of shared data across different caches. Background and / or dedicated synchronization needs to be executed in order to keep consistency. Timing vs. potential inconsistency is important in this context and the relationship analysis information can be employed to identify the *least* amount of synchronization points. Data consistency is covered substantially in literature though and will not be elaborated here (e.g. [14] [15]).
- Concurrent usage of access limited resources (e.g. hard-drive) pose issues on consistency and cause delays in the executing process. In order to reduce delay, the process is often handled by separate threads – in the case of multi-core processors, these threads can be handled like separate processes with the additional relationship information in the respective process graph.
- Queuing and scheduling is in principle no different to other OS [8] – however self-adapting microkernels have the additional advantage that they can rearrange themselves to process queues faster, given that they do not compete for restricted / limited resources.
- Cross-segment communication, as opposed to the single-core approach, requires dedicated communication points, channeling of messages, as well as their queuing etc. Similar to limited resources, data consistency etc. communication between segments may cause delays due to dependencies.

The main issue in executing segmented code and that also causes problems in manual development of distributed programs consists in the delays caused by communication between threads – partially due to latency, but also due to the fact that processes do not send / require information exchange at exactly the same point, so that delays in response, respectively in reception. MPI (Message-passing Interface) [10] is one of the few programming models dedicated to handling the communication model between blocks and similar principles must be applied in the case of automated segmentation.

Efficiency may be slightly increased by executing other processes whilst the respective thread(s) are put into a waiting state – accordingly, the amount of communication has to be kept at a minimum. In segmented (as opposed to parallelised) code, the main communication within a single process consists in passing the execution environment between blocks, and system calls. As opposed to this, cross-process communication is comparatively seldom.

5.4 Self-adaptive Microkernels

As noted, the main issue to be addressed by the OS (respectively the kernel), consists in reducing the communication and the context switching overhead, respectively keeping it at a minimum. Since the two main causes for this overhead consists in passing the execution point between code segments and making system calls – and thus implicitly accessing resources, including the virtual memory – the most strongly related code parts should be made locally available, whereas lower-level cache is preferable over higher-level one, as latency increases over distance (level).

The segmentation must therefore find the best distribution of code blocks according to size of cache and their latency – in other words, frequent invocations and strong relationships should be located closer than loosely coupled blocks. This does not only apply to process specific code and data, but implicitly also to system calls – in particular since essential capabilities (virtual memory, messaging etc.) are required by almost all processes to execute smoothly in a potentially dynamic environment where locations (in particular in memory) are subject to change.

In the classical OS approach, as noted, the main kernel instance (located on any one core) is responsible for handling such requests, leading to additional messaging overhead, conflicts and extensive delays. With the more advanced dynamic approach as suggested here, the kernel can provide *partial* functionalities to the individual core's environment, where it sees fit. This segmentation is basing on the relationship information as described above – however, since the kernel is more sensitive to execution faults and since it also requires that specific functionality is available and cannot be routed to another code location, such as the capability to route in the first instance, some segments need to be made available together. Furthermore, since the virtual memory is enacted by the kernel itself, relationship information is generally not maintained about the kernel in order to reduce overhead.

Instead, the kernel is structured in a fashion that adheres to the main principles of SOA: atomic, logical functionality groups; minimal size; common interfaces and protocol-independent communication. By identifying the direct entry points of the process into the system kernel (i.e. system procedure calls), the segmentation method can identify the system capabilities that need to be provided in addition to base capabilities, such as virtual memory and communication handling. Depending on the system calls needed by the process, additional segments can be identified that need / should be provided with the sub-kernel in the respective core's cache – the primary restriction consisting in the size of the cache.

Sub-kernels will only maintain memory information related to the specific processes, in order to reduce the memory size required. Similarly, only essential, frequently required functionalities will be hosted in the same cache. The according selection of kernel methods bases primarily on predefined architectural relationship similar to the one depicted in Figure 5 – the fully detailed kernel architecture relation graph will be published in a separate document, as it exceeds the scope of the current paper.

Context switches are particularly critical with OS methods, as no higher-level management system (i.e. the kernel) can supervise the process at this level. As switches on this level add to the delays caused by context switches per core, the amount of changes in the sub-kernel infrastructure per core should be kept to a minimum. Implicitly, the distribution of processes across cores does not only depend on relationships between segments and the size restrictions of the according cache, but more importantly on the functional distribution of sub-kernel segments. In other words, the relationship to system procedure calls and the according distribution across cores plays an essential role in the segmentation process, whereby the amount of switches between sub-kernel routines should be kept to a minimum.

Each system procedure call can therefore lead to one of the following three types of invocation:

1. Local processing using the cache of the respective core – this is the most efficient and fastest call, but leads to the same consistency issues as segmented processes do
2. Local processing with context switching – in this case the call is executed by the same core that processes the invoking procedure, but must load the system procedure from central memory (or another location). This reduces the consistency problem, as the context switches can update the memory, but it leads to increased delays in the execution of the invoking procedure
3. Call forwarding to the main kernel's core – system procedure calls can also be forwarded to the main kernel instance, just like in monolithic instances. Obviously this loses the advantage coming from a distributed kernel, namely obstructing message queues and concurrent call handling. By reducing the average number of "centralised" system calls, however, the risk of conflicts decreases accordingly (cf. Section 3). Since such call handling comes at the cost of higher latency, it is generally recommended to reserve this for background calls (that can be executed in parallel and may be identified in the dependency graph). In all cases, the OS must be able to precedence "active" processes over "waiting" ones, e.g. through an event-based system – a detailed discussion of these mechanisms will be published separately.

6   Local Private Clouds (or Micro-Clouds)

As has been mentioned in the initial chapters, current approaches towards cloud systems all take a high-level approach towards resource management, i.e. they assume that the operating system handles simple multi-core platforms and that main cloud features act over multiple instances (PCs, Servers) rather than over multiple cores as such. Implicitly, most cloud systems only address horizontal elasticity – process / data replication on multiple systems – and only little vertical elasticity – extending the amount of resources vested into a single instance, though notably the according scale will have to be applied to all horizontal replications too.

The biggest business motivation for outsourcing to clouds at the moment being that equipment and maintenance of a local resource infrastructure (private cloud) is too costly. However, such assessments forget about the current development in current Microsystems leading to unprecedented resource availability even in desktop PCs. This poses three issues: 1) outsourcing to public clouds will only be of interest for large scale applications, 2) applications and services must foresee their own (vertical) scalability already at development time, whereas only little "common" programming models are available to this end, and 3) scalable execution on local infrastructures requires new OS models.

This paper presented an approach to exploit the specific features of multi-core systems in a way that enables cloud-specific capabilities on a single (multi-core) machine:

6.1 Elasticity in Self-managed Microkernels

The core feature of selfmanaged microkernels as presented in this paper consists in its capability to adjust the distribution of code and data segments according to resource requirements and availability. By updating the relationship graph frequently and relating individual graphs (per process) with one another, the system can adjust the vertical scale to reflect the current requirement of the process in alignment with other processes and resource availability. Since the principle of service oriented operating systems also enables enhanced programming models, vertical scalability can both be exploited for more efficient data throughput, as well as for multiple instantiation of individual threads with shared, as well as distributed memory. Such threads can be dynamically instantiated and destroyed by the system, but the process itself must still be capable to deal with a dynamic number of concurrent threads. Optimally parallelizable code, i.e. algorithms that execute calculations on separate data instances and which results' are integrated only after execution, are ideal for such usage – typical examples for such applications are 3d renderers, protein folding etc. [11] [12] [13].

Horizontal scalability in a multi-core environment is only limited by the number of cores – similar to the limitation of yesterday's web servers that merged multiple motherboards ("blades") into a single interface. As discussed, multiple instantiation automatically leads to the problem of consistency maintenance, which has to be compensated by complex data management mechanisms which lead to additional latencies, as they act on a higher level than the processes themselves. Even though service oriented operating systems cannot handle complex differentiation and merging strategies, they can nonetheless support data consistency management through background synchronization thus ensuring that multiple instances have access to principally the same data body.

6.2 Open Issues

Service-oriented operating systems and self-managed microkernels are still research issues and as such, many challenges remain incompletely solved, such as security aspects and reliability:

Security: since service oriented operating systems act below the level of virtual machines (but on top of virtual resources), they implicitly do not support segregation into secure, individual execution environments. All top layer security can be provided in the same fashion as in classical, non-SOA operating systems, though kernel-near security (message encryption etc.) may need further investigation, considering the dynamic distribution of processes and sub-kernel modules across cores.

Reliability: self-managed microkernels can principally increase reliability through improved data and code management which allows even dynamic (re)distribution of code, thus dealing with potential issues. However, main reliability issues arise from hardware faults which cannot be foreseen, therefore typically being addressed by means of replication mechanisms. Though service oriented OS support replication mechanisms, it is typically the whole system that goes down and not just a single core, so that cross-system mechanisms need to be employed. In [9] we discuss the principles of a distributed virtual memory to enable distributed execution and indicate how replication across systems may be realized – however, such mechanisms are still subject to research.

6.3 Summary

The self-managed microkernel approach as presented in this paper is taking cloud concepts to a core level in future tightly coupled systems, thus providing elasticity for large scale systems, as well as means to deal with dynamic and heterogeneous infrastructures. This will not only allow common users and providers to make use of cloud features in simple, smaller sized infrastructures, but also enable new means to write and execute distributed applications in dynamic environments.

Multicore systems for common usage are comparatively new on the market and distributed computing platforms so far have mostly been an issue for high performance computing developers. With the trend of integrating more and more cores into a single system, the average developer is now faced with similar issues than HPC programmers were before and who have realized their own specific programming models to realize these issues. The self-managed microkernel approach simplifies this problem by providing new means to develop distributed applications that allow for a certain degree of self-management, namely cloud capabilities.

At the same time, many issues have not yet been fully researched in this area and since furthermore most approaches only consist of conceptual models so far, actual benchmarks still have to validate the approach and, what is more, define the fine-grained parameters to identify cut-off points in code / data segmentation, as well as the according dynamicity.

Business benefits for such a system are obvious, yet not all of the according requirements have been addressed so far, since many of them require that a stable base system exists first. It is e.g. not sensible to elaborate authorization mechanisms yet, when not all implications from code segmentation have been fully elaborated – as such, security could be tightly coupled with the main kernel instance, or be dynamically distributed like other sub-kernel modules.

References

1. Saabeel, W., Verduijn, T., Hagdorn, L., Kumar, K.: A Model for Virtual Organisation: A structure and Process Perspective. Electronic Journal of Organizational Virtualness, 1–16 (2002)
2. Schubert, L., Wesner, S., Dimitrakos, T.: Secure and Dynamic Virtual Organizations for Business. In: Cunningham, P., Cunningham, M. (eds.) Innovation and the Knowledge Economy - Issues, Applications, Case Studies, pp. 1201–1208. IOS Press, Amsterdam (2005)
3. Intel, Intel White Paper. An Introduction to the Intel® QuickPath Interconnect (2009), http://www.intel.com/technology/quickpath/introduction.pdf
4. Lameter, C.: Extreme High Performance Computing or Why Microkernels Suck. In: Proceedings of the Linux Symposium (2007)
5. Wray, C.: Ramtron Announces 8-Megabit Parallel Nonvolatile F-RAM Memory (2009), http://www10.edacafe.com/nbc/articles/view_article.php?section=ICNews&articleid=714760
6. Gropp, W.: Using MPI: Portable Parallel Programming with the Message-passing Interface. MIT Press, Cambridge (2000)
7. Schubert, L., Kipp, A., Wesner, S.: Above the Clouds: From Grids to Resource Fabrics. In: Tselentis, G., Domingue, J., Galis, A., Gavras, A., Hausheer, D., Krco, S., et al. (eds.) Towards the Future Internet - A European Research Perspective, pp. 238–249. IOS Press, Amsterdam (2009)
8. Tanenbaum, A.S.: Modern Operating Systems. Prentice Hall PTR, Upper Saddle River (2001)
9. Schubert, L., Kipp, A.: Principles of Service Oriented Operating Systems. In: Vicat-Blanc Primet, P., Kudoh, T., Mambretti, J. (eds.) Networks for Grid Applications, Second International Conference, GridNets 2008. Lecture Notes of the Institute for Computer Sciences, Social Informatics and Telecommunications Engineering, vol. 2, pp. 56–69. Springer, Heidelberg (2009)
10. Gropp, W.: Using MPI: Portable Parallel Programming with the Message-passing Interface. MIT Press, Cambridge (2000)
11. Anderson, D.: Public Computing: Reconnecting People to Science. In: Conference on Shared Knowledge and the Web. Residencia de Estudiantes, Madrid, Spain (2003)
12. Menzel, K.: Parallel Rendering Techniques for Multiprocessor Systems. In: Computer Graphics, International Conference, pp. 91–103. Comenius University Press (1994)
13. Foster, I.: Designing and Building Parallel Programs: Concepts and Tools for Parallel Software. Addison-Wesley, Reading (1995)
14. Tanenbaum, A.: Modern Operating Systems. Prentice-Hall, Englewood Cliffs (1992)
15. Deitel, H.: An Introduction to Operating Systems. Addison-Wesley, Reading (1990)
16. Lameter, C.: Extreme High Performance Computing or Why Microkernels Suck. In: Proceedings of the Linux Symposium (2007)

Proactive Software Rejuvenation Based on Machine Learning Techniques

Dimitar Simeonov[1] and D.R. Avresky[2]

[1] IRIANC
simeonov.dimitar@gmail.com
[2] IRIANC
autonomic@irianc.com

Abstract. This work presents a framework for detecting anomalies in servers leading to crash such as memory leaks in aging systems and proactively rejuvenating them.

Proactive VM-rejuvenation framework has been extended with machine learning techniques. Utilization of the framework is allowing the effect of software failures virtually to be reduced to zero downtime. It can be applied against internal anomalies like memory leaks in the web servers and external as Denial of Service Attacks. The framework has been implemented with virtual machines and a machine learning algorithm has been realized for successfully determining a decision rule for proactively initiating the system rejuvenation. The proposed framework has been theoretically justified and experimentally validated.

Keywords: proactive rejuvenation, virtualisation, machine learning techniques, feature selection, sparsity, software aging (memory leaks), validation.

1 Introduction

All computer systems may fail after some amount of time and usage. This is especially true for web servers. The availability is one of the most important characteristic of the web servers. Computer systems, which are prone to failures and crashes, can be realized with a higher availability if their mission critical parts are replicated. There are many practical examples of such systems - RAID, e-mail servers, computing farms. In this paper, it is shown how the software replication and rejuvenation can be used for increasing the availability of a software application with a critical workload. Software replication and rejuvenation can be performed by virtual machines easily, cheaply and effectively. The virtualization allows us to create a layer of an abstraction between software and hardware, which provides some independence of the underlying hardware.

Any anomalies, with a similar behavior that are leading to a system's crash, can be effectively predicted by a machine learning algorithm. For example, memory leaks exhibit a similar behavior every time they occur, and therefore, such behavior can be predicted with a high accuracy. With an accurate prediction and an efficient recovery mechanism, the software system's availability can be increased significantly.

D.R. Avresky et al. (Eds.): Cloudcomp 2009, LNICST 34, pp. 186–200, 2010.
© Institute for Computer Sciences, Social-Informatics and Telecommunications Engineering 2010

2   Related Work

Different methods and models have been presented for estimating software aging in web servers and resource exhaustion in operational software systems in [17], [18] and [19]. Software rejuvenation has been introduced as an efficient technique for dealing with this problem in [14] and further developed in [23]. Virtualization has been effectively used in [1] for improving software rejuvenation. Virtual machines are widely used for increasing the availability of web servers [16]. In [5], [11] and [24] different techniques for increasing availability of complex computing systems have been introduced. Recently, a comprehensive model for software rejuvenation has been developed for proactive detection and management of software aging ([15], [17], [20], [21] and [22]). Different techniques for analyzing the application performance due to anomalies for enterprise services are presented in [6], [10], [12] and [13].

In this paper a comprehensive method for a proactive software rejuvenation for avoiding system crashes due to anomalies, such as memory leaks, is presented. It is theoretically justified and experimentally validated. Based on the training data, obtained by the proposed framework, a close predictor of the actual remaining time to crash of a system has been accurately estimated. Such prediction has been used as a decision rule for initiating software rejuvenation.

3   Proactive VM-Rejuvenation Framework

The VM-REJUV framework has been developed in [1] in attempt to solve the problem of aging and crashing web servers. Current paper proposes an extension to the VM-REJUV framework that allows to predict the right time for activating the rejuvenation mechanism.

The VM-REJUV framework consists of three virtual machines called for simplicity VM1 (VM-master), VM2(VM-slave) and VM3(VM-slave). VM1 contains the controlling mechanism of the application. VM2 and VM3 are identical and contain the application susceptible to anomalies. VM1 is like a mini-server to which VM2 and VM3 are connected. They regularly send information about their parameters to VM1. This information is analyzed and only one of VM2 and VM3 is allowed to be active. VM1 activates the spare copy to become active and to start handling the workload when the active machine will be crashing soon or stop reporting data.

The VM-REJUV framework can be extended into Proactive VM-rejuvenation framework to contain an arbitrary number of virtual machines with the functionality of VM2 and VM3. Figure 1 shows the organization of Proactive VM-rejuvenation framework.

3.1   VM-Master and VM-Slave Components and Communication

VM-master needs to be always on. It creates a local server to which VM-slaves are connected. Each VM-slave can be in one of the possible states: starting up, ready, active and rejuvenating. All virtual machines have the following properties:

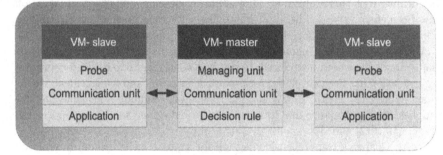

Fig. 1. Proactive VM-rejuvenation framework

- There is at least one active VM-slave (if possible.)
- All VM-slaves are functioning according to same rules.
- If the VM-master decides that the active VM-slave will crash soon it sends a control message to a ready VM-slave to become active. When the new VM-slave becomes active the old one is forced to rejuvenate.

3.2   VM-Master Components

Decision rule
The decision rule is a function from the history of parameters of a VM-slave to a binary value YES/NO. It is obtained off-line by the developed machine learning technique and is hard-coded in the VM-master. If the value is YES then the corresponding VM-slave needs to be rejuvenated.

Managing unit
The managing unit holds information about which VM-slaves are currently connected and what is their most recent status. When the Decision Rule decides that a VM-slave needs rejuvenation and informs the Managing unit, it starts rejuvenation at a suitable moment.

Communication unit
The communication unit is responsible for receiving VM-slave parameters and responding with simple commands for activating the application in a VM-slave. The communication can be performed using either TCP-IP or VMCI protocols (provided by VMware.)

3.3   VM-Slave Components

Probe
The probe collects system parameters of the VM-slave such as but not limited to a memory distribution and a CPU load.

Communication unit

The communication unit receives orders about the execution of the application from the VM-master and follows them. This way it serves as a managing unit as well. Another duty of the communication unit is to report the system parameters that has been collected by the probe.

Application

The application can be virtually any legacy code. It can be an Apache web server, a protein folding simulation or any other program.

4 Machine Learning Framework

The VM-REJUV framework presented in [1] relies simply on selecting a level of the current CPU utilization of a VM-slave to decide whether it needs to be rejuvenated. This has been shown to be effective for detecting memory leaks but has some limitations and drawbacks ([10]).

First, it discards a lot of the parameters of the VM-slave system, which may be used for further refining the decision rule. Therefore, there is no warranty that any empirically chosen level will be good for all scenarios. Some attacks and exploits may be keeping the CPU utilization high enough to prevent the rejuvenation of the VM-machine.

Second, it doesn't keep any track of previous times. Some attacks are recognizable only if one considers several consecutive moments in time combined.

The proposed solution in this paper is eliminating these drawbacks. The machine learning technique for deriving an adequate decision rule that has been developed in this paper is extending the capabilities of the Proactive VM-rejuvenation framework to predict anomalies leading to the system crash. It is presented in Figure 2 and consists of five steps.

1. Training Data Collection
   To be able to detect anomalies (memory leaks) in advance, the system needs to have information about the symptoms of such anomalies. Such data can be obtained by exposing the system to the anomalies several times and recording the system parameters through the time.
2. Data Labeling
   The system parameters record needs to be tagged with the remaining time to the crash. This means for an every moment in time, in which the system parameters are recorded, an additional parameter is added i. e., the time remaining to crash. Note that this value cannot be known in advance. The goal of this framework is to be able to extract a good prediction for the time to crash from the rest of the parameters. Such prediction can be used in the decision rule.
3. Data Aggregation
   The system parameters for a certain period of time are collected and combined in what is called an aggregated datapoint. To such datapoint are added additional parameters, which describe the dynamics of the parameters during the time period. For example, the average slope of each parameter is

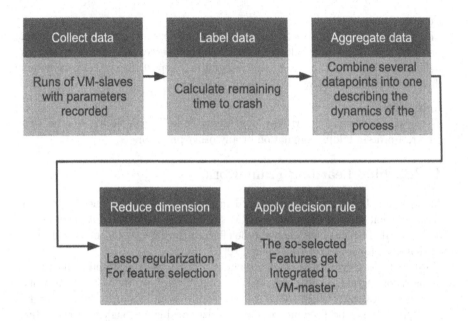

Fig. 2. ML framework

an aggregated datapoint. This aggregation increases the number of parameters to consider many-fold, and each parameter constitutes an additional dimension in the representation of the problem. Considering all of them is not the most efficient approach as some of them may be irrelevant to a certain anomaly. Also to provide convergence guarantees for a decision rule in a certain dimension, the higher dimension, the higher number of training points is required. By reducing the dimension of aggregated datapoints the convergence becomes possible and tractable.

4. Feature selection
    A sparse regression, also known as Lasso regularization([9]), is performed to reduce the number of important parameters to a certain number, which can be controlled. Lasso regularization is explained further in the paper.

5. Decision rule application
    The solution of a Lasso regularization is a parse set of weights of the parameters in the aggregated datapoint. Application of the decision rule can be implemented by calculating aggregated datapoint on the fly and taking the dot product of it and the weights obtained by Lasso regularization.
    More sophisticated machine learning methods with higher degree kernels can be applied to the reduced dimensionality datapoints. These could be Support Vector Machines (SVM) and Regularized Least Squares (RLS) ([7]). This step might not be necessary in some cases but in other it might further boost the efficiency of the decision rule. Because Lasso regularization only tries to find a linear regression, this step might be necessary for some problems and anomalies that might have a non-linear behavior.

5   Lasso Regularization

A machine learning task is equivalent to learning a function or a close approximation to it, given the values of the function at some points ([3],[4]). These values will be called training data. There could be many functions, which satisfy the training data or have a small difference. A measure of how well a function matches the training data is the Empirical Risk([2]). Therefore, a function that minimizes the Empirical Risk might look like a good candidate function. However, such functions have the drawback that they overfit the training data i. e., these functions adjust themselves to the training data for the cost of making themselves more complicated, which leads to them having uncontrollable and hard to predict behavior if evaluated at other points. Therefore, a machine learning tries to regularize such functions by assigning some penalty to their complexity i. e., the more complicated the function, the higher is the penalty.

The most common and widely known regularization technique is Tikhonov regularization([8]). It selects the function to be learned by the following rule:

$$f = \arg\min_{f \in H} \frac{1}{m} \sum_{k=1}^{m} V(f(X_k), Y_k) + \lambda ||f||_H \qquad (1)$$

In this formula H is the space of all functions that are considered (usually some Hilbert space with a defined norm, usually L2 norm), m is the size of the training data, (X_k, Y_k) is the format of the training data - X_k is a vector of parameters and Y_k is a scalar or a vector of values that somehow depend on the parameters (in this paper Y_k is the remaining time to crash), V is a loss function that penalizes empirical errors. λ is a parameter, which controls how much to regularize and how important is minimizing the empirical risk. Usually, the best value for λ is selected through a cross-validation.

Lasso Regularization differs slightly from Tikhonov regularization and the difference is that the norm on the function is not given by the Hilbert Space the function is in, but is the L1 norm. The function selection rule takes the form:

$$f(x) = < \beta, x > \qquad (2)$$

where x can be any vector variable of parameters. The vector β is derived by:

$$\beta = \arg\min_{\beta \in \mathbb{R}^{dim(X_k)}} \frac{1}{m} \sum_{k=1}^{m} (< \beta, X_k > -Y_k)^2 + \lambda ||\beta||_{L1} \qquad (3)$$

The functions that Lasso regularization considers are restricted to linear functions but it has the property that the selected weight vector β is sparse, i.e. the majority of its coordinates are zeros. An intuition about this can be observed in Figure 3:

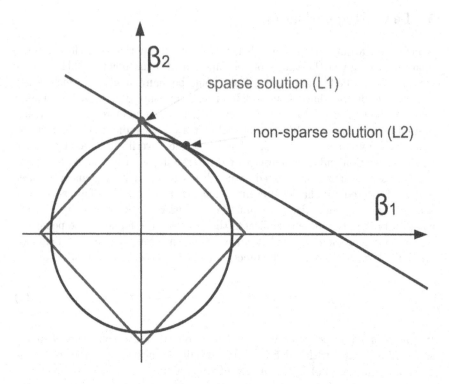

Fig. 3. Sparsity of Lasso regularization

At Figure 3 β_1 and β_2 represent the different coordinates of β. The sloped violet line represents space of solutions with equal empirical risk. Then, among them, one needs to chose the solution that minimizes the regularization penalty. For Tikhonov regularization (red) the regularization penalty is the L2 distance between a solution and the origin of the coordinate system. Therefore, the best solution is at a tangent point between a circle centered at the origin and the sloped line. For Lasso regularization the penalty is the L1 distance between a solution and the origin. Therefore, the best solution is at a tangent point of L1-ball (green rhomboid) and the line, which will happen to be at a some subset of the axes i. e., therefore, it will be sparse. Similar arguments in higher dimensions justify the sparsity of Lasso regularization in general.

6   Experimental Setup

Two laptops Dell M1530 with 4GB RAM and 2GHz Core Duo processor have been used for performing the experiments and the Proactive VM-Rejuvenation Framework has been installed on each of them. The operating system was Linux (Ubuntu 8.04). The virtual machines were created and maintained with VMWare Workstation 6.5, but this is not necessary - they could be managed with any other virtualization software. There was one VM-master and two VM-slaves. They were communicating to each other via VMCI protocol, but of course other forms of communication such as TCP-IP are possible. All the software in VM-master and VM-slaves was self-written or built-in in Ubuntu.

In order to demonstrate the scalability of the proposed Proactive VM-rejuvenation framework, as shown in Fig 1, it has been has implemented with a possibility to introduce multiple VM machines, independent of the available hardware. This approach also demonstrates the minimal hardware requirements. Still, the Proactive VM-rejuvenation framework can scale horizontally, to many physical machines. VM-masters and VM-slaves could be replicated multiple times, if the VM-masters can synchronize their actions, for example with a common database.

The Managing unit in the VM-master, the Communication units in the VM-master and VM-slaves, the Probe and a sample Application were self-written and are in the range of few thousands lines of C code. For the decision rule were used some freely available libraries of implementations of Lasso regularization.

The Probe collects parameters about a VM-slave, combines them in a strictly defined form and sends the data to the VM-master on a regular interval. In the experiment performed this interval was set to one second. The form of the data is the following:

```
Datapoint:
Memory: 515580 497916 17664 0 17056 268692
Swap: 409616 0 409616
CPU: 52.380001 0.070000 3.090000 0.260000 0.000000 44.200001
```

Such datapoint contains information about the memory distribution and CPU activity.

The Application in the VM-slaves had the capability to produce memory leaks. Its only task was to accumulate them.

The Communication units were responsible for transmitting data between the Probe and the Communication unit in the VM-slave and for transmitting the commands from the Communication unit of the VM-master to the Communication unit of the VM-slave.

Besides communication with the VM-master, the Communication unit of the VM-slave is responsible for only executing simple commands like START and STOP the application.

The data collection per each laptop has been conducted for 63 runs, each of them consisted of approximately 15-30 minutes of parameter history recorded every second. That data was aggregated and labeled with a simple self-written Python script. The Lasso regularization was performed using freely available implementations of Lasso regularization.

Rejuvenation

For rejuvenation was used a restart of the virtual machine. Another approach would be to simply restart the process of the application. However, this would not completely restore the original state of the system when the application was started. For example if the application has used the swap space this would not be cleared after a process restart but would be after a virtual machine restart. The only way that it can be guaranteed that the system parameters will be the same at the start of the application is through a virtual machine restart.

7   Results

Figure 4 shows some of the values of the parameters combined in the aggregation step, change with a respect to the time before crash for one particular run. These parameters describe the memory distribution, the swap memory distribution (on the left) and the CPU load distribution (on the right). These are presented for one of 30 instances used for the aggregation, correspondingly at time 15 seconds. The values of the parameters are in parameter units. For example, for memory parameters the units are KB and for CPU parameters the units are % (percent).

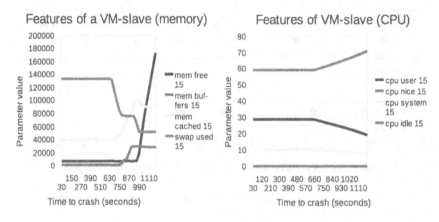

Fig. 4. Variation of all parameters over time

Figure 5 shows some additional parameters(the average slopes) that were calculated for aggregation. For Figure 5 the values of the parameters are shown in parameter units per time. For example, for memory parameters the units are KB/s and for CPU parameters the units are %/s (percent per second).

However, some problems with the probes have been observed in the cases when a certain level of memory leaks have been reached. Unfortunately, this holds for all runs and consists of repeating the old system parameters without a change. It can be observed at figures 4 and 5 as flattening of all parameter plots approximately 600 seconds before the actual crash. However, this outrage of the Probe module does not change the effectiveness of the machine learning method. This is explained later in the paper at Figure 8.

Another specific of Lasso regularization is that the algorithm is not guaranteed to converge to the global minimum for β, but may end up with a local minimum solution. This is due to the fact that Lasso regularization is a convex relaxation

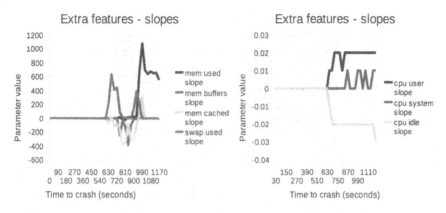

Fig. 5. Variation of extra calculated parameters (slopes) over time

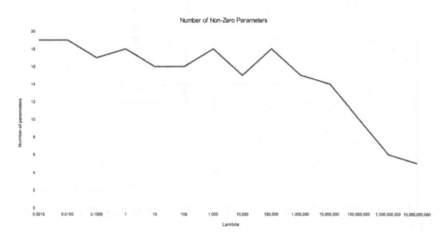

Fig. 6. Variation of the number of non-zero parameters with respect to λ

of a NP-hard problem. Yet, the solution that the algorithm provides is good enough in the sense that it exhibits important properties such as a sparsity and a good regression solution. This is illustrated in Figure 6, by showing the number of the parameters in the sparse solution with respect to lambda. The general trend is to decrease the number of parameters, even though this doesn't happen strictly monotonously. After aggregating the datapoints Lasso regularization was performed on them, and the weights selected for the parameters for few values of λ are presented in Figure 7. Many of the parameter weights are zeros, which is expected since the method provides a sparse solution. The sparsity of the solution can be adjusted by the value of λ.

For example, in the case $\lambda = 10$, only 5 out of 39 parameters were given high non-zero weights. All other parameters had weights smaller than 0.01. These five parameters are shown in Table 1:

Table 1. Most important parameters after feature selection for $\lambda = 10$

Parameter name	Weight
mem_used_slope	-0.70
swap_used_slope	0.89
cpu_user_15sec	12.01
cpu_idle_15sec	17.52
cpu_user_30sec	9.12

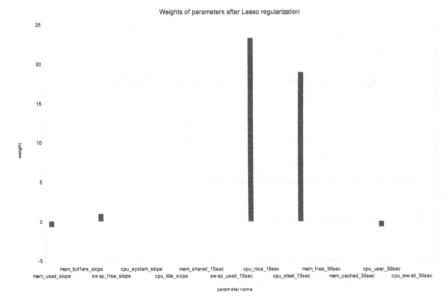

Fig. 7. Selected weights for the parameters after Lasso regularization for several values of λ

Decision Rule

When the weights of the parameters were multiplied to the values of the parameters at each datapoint and summed the result is a close predictor of the actual remaining time to crash. For that datapoint, the calculated remaining time to the crash is incorporated in a decision rule. Figure 8 is an example of the correspondence between a predicted and actual remaining time on one of the runs. The training was done over all runs, and the figure presents only one of the runs. The ground truth is the dashed line called "Actual time", and the predicted remaining time for various values of λ is described by the other lines in Figure 8. The predicted times were calculated by using parameter weights, in the format shown in Figure 7, multiplied to the parameter values in the format shown in Figures 4 and 5 to obtain time to crash value and then summed up. This is equivalent to taking the dot product between the weights vector $\boldsymbol{w}$ and the parameters vector $\boldsymbol{p}$.

$$\boldsymbol{w}.\boldsymbol{p} = t_{predicted} \tag{4}$$

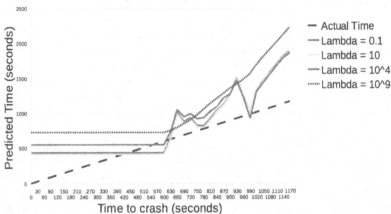

Fig. 8. Comparison between actual remaining time and prediction based on the machine learning algorithm for various values of lambda

The results are presented in Figure 8, which shows that the predicted time for all values of λ is a good approximation of the ground truth. The abscissa shows the remaining time to crash, and the ordinate shows the predicted time in seconds.

Usually, the best value of λ is selected through cross-validation. However, in this case, another property of a good solution is its sparsity. Hence, the value of lambda can be varied to achieve a small number of parameters, which would lead to efficiency from implementation point of view. As can be observed in Figure 8 the quality of the solution doesn't vary greatly as λ varies. The predicted remaining times are for values of λ with multiplicative difference in the order of 10^{13}.

Such predictor was used as a decision rule. If the predicted remaining time is under some safe limit (1000 seconds - more than the minimal predicted time), as in Figure 8, the decision rule is activated and it informs the managing unit of the VM-master that the corresponding VM-slave needs to be rejuvenated. The decision rule was hard coded, since all the learning was done off-line, as it requires the data labeling step of the ML framework, which can be performed only after the data is once collected.

The framework with one VM-master and two VM-slaves, with properly set a decision rule and a bug-free implementation was able to continue changing the load from one VM-slave to another without a server crash. The Proactive VM-rejuvenation framework with a properly devised decision rule flawlessly was able to run for a couple of weeks and switch the activity of VM-slaves every 15-30 minutes. Additional difficulties to that aim were the varying rejuvenation times. Many times all that was needed for the rejuvenation was simply a restart of the virtual machine. However, in some cases was necessary the OS to perform a hard-disk check and this required an additional time to be taken into account during the rejuvenation process.

8 Conclusion

Proactive VM-rejuvenation framework for selecting critical parameters for detecting anomalies in web servers has been presented in the paper. The ability to add arbitrary number of backup virtual machines and reliably to predict the remaining time to crash with the use of machine learning techniques is described. An algorithm for a feature selection, based on machine learning for reducing the complexity and dimensionality of the problem, has been developed. The framework has been implemented with virtual machines and a machine learning algorithm has been realized for successfully determining a decision rule for proactively initiating the system rejuvenation. The proposed framework has been theoretically justified and experimentally validated. These are real problems for the Internet today and the future cyber infrastructure. The proposed machine learning method is general and can be applied for a wide range of anomalies.

9 Future Work

One opportunity for extension is to apply other machine learning techniques on the top of Lasso Regularization. Such techniques could be Regularized Least Squares (RLS) or Support Vector Machines (SVM). They could be used with a non-linear kernel and learn more complicated behavior. This would reduce the number of false positives and false negatives of the decision rule significantly.

Another opportunity for example is to learn to defend against more than one type of anomaly. If decision rules against memory leaks and denial of service attack can be learned, both of them can be used simultaneously. In this case, whenever any anomaly occurs, the rejuvenation of the VM-slave will be initiated.

Each virtual machine can implement a simplified version of the proposed framework that includes the embedded decision rule and the probe for monitoring the parameters in a real time. These virtual machines can be provided to the clients on demand across the network.

References

1. Silva, L., Alonso, J., Silva, P., Torres, J., Andrzejak, A.: Using Virtualization to Improve Software Rejuvenation. In: IEEE Network Computing and Applications, Cambridge, USA (July 2007)
2. Bousquet, O., Boucheron, S., Lugosi, G.: Introduction to Statistical Learning Theory. In: Bousquet, O., von Luxburg, U., Rätsch, G. (eds.) Machine Learning 2003. LNCS (LNAI), vol. 3176, pp. 169–207. Springer, Heidelberg (2004)
3. Poggio, T., Smale, S.: The Mathematics of Learning: Dealing with Data. Notices of the AMS (2003)
4. Bishop, C.: Pattern Recognition and Machine Learning. Springer, Heidelberg (2007)

5. Chen, M., Accardi, A., Kiciman, E., Lloyd, J., Patterson, D., Fox, A., Brewer, E.: Path-based failure and evolution management. In: Proc. of the 1st Symposium NSDI 2004 (2004)
6. Cherkasova, L., Fu, Y., Tang, W., Vahdat, A.: Measuring and Characterizing End-to-End Internet Service Performance. Journal ACM/IEEE Transactions on Internet Technology, TOIT (November 2003)
7. Evgeniou, T., Pontil, M., Poggio, T.: Regularization Networks and Support Vector Machines. Advances in Computational Mathematics (2000)
8. Cucker, F., Smale, S.: On the mathematical foundations of learning. Bulletin of the American Mathematical Society (2002)
9. Tibshirani, R.: Regression selection and shrinkage via the lasso. J. R. Stat. Soc. Ser. B 58, 267–288 (1996)
10. Cherkasova, L., Ozonat, K., Mi, N., Symons, J., Smirni, E.: Towards Automated Detection of Application Performance Anomaly and Change. HPlabs 79 (2008)
11. Cohen, I., Zhang, S., Goldszmidt, M., Symons, J., Kelly, T., Fox, A.: Capturing, Indexing, Clustering, and Retrieving System History. In: Proc. of the 20th ACM Symposium SOSP 2005 (2005)
12. Mi, N., Cherkasova, L., Ozonat, K., Symons, J., Smirni, E.: Analysis of Application Performance and Its Change via Representative Application Signatures. In: NOMS 2008 (2008)
13. Zhang, Q., Cherkasova, L., Mathews, G., Greene, W., Smirni, E.: R-Capriccio: A Capacity Planning and Anomaly Detection Tool for Enterprise Services with LiveWorkloads. In: Cerqueira, R., Campbell, R.H. (eds.) Middleware 2007. LNCS, vol. 4834, pp. 244–265. Springer, Heidelberg (2007)
14. Huang, Y., Kintala, C., Kolettis, N., Fulton, N.: Software Rejuvenation: Analysis, Module and Applications. In: Proceedings of Fault-Tolerant Computing Symposium, FTCS-25 (June 1995)
15. Castelli, V., Harper, R., Heidelberg, P., Hunter, S., Trivedi, K., Vaidyanathan, K., Zeggert, W.: Proactive Management of Software Aging. IBM Journal Research & Development 45(2) (March 2001)
16. Rosenblum, M., Garfinkel, T.: Virtual Machine Monitors: Current Technology and Future Trends. IEEE Internet Computing 38(5) (May 2005)
17. Vaidyanathan, K., Trivedi, K.: A Comprehensive Model for Software Rejuvenation. IEEE Trans. on Dependable and Secure Computing 2(2) (April 2005)
18. Vaidyanathan, K., Trivedi, K.S.: A Measurement- Based Model for Estimation of Resource Exhaustion in Operational Software Systems. In: Proc. 10th IEEE Int. Symp. Software Reliability Eng., pp. 84–93 (1999)
19. Li, L., Vaidyanathan, K., Trivedi, K.: An Approach for Estimation of Software Aging in a Web-Server. In: Proc. of the 2002 International Symposium on Empirical Software Engineering, ISESE 2002 (2002)
20. Gross, K., Bhardwaj, V., Bickford, R.: Proactive Detection of Software Aging Mechanisms in Performance Critical Computers. In: Proc. 27th Annual IEEE/NASA Software Engineering Symposium (2002)
21. Kaidyanathan, K., Gross, K.: Proactive Detection of Software Anomalies through MSET. In: Workshop on Predictive Software Models (PSM 2004) (September 2004)
22. Gross, K., Lu, W.: Early Detection of Signal and Process Anomalies in Enterprise Computing Systems. In: Proc. 2002 IEEE Int. Conf. on Machine Learning and Applications, ICMLA (June 2002)

23. Silva, L., Madeira, H., Silva, J.G.: Software Aging and Rejuvenation in a SOAP-based Server. In: IEEE-NCA: Network Computing and Applications, Cambridge USA (July 2006)

24. Candea, G., Brown, A., Fox, A., Patterson, D.: Recovery Oriented Computing: Building Multi-Tier Dependability. IEEE Computer 37(11) (November 2004)

25. Oppenheimer, D., Brown, A., Beck, J., Hettena, D., Kuroda, J., Treuhaft, N., Patterson, D.A., Yellick, K.: ROC-1: Harware Support for Recovery-Oriented Computing. IEEE Transactions on Computers 51(2) (2002); Special issue on Fault Tolerant - Embedded Systems, Avresky, D., Johnson, B.W., Lombardi, F. (Guest eds.)

Dynamic Load Management of Virtual Machines in Cloud Architectures

Mauro Andreolini, Sara Casolari, Michele Colajanni, and Michele Messori

Department of Information Engineering
University of Modena and Reggio Emilia, Italy
{mauro.andreolini,sara.casolari,michele.colajanni,
michele.messori}@unimore.it

Abstract. Cloud infrastructures must accommodate changing demands for different types of processing with heterogeneous workloads and time constraints. In a similar context, dynamic management of virtualized application environments is becoming very important to exploit computing resources, especially with recent virtualization capabilities that allow live sessions to be moved transparently between servers. This paper proposes novel management algorithms to decide about reallocations of virtual machines in a cloud context characterized by large numbers of hosts. The novel algorithms identify just the real critical instances and take decisions without recurring to typical thresholds. Moreover, they consider load trend behavior of the resources instead of instantaneous or average measures. Experimental results show that proposed algorithms are truly selective and robust even in variable contexts, thus reducing system instability and limit migrations when really necessary.

1 Introduction

Existing data centers are characterized by high operating costs, inefficiencies, and by myriads of distributed and heterogeneous servers that add complexity in terms of security and management. In order to improve data center efficiency, most enterprises are going to consolidate existing systems through virtualization solutions up to cloud centers. Logically pooling all system resources and centralizing resource management allow to increase overall utilization and lowering management costs. There are various approaches to virtualization (hardware virtualization up to micro-partitioning, operating system virtualization, software virtualization), but consolidation and virtualization by themselves do little to improve application performance. The question is whether huge increases in terms of system utilization correspond to an actual better efficiency or they are due to applications running poorly in those virtual environments.

Consolidation and virtualization deliver more computing resources to the organizations, but failure to tune applications to run on virtualized resources means that un-tuned applications are wasting processing cycles. In order to avoid to waste computing and storage resources it is necessary to optimize management

D.R. Avresky et al. (Eds.): Cloudcomp 2009, LNICST 34, pp. 201–214, 2010.
© Institute for Computer Sciences, Social-Informatics and Telecommunications Engineering 2010

of these novel cloud systems architectures and virtualized servers. Overall performance analysis and runtime management in these contexts are becoming extremely complex, because they are a function not only of guest applications, but also of their interactions with other guest machines as they contend for processing and I/O resources of their host machine. We should consider that these modern cloud infrastructures must accommodate varying demands for different types of processing within certain time constraints, hence dynamic management of virtualized application environments is becoming very important. Indeed, automated workload management and balancing facilities can also lead to performance improvements while greatly reducing management cost. For these reasons, all recent virtualization management capabilities allow loads and live sessions to be moved transparently between processors or even servers, thus allowing applications to exploit unused computing resources regardless of whether those resources are located on local or remote servers. Dynamic capacity management can increase productivity but it requires continuous monitoring services and innovative runtime decision algorithms that represent the focus of this paper. In particular, we propose quite innovative algorithms for deciding when a physical host should migrate part of its load, which part of the load must be moved, and where should be moved. The difficulty of answering to these questions is also due to the observation that the performance measures referring to cloud system resources are characterized by spikes and extreme variability to the event that it is impossible to identify stable states if not for short periods.

The paper is organized as follow. Section 2 evidences main contributions to the state of the art. Section 3 describes the operating context and outlines the main phases of the proposed management algorithms. Section 4 considers the problem of identifying when a host really requires a load migration because of its critical state conditions, and proposes an innovative selection algorithm. Section 5 is devoted to the identification of the virtual machines that is convenient to migrate and of the physical hosts that can receive them. Section 6 concludes the paper with some final remarks and future work.

2   Related Work

There are several proposals for live migration of virtual machines in clusters of servers, and the most recent techniques aim to reduce downtime during migration. For example, the solution in Clark et al. [6] is able to transfer an entire machine with a downtime of few hundreds of milliseconds. Travostino et al. [7] migrate virtual machines on a WAN area with just 1-2 seconds of application downtime through lightpath [8]. Unlike these solutions that are based on a pre-copy of the state, Hines et al. [9] propose a post-copy which defers the transfer of a machine memory contents after its processor state has been sent to the target host. Migration techniques through Remote Direct Memory Access (RDMA) further reduce migration time and application downtime [10]. Although these mechanisms are rapidly improving, live migration remains an expensive operation that should be applied selectively especially in a cloud context characterized by thousands of physical machines and about one order more of virtual machines. The focus of this paper on decision and management algorithms differentiates our work from literature on migration mechanisms. We evidence three main phases of the migration management process: to decide when a dynamic redistribution of load is necessary; how to choose which virtual machines is convenient to migrate; to place virtual machines to other physical machines.

Khanna et al. [4] monitor the resources (CPU and memory) of physical and virtual machines. If a resource exceeds a predefined threshold and some SLA is at risk, then the system migrates a virtual machine to another physical host. Sandpiper [11] is a mechanism that automates the task of monitoring and detecting hotspots; Bobroff et al. [12] propose an algorithm for virtual machine migration that aims to guarantee probabilistic SLAs. All these works decide when a dynamic redistribution of load is necessary through some threshold-based algorithms. We propose a completely different approach that decides about migration by avoiding thresholds on the server load, but considering the load profile evaluated through a CUSUM-based stochastic model [1].

The issues about to choose which virtual machines is convenient to migrate and where to place virtual machines have been often addressed through some global optimization approach. Entropy [13] decides about a dynamic placement of virtual machines on physical machines with the goal of minimizing the number of active physical servers and the number of migrations to reach a new configuration. Nguyen Van et al. [14] use the same approach but they integrate SLAs. Sandpiper [11] proposes two algorithms: a black-box approach that is agnostic about operating system and application; a gray-box approach that exploits operating system and application level statistics. It monitors CPU, memory and network resources to avoid SLA violations. The gray-box can also analyze application logs. The scheme proposed by Khanna et al. [4] moves the virtual machines with minimum utilization to the physical host with minimum available resources that are sufficient to host that virtual machines without violating the SLA. If there is no available host, it activates a new physical machine. Similarly, if the utilization of a physical machine falls below a threshold, the hosted servers are migrated elsewhere and the physical machine is removed from the pool of available hosts. Stage et al. [5] consider bandwidth consumed during migration. They propose a system that classifies the various loads and consolidate more virtual machines on each host based on typical periodic trends, if they exist. The paper in [12] adopts prediction techniques and a bin packing heuristic to allocate and place virtual machines while minimizing the number of activated physical machines. The authors propose also an interesting method for characterizing the gain that a virtual machine can achieve from dynamic migration. Our proposals differ from all these global optimization models that are applicable at runtime when there is a small set of machines to consider, but they cannot work in a cloud context characterized by thousands of physical machines. For these reasons, we analyze separately each physical host and its related virtual machines with the main goal of minimizing migrations just to the most severe instances. Instead of distributing the load evenly across a set of physical machines in order to get an optimal resource utilization, we think that in a cloud context exposed to unpredictable demand and heterogeneous workload, a load sharing approach for migration of virtual machine is more realistic, in that it is possible to share the load across multiple servers, even if in an unequal way.

3   Management Algorithms for Load Migration

A typical cloud architecture consists of a huge set of physical machines (*host*), each of them equipped with some virtualization mechanisms, from hardware virtualization up to micro-partitioning, operating system virtualization, software virtualization. These mechanisms allow each machine to host a concurrent execution of several virtual machines (*guest*) each with its own operating system and applications.

To accommodate varying demands for different types of processing, the most modern cloud infrastructures include dynamic management capabilities and virtual machine mobility that is, the ability to move transparently virtual machines from one host to another. By migrating a guest from an overloaded host to another not critical host, it is possible to improve resource utilization and better load sharing. Independently of the migration techniques, they share a common management model: any decision algorithm for migration has to select one or more *sender* hosts from which some virtual machines are moved to other destination hosts, namely *receivers*. This paper addresses the main issues related to migration decisions, that is, it aims to answer to the following questions: when it is necessary to activate a migration, which guests of a sender host should migrate, and where they should be moved.

We are aware that any dynamic guest migration remains an expensive operation that consumes resources of the sender and receiver hosts as well as network bandwidth because of transfers of large chunks of data representing the memory state of the guests. In a cloud architecture with thousands of hosts, an abuse of guest migrations would devastate system and application performance. Hence, we should recur to migration in few severe instances during the cloud platform operations. In other words, a good algorithm for governing of dynamic migrations in a cloud architecture must guarantee a *reliable classification* of the host behavior (as sender, receiver and neutral) that can reduce the number of useless guests migrations, and a *selective precision* in deciding which (few) guests should migrate to another host.

The load state of a host is obtained through a periodic collection of measures from server monitors. These measures are typically characterized by noises and non stationary effects in the short-medium term, while there is some periodic behavior in a long term vision (day, week) that we do not consider in this paper. Figure 1 shows four load profiles (concerning host CPU utilizations) in a cloud architecture where physical machines host any type of virtual machines and applications, such as Web sites, databases, access controls, CMSes, mail servers, management software. In a similar context, the traditional threshold-based approach [4, 11] that classifies a host as a sender or receiver because its

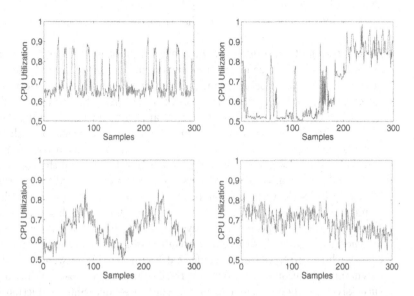

Fig. 1. Load profiles of hosts in a cloud architecture

load is beyond or below some given lines cannot work. This problem is even more serious in a cloud context with thousands of hosts where, at a checkpoint, a threshold may signal hundreds of senders and, at the successive checkpoint, the number of senders can become few dozen or, even worse, remain in the order of hundreds but where most servers are different from those of the previous set. The decision about which guests is useful to migrate from one server to another is affected by similar problems if we adopt some threshold-based method.

The primary goal of this paper is to provide robust and selective reallocations of guests in a context of thousands of hosts, under the consideration that high performance and low overheads are guaranteed only if we are able to limit the number of migrations to few really necessary instances. To this purpose, we propose novel algorithms for dynamic load management in a cloud architecture that take decisions without fixed thresholds and that consider trend behavior instead of instantaneous or average load measures.

The proposed management algorithm is activated periodically (typically in the order of few minutes) and, at each checkpoint, it aims at defining three sets: sender hosts, receiver hosts, and migrating guests, where their cardinalities are denoted as S, R, and G, respectively. Let also N be the total number of hosts. We have to guarantee that $N \geq S + R$, and that the intersection between the set of sender hosts and of receiver hosts is null. The algorithm is based on the following four phases.

- **Phase 1: Selection of sender hosts.** The first action requires the selection of the set of sender hosts that require the migration of some of their guests. We describe our strategy that is based on the CUSUM models [1] in Section 4.

The idea is to have a selective and robust algorithm so that the cardinality S of the set of senders is much smaller than the total number of hosts that is, $S \ll N$.

- **Phase 2: Selection of guests.** Once selected the senders, we have to evaluate how many and which guests it is convenient to migrate. To this purpose, in Section 5 we propose an algorithm that is able to select the most critical guests for each server on the basis of a *load trend-based* model instead of traditional approaches based on instantaneous or average load measures. Even for this phase, the goal is to limit the number of guests for each host that should migrate, so that $G < (N - S)$. If this does not occur after the first evaluation, the guest selection proceeds iteratively until the constraint is satisfied. (It is worth to observe that no experiment required an iteration.)

- **Phase 3: Selection of receiver hosts.** Once selected the guests that have to migrate, we have to define the set of receiver hosts. To this purpose, we do not propose any specific innovative algorithm. From our past experience in other geographically distributed architectures and initial experiments on cloud architectures, we can conclude that the major risk we want to avoid is a dynamic migration that tends to overload some receiver hosts so that at the successive checkpoint a receiver may become a sender. Similar fluctuations devastate system performance and stability. Hence, our idea is to set $R = G$ so that each receiver host receives at most one guest. The selected receivers are the R hosts that exhibit the lowest load computed on the basis of the trend model described in Section 5.

- **Phase 4: Assignment of guests.** The guests selected in the Phase 2 are assigned to the receivers through a classical greedy algorithm where we begin to assign the most onerous guests to the lowest loaded hosts. (It is worth to observe that in actual cloud architectures there are other architectural and application constraints that should be satisfied in the guest migration phase. These constraints limit the combinations of possible assignments to different sets thus reducing the computational cost of sorting.)

The most innovative contribution of this paper is on the first two phases that represent the core of the following two sections. In the other two phases, we adopt more traditional algorithms not deserving an accurate treatment in this paper.

4   Selection of Sender Hosts

The identification of the set of sender hosts represents the most critical problem for the dynamic management of a cloud architecture characterized by thousands of machines. The fundamental idea to determine selective and robust detections is to pass from more or less sophisticated threshold-based models, that consider the amount of load of a host in a certain interval, to a model that analyzes the load profile of the resources. The goal is to signal only the hosts subject to *significant state changes* of their load, where we define a state change *significant* if it

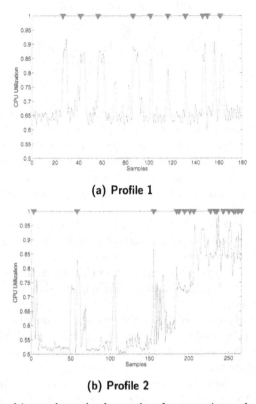

(a) Profile 1

(b) Profile 2

Fig. 2. CPU load in two hosts (each sample refers to an interval of 1 minute)

is intensive and persistent. To determine abrupt modifications of a host load profile, we propose a reliable and robust detection model especially useful when the
application context consists of large numbers of hosts subject to: many instantaneous spikes, non-stationary effects, and unpredictable and rapidly changing
load.

As examples, Figure 2(a) and Figure 2(b) show two typical profiles of the CPU
utilization of two hosts in a cloud architecture. The former profile is characterized
by a stable load with some spikes but there is no *significant state change* in terms
of the previous definition. On the other hand, the latter profile is characterized
by some spikes and by two significant state changes around sample 180 and
sample 220. A robust detection model should arise no alarm in the former case,
and just two alarms in the latter instance. In a similar scenario, it is clear that
any detection algorithm that takes into consideration an absolute or average load
value as alarm mechanism tends to cause many false alarms. This is the case of
threshold-based algorithms [4,11] that are widely adopted in several management
contexts. Just to give an example, let us set the load threshold to define a sender
host to 0.8 of its CPU utilization (done for example in [15]). In the Figures 2,
the small triangles on the top of the two figures denote the checkpoints where

Table 1. Evaluation of ARL

h	1	2	3	4	5	6	7	8	9	10
ARL_0	6	20	59	169	469	1286	3510	9556	25993	70674
ARL_1	2	4	6	8	10	12	14	16	18	20

the threshold-based detection algorithm signals the host as a sender. There are 10 signals in the former case and 17 in the latter case instead of the expected 0 and 2. This initial result denotes a clear problem with a critical consequence on performance: we have an excessive number of guest migrations even when not strictly necessary. If we extend this example to a cloud context characterized by thousands of hosts, then we can understand why dynamic guest migration is not yet so popular.

Our detection model takes a quite different approach that evaluates the entire load profile of a resource and aims to detect abrupt and permanent load changes. To this purpose, we consider a stochastic model based on the CUSUM (Cumulative Sum) algorithm [1] that works well even at runtime. Other anomaly detection techniques based on pattern matching and data mining are preferable for off-line approaches.

The CUSUM algorithm has been shown to be optimal in that it guarantees minimum mean delay to detection in the asymptotic regime when the mean time between false alarms goes to infinity [2]. We consider the one-sided version of the CUSUM algorithm that is able of selecting increasing changes of the load profile in face of variable and non-stationary characteristics. The samples of the loads deriving from the host monitors denote a time series $\{y_i\}$, $i = 1, \ldots, n$, characterized by a target value $\widehat{\mu}_i$ that is computed as the exponentially weighted average of prior data:

$$\widehat{\mu}_i = \alpha y_i + (1 - \alpha)\widehat{\mu}_{i-1} \tag{1}$$

where $0 < \alpha \leq 1$ is typically set to $1/(1 + 2\pi * f)$, and f is the cutoff frequency of the EWMA model [3]. The CUSUM algorithm detects abrupt increases from the target value $\widehat{\mu}_i$ by evaluating the following test statistics:

$$d_0 = 0; \quad d_i = \max\{0, d_{i-1} + y_i - (\widehat{\mu}_i + K)\} \tag{2}$$

which measures positive deviations from a nominal value $\widehat{\mu}_i$. A counter d_i accumulates all deviations of the measures y_i from the target value $\widehat{\mu}_i$ that are greater than a pre-defined constant K; the counter d_i is reset to 0 when they become negative. The term K, which is known as the allowance or slack value, determines the minimum deviation that the statistics d_i should account for. The suggested default value in literature is $K = \frac{\Delta}{2}$, where Δ is the minimum shift to be detected [2]. A change in the load profile of a host is signaled when d_i exceeds $H = h\sigma_y$, where h is a design parameter and σ_y is the standard deviation of the observed time series.

The choice of the parameter h influences the performance of the CUSUM algorithm in terms of the so called *Average Run Lengths* (ARL), where ARL_0

denotes the average number of samples between false alarms when no significant change has occurred in the load, and ARL_1 denotes the average number of samples to detect a significant change when it does occur. Ideally, ARL_0 should be very large because we want to limit false alarms, while ARL_1 should be rather small because we do not want an excessive delay to signal a significant load change. We know and show in Table 1 that both ARL_0 and ARL_1 tend to grow for increasing values of h, although ARL_0 shows an exponential increment, and ARL_1 a linear increment as a function of h. Hence, the best choice of h is a compromise because too large values would improve ARL_0 but would deteriorate ARL_1 performance. As the reference value proposed in literature [2] is $h = 5$, we initially consider the so called *Baseline CUSUM* having $H = 5\sigma_y$. The performance of this algorithm is shown in Figures 3, where each small triangle denotes a point in which a host is signaled as a sender. If we compare the results in Figure 3 with those in Figure 2 (referring to a threshold-based algorithm), we can appreciate that the total number of detections is significantly reduced because it passes from 27 to 11. In particular, the Baseline CUSUM is able to avoid detections due to load oscillations around the threshold value. On the other hand, it is unable to address completely the issue of unnecessary

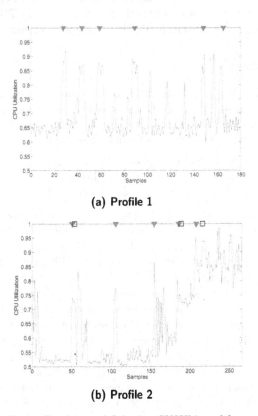

(a) Profile 1

(b) Profile 2

Fig. 3. Baseline and Selective CUSUM models

detections related to short-time spikes, such as those occurring at samples 30, 45, 55 and 90 in Figure 3(a).

To have even a more robust and selective detection algorithm suitable for cloud contexts, we propose a modified version of the Baseline CUSUM model, namely *Selective CUSUM*, that chooses h with the goal of maximizing ARL_0 under some temporal constraints X related to the average delay necessary to signal a significant load change. From this temporal constraint X, that is expressed in terms of samples and ARL_1, we can select the upper bound for h by referring to the Table 1. This is not the best value for X because the choice always depends on the application context. For example, if in our platform we consider that a maximum acceptable delay for detecting a significant load change is around 15 minutes, by considering that samples are taken every minute, we have that $X = 15$. From Table 1, we can easily get that a value of $h \in [7, 8]$ exhibits an $ARL_1 \sim 15$. Hence, a good choice for characterizing the Selective CUSUM is to set $h = 7$.

In Figures 3, the three small boxes on the top denote the activations signaled by the Selective CUSUM. We can appreciate that this algorithm determines robust and selective detections of the sender hosts: indeed, it is able to remove any undesired signal caused by instantaneous spikes in Figure 3(a), and to detect only the most significant state changes at samples 55, 185, 210 in Figure 3(b), actually just one more (at sample 55) than the optimal selection of two signals.

5   Selection of Guests

When a host is selected as a sender, it is important to determine which of its guests should migrate to another host. As migration is expensive, our idea is to select few guests that have contributed to the significant load change of their host. For each host, we apply the following three steps:

1. evaluation of the load of each guest;
2. sorting of the guests depending on their loads;
3. choice of the subset of guests that are on top of the list.

The first step is the most critical, because we have several alternatives to denote the load of a guest. Let us consider for example the CPU utilization of five virtual machines (A-E) in Figure 4 obtained by the VMware monitor.

The typical approach of considering the CPU utilization at a given sample as representative of a guest load (e.g., [4, 11]) is not a robust choice here because the load profiles of most guests are subject to spikes. For example, if we consider samples 50, 62, 160, 300 and 351, the highest load is shown by the guest B, albeit these values are outliers of the typical load profile of this guest. Even considering as a representative value of the guest load the average of the past values may bring us to false conclusions. For example, if we observe the guests at sample 260, the heaviest guest would be A followed by E. This choice is certainly preferable to a representation based on absolute values, but it does not take into account an important factor of the load profiles: the load of the guest E is rapidly decreasing while that of the guest A is continuously increasing.

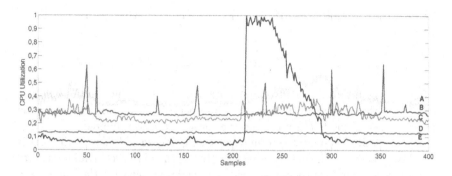

Fig. 4. Profiles of guest machines

Our idea is that a guest selection model should not consider just absolute or average values, but it should also be able to estimate the *behavioral trend* of the guest profile. The behavioral trend gives a geometric interpretation of the load behavior that adapts itself to the non stationary load and that can be utilized to evaluate whether the load state of a guest is increasing, decreasing, oscillating or stabilizing. Consequently, it is possible to generate a load representation of each guest based on the following geometric interpretation. Between every pair of the m consecutive selected points in the time series $\{y_i\}$, $i = 1, \ldots, n$, we compute the *trend coefficient* α_j, with $0 \le j \le m - 1$, of the line that divides the consecutive points $y_{i-j|\frac{n}{m}|}$ and $y_{i-(j+1)|\frac{n}{m}|}$.

$$\alpha_j = \frac{y_{i-j|\frac{n}{m}|} - y_{i-(j+1)|\frac{n}{m}|}}{|\frac{n}{m}|}; 0 \le j \le m - 1; i < m \tag{3}$$

In order to quantify the degree of variation of the past data values, we consider a weighted linear regression of the m trend coefficients:

$$\bar{\alpha}_i = \sum_{j=0}^{m-1} p_j \alpha_j; \quad \sum_{j=0}^{m-1} p_j = 1 \tag{4}$$

where $\alpha_0, \ldots, \alpha_{(m-1)}$ are the trend coefficients that are weighted by the p_j coefficients. This is the most general formula that can pass from not weighted p_j values to weighted coefficients obtained through some decay distributions. In this paper, we consider a geometric distribution of the weights p that gives more importance to the most recent trend coefficients. The absolute value of the j-th trend coefficient $| \alpha_j |$ identifies the intensity of the variation between two consecutive measures $y_{i-j|\frac{n}{m}|}$ and $y_{i-(j+1)|\frac{n}{m}|}$. The sign of α_j denotes the direction of the variation: a plus represents an increase between the $y_{i-j|\frac{n}{m}|}$ and $y_{i-(j+1)|\frac{n}{m}|}$ values, while a minus denotes a decrease. A load representation of the guest g at sample i-th, denoted by L_i^g (for g spanning the entire set of guests hosted by the considered physical machine), is the result of a linear combination between the quantitative trend, $\bar{\alpha}_i$, and the actual load value, $y_0, \ldots, y_{n-1}$, that is:

$$L_i^g = \bar{\alpha}_i + \sum_{j=0}^{n-1} q_j y_{i-j}; \quad \sum_{j=0}^{n-1} q_j = 1 \qquad (5)$$

After having obtained a load representation L_i^g for each guest g, we can sort them from the heaviest to the lightest. This operation is immediate because the total number of guests U running on the considered host is limited.

The third final step must determine which guest(s) should migrate to another host. We recall that the idea is to select only the guests that contribute more to the host load. To this purpose, we estimate the relative impact of the load of each guest on the overall load and we compute $\gamma_i^g = \frac{L_i^g}{\sum_{j=1}^{U} L_i^j}$ for $i = 1, ..., U$, where U is the total number of guests in the host i. As we have already sorted the guests in a decreasing order based on L_i^g values, the order is preserved when we consider the γ_i^g values. The idea is to select for migration the minimum number of guests with the highest relative loads. This is an arbitrary choice, but we found convenient to consider, as an example, the guests that contribute to one-third of the total relative load. To give an idea, let us consider two hosts H_1 and H_2 characterized by the following γ_i^g values: $(0.25, 0.21, 0.14, 0.12, 0.11, 0.10, 0.03, 0.02, 0.01)$, and $(0.41, 0.22, 0.20, 0.10, 0.04, 0.02, 0.01)$, respectively. In H_1, we select the first two guests because the sum of their relative loads 0.46 exceeds one-third. On the other hand, in H_2 we select just the first guest that alone contributes to more than one-third of the total load.

As we want to spread the migrating load to the largest number of receiver hosts, we want that no receiver should get more than one guest that is, $G = R$. Hence, we have to guarantee that the number of guests we want to migrate is $G < (N - S)$. Typically, this constraint is immediately satisfied because S is a small number, $S \ll N$, and typically $G \leq 2S$. However, if for certain really critical scenarios it results that $G > (N - S)$, we force the choice of just one guest for each sender host. This should guarantee a suitable solution because otherwise we have that $S > R$ that is, the entire cloud platform tends to be overloaded. Similar instances cannot be addressed by a dynamic migration algorithm but they should be solved through the activation of standby machines [4] that typically exist in a cloud data center. It is also worth to observe that all our experiments were solved through the method based on the one-third of the total relative load with no further intervention.

6   Conclusion

Dynamic migrations of virtual machines is becoming an interesting opportunity to allow cloud infrastructures to accommodate changing demands for different types of processing with heterogeneous workloads and time constraints. Nevertheless, there are many open issues about the most convenient choice about when to activate migration, how to select guest machines to be migrated, and the most convenient destinations. These classical problems are even more severe in a cloud context characterized by a very large number of hosts. We propose novel algorithms and models that are able to identify just the real critical host and guest devices, by considering the load profile of hosts and the load trend behavior of the guest instead of thresholds, instantaneous or average measures that are typically used in literature.

Experimental studies based on traces coming from a cloud platform supporting heterogeneous applications on Linux and MS virtualized servers show significant improvements in terms of selectivity and robustness of the proposed algorithm for sender detection and selection of the most critical guests. These satisfactory results are encouraging us to integrate the proposed models and algorithms in a software package for dynamic management of virtual machines in cloud architectures. On the other hand, we should consider that a cloud architecture consists of heterogeneous infrastructures and platforms, guests that must not migrate or that can migrate only within certain subsets of hardware and operating systems. These real constraints are not taken into account in this paper, but we are working to include them in a future work.

References

1. Page, E.S.: Estimating the point of change in a continuous process. Biometrika 44 (1957)
2. Montgomery, D.C.: Introduction to Statistical Quality Control
3. Kendall, M., Ord, J.: Time Series. Oxford University Press, Oxford (1990)
4. Khanna, G., Beaty, K., Kar, G., Kochut, A.: Application Performance Management in Virtualized Server Environments. In: Proc. of Network Operations and Management Symp. (2006)
5. Stage, A., Setzer, T.: Network-aware migration control and scheduling of differentiated virtual machine workloads. In: Proc. of 31st Int. Conf. on Software Engineering (2009)
6. Clark, C., Fraser, K., Steven, H., Gorm Hansen, J., Jul, E., Limpach, C., Pratt, I., Warfield, A.: Live Migration of Virtual Machines. In: Proc. of the 2nd ACM/USENIX Symp. on Networked Systems Design and Implementation (2005)
7. Travostino, F., Daspit, P., Gommans, L., Jog, C., de Laat, C., Mambretti, J., Monga, I., Van Oudenaarde, B., Raghunath, S., Wang, P.Y.: Seamless live migration of virtual machines over the MAN/WAN. Future Gener. Computer System 22(8) (2006)
8. DeFanti, T., de Laat, C., Mambretti, J., Neggers, K., St. Arnaud, B.: TransLight: a global-scale LambdaGrid for e-science. Communications of the ACM (2003)
9. Hines, M.R., Gopalan, K.: Post-copy based live virtual machine migration using adaptive pre-paging and dynamic self-ballooning. In: Proc. of the ACM SIGPLAN/ SIGOPS Int. Conf. on Virtual execution environments (2009)
10. Wei, H., Qi, G., Jiuxing, L., Panda, D.K.: High performance virtual machine migration with RDMA over modern interconnects. In: Proc. of the IEEE Int. Conf. on Cluster Computing (2007)
11. Wood, T., Shenoy, P., Venkataramani, A., Yousif, M.: Black-box and Gray-box Strategies for Virtual Machine Migration. In: Proc. of the 4th USENIX Symp. On Networked Systems Design and Implementation (2007)

12. Bobroff, N., Kochut, A., Beaty, K.: Dynamic Placement of Virtual Machines for Managing SLA Violations. In: Proc. of the 10th IFIP/IEEE International Symp. On Integrated Network Management (2007)
13. Hermenier, F., Lorca, X., Menaud, J.-M., Muller, G., Lawall, J.: Entropy: a Consolidation Manager for Cluster. In: Proc. of the Int. Conf. on Virtual Execution Environments (2009)
14. Nguyen Van, H., Dang Tran, F.: Autonomic virtual resource management for service hosting platforms. In: Proc. of the Workshop on Software Engineering Challenges in Cloud Computing (2009)
15. VMware Distributed Power Management Concepts and Use

Cloud Computing Platforms

Track Session 4

Dynamic Service Encapsulation

Alexander Kipp[1], Lutz Schubert[1], and Christian Geuer-Pollmann[2]

[1] HLRS–Höchstleistungsrechenzentrum Universität Stuttgart,
Nobelstraße 19, 70569 Stuttgart, Germany
{kipp,schubert}@hlrs.de
[2] European Microsoft Innovation Center (EMIC) GmbH,
Ritterstrasse 23, 52072 Aachen, Germany
Christian.Geuer-Pollmann@microsoft.com

Abstract. Service Provisioning over the internet using web service specifications becomes more and more difficult as real business requirements start to shape the community. One of the most important aspects relates to dynamic service provisioning: whilst the straight forward web service usage would aim at exposing individual resources according to a fixed description, real organizations would want to expose a flexible description of their complexly aggregated products. This paper presents an approach towards reducing the technological overhead in virtual service exposition over the internet, thus allowing for more flexibility. It therefore introduces a dynamic gateway structure that acts as virtual endpoint to message transactions and can encapsulate complex business process on behalf of the provider.

Keywords: Business communication, Communication standards, Communication system control, Communication system operations and management.

1 Introduction

Today's eBusiness scenarios require a consequent realization of the Service Oriented Architecture (SOA) paradigm. Such a consequent realization provides benefits for both sides, the service providers as well as for the service consumers. Service provider can easily provide their "products" in such a way that potential service consumers can integrate these services in their own products. This is done in an abstract manner which means in particular that no implementation details of the underlying service implementation need to be considered.

Service virtualisation goes even one step further. Here operational, integration and life cycle issues are faced which is critical regarding the success of SOA [1].

Service virtualization has already taken place in our everyday life. An example for such a virtual service is a banking service providing functionality allowing a client to execute financial transactions. Therefore in the background several underlying services are needed, like a transaction manager and a database system. The user of the banking service does not recognize these underlying subsystems since he only sees the interface of the banking service. Via this interface the complexity of the underlying infrastructure is hidden from the current user. Another example is a DNS

D.R. Avresky et al. (Eds.): Cloudcomp 2009, LNICST 34, pp. 217–230, 2010.
© Institute for Computer Sciences, Social-Informatics and Telecommunications Engineering 2010

or virtual network capabilities. Without virtualization it would not be possible to handle such complex systems at all. Altogether virtualization can be seen as a more abstract view of the corresponding services and the underlying service infrastructure.

In modern eBusiness scenarios it is necessary to decouple service implementations and the corresponding service interfaces. The main reasons therefore are that such a decoupling increases fundamentally the maintainability of services as well as the flexibility of both, service providers and service consumers.

Actually Web services provide an infrastructure towards a SOA paradigm [17] but still have some gaps regarding the needed dynamicity in eBusiness and collaborative working scenarios [16]. An example of the latter one is the research project CoSpaces [2]. This projects aims to develop a framework allowing dynamic collaboration sessions for engineering teams being distributed all over the world. The issues being faced within this project are to bring together the involved people within such a collaborative working session as well as the corresponding applications. So a consequent realization of the SOA paradigm is here also very important. In this paper we provide an approach towards virtual services allowing a decoupling of service implementations from the corresponding service interfaces.

2   eBusiness and Web Services

In current eBusiness scenarios an abstract integration of collaboration partners is one of the main issues to be faced. In particular this means that partners within a collaboration want to consume the provided "product" of a partner without taking into account the corresponding service infrastructures. Web Services provide a first step towards such an approach. Web service technologies allow the consumption of services without the need to take into account the underlying service implementation. This is done by providing a standardized interface of these services (WSDL). These interfaces are integrated in the customers' code allowing him to consume the corresponding services. This interface just describes the functionality of the service in a syntactical manner. To announce a "product" consisting of the composition of several services enforces a more abstract view of the underlying services. One of the main disadvantages of the web service approach is that in the case of a change in a web service interface description the corresponding client code has also to be adapted to these changes.

Therefore abstract entities [3] have been introduced describing such a level of abstraction in a first instance. These abstract entities allow the integration of partners in an eBusiness process by assigning roles to partners and access the corresponding services or products via these abstract entities. This allows the design of collaborative eBusiness scenarios without the burden of taken into account the complexity of the underlying service infrastructures and the corresponding service implementations.

The main goals from an eBusiness perspective are

- The easy encapsulation and usage of services being distributed all over the world
- The easy composition of services in order to provide a "new product"

To realise these goals a new kind of infrastructure is needed with the goal to ease the maintenance of the underlying service infrastructures. In particular, changes of an interface or the service infrastructure should not affect the corresponding client applications. Additionally, service provider should also be able to easily adapt their infrastructures without affecting the corresponding interfaces and consequently the client applications consuming these services. The approach being presented in the following section is also going to ease the provision of new products regarding the currently available services.

3 A Dynamic WS Interface

Currently WSDLs describe a static interoperable interface to a service which is used in static manner. The interface is once proposed and linked in a static manner in the corresponding client code. This static approach does not provide the needed flexibility in a dynamic eBusiness scenario.

To provide such an adaptive and dynamic infrastructure just a contract should be proposed describing the name of this "virtual" service as well as the available operations and what they mean in particular. Additionally it should be mentioned how these operations can be invoked.

Service virtualization provides such an infrastructure by not directly proposing a static interface in the means of WSDL, instead a kind of contract is proposed describing the available functionality and how these services can be invoked as well as which information is needed to invoke these services. The introduced middleware maps in the next step after having intercepted an invocation of such a virtual service endpoint the calls to the corresponding service implementations.

The next sections are going to reflect this new approach in detail.

The New Gateway Architecture

In this section the Architecture of the new gateway is introduced and described in more detail. As mentioned before there is a concrete need in service virtualization and so consequently in an abstraction layer. This abstraction layer operates as an intermediary service between the service consumer and the service implementation by capturing the corresponding messages and mapping them to the corresponding services. This mapping also includes the necessary transformations since the virtualization gateway does not focus on a specific interface description.

Beside the mapping of messages to the corresponding service implementations within the service virtualization layer the following jobs can also be realised within this layer since the gateway describes a single point of entry to use the underlying services. This is preferable since most of the SOA infrastructures are some kind of "grown" nature with the restriction that some already existing implementations may not be compatible with current standards in interface definitions and messaging. So the gateway also provides functionality to encapsulate services.

In particular, this includes:

- *Policy enforcement*: The gateway acts as a policy enforcement point since it allows the definition of criteria that must be fulfilled before a potential service consumer is authorized to access a specific service. For example, it is possible to distinguish service consumers based on their reputation, e.g. in good and "not so" good customers.

Based on their reputation, the customers' requests are forwarded to services with different SLAs, such as "gold" services or "standard" services, where the "gold" rated services e.g. could provide a better quality of service as the "standard" services.

- *Message security, identity and access management:* In an ideal world, all deployed client applications and web services support the corresponding specifications like WS-Security, WS-Trust and WS-Federation. Ideally, each client application should be able to fetch security tokens that are necessary for service access, and each deployed service should be able to authorize an incoming request using a claims-based security model with fine-grained authorization. Unfortunately, many applications in production today do not yet adhere to these principles, and the gateway can serve as a migration path towards broader adoption of the claims-based access model. The customer-side gateway can authenticate internal requestors, request security tokens on their behalf and protect the outgoing messages. A service-side gateway can act as a policy-enforcement point to authenticate and authorize incoming callers. For example the gateway can establish a secure connection to the service consumer while the concrete client application does not support any secure data transmission.

- *Protocol translation:* Since standards in the area of web services are always a matter of change, the reflection of current needs of service consumers as well as of service provider are an essential criterion for such an infrastructure. In particular, the change of an addressing standard like WS-Addressing forces the adaption of the service implementations at the service provider side as well as the corresponding client applications consuming these services. In such a scenario the gateway allows the adaption of the corresponding service calls to the most current standards without affecting the concrete service implementation.

- *Transformation:* Since the gateway provides an universal interface for the underlying services a transformation has to be done before the message is forwarded to the corresponding service.

- *Filtering and information leakage protection:* The gateway can detect and remove private information from a request, offering a hook to install information leakage detection and prevention mechanisms.

- *Load balancing & fail over:* The gateway can act as a load balancer. If e.g. one service is currently heavy in use the gateway may decide to forward requests to this service to an equivalent one.

- *Routing:* If several equivalent services are available the routing of the messages to these services can be handled in this abstraction layer.

- *Login monitoring:* Often it is interesting for a service provider to see which version of a service is still used by the customers. Via the gateway this information is also available.

Figure 1 shows the structure of such a gateway. This structure enables service provider to *encapsulate* and *hide* their infrastructure in a way that also allows for *virtualization of products*. With the gateway being extensible, it provides the basis to non-invasively enact *security, privacy* and *business policies* related to message transactions. With the strong SOA approach pursued by the virtualization gateway, the structure furthermore meets the requirements of *minimal impact* and *maximum deployment flexibility*; through its filters, it furthermore supports the *standardized messaging support*. The gateway is

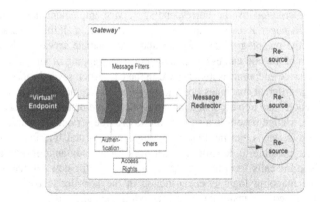

Fig. 1. Gateway Structure

furthermore constructed in a way that allows for participation in *multiple collaborations* at the same time without requiring reconfiguration of the underlying infrastructure.

The gateway of a service provider acts as the virtualization endpoint of the services exposed by the respective organization. Its main task consists in intercepting incoming and outgoing messages to enforce a series of policies related to access right restrictions, secure authentication etc. (cp. Figure 2) thus ensuring that both provider and collaboration specific policies are maintained in transactions.

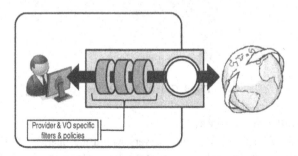

Fig. 2. The Gateway Principle

As a virtual endpoint, the gateway is capable of redirecting messages from virtual addresses to actual, physical locations (local or in the Internet), thus simplifying endpoint management from client side, i.e. applications / client services are not affected by changes in the collaboration, such as replacement of providers etc. An intrinsic handler in the gateway channel hence consists in an endpoint resolution mechanism that identifies the actual destination of a given message.

Figure 3 shows the conceptual overview of such an approach. In particular, the virtualization manager of a service provider announces a virtual service interface definition (WSDL). This virtual interface is also announced by the web server of the service provider to receive external service calls via the included virtual methods. These calls to the virtual interface are forwarded to the virtualization manager. In the following proceeding the virtualization manager transforms the incoming virtual message to a message that can be interpreted by the corresponding service implementation. Therefore the virtualization manager accesses a knowledge base containing all the necessary information like e.g. the mapping of the virtual name to a concrete service endpoint and the transformation of method names and parameters. The mapping of virtual service names to concrete service endpoints is also needed in the case when several service implementations on e.g. different machines hosting the same service are available as well as to avoid the client to take into account concrete service implementation aspects.

Via the knowledge base it is also possible to provide services dynamically. On the one hand new services can be announced via a new virtual interface. On the other hand it is also possible to develop new services for already announced virtual interfaces and map the calls from the old virtual interface to the new service implementations. So the mapping logic is encapsulated in the knowledge base providing the information needed to transform the corresponding message calls.

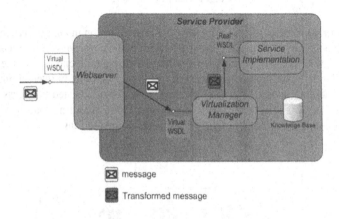

message

Transformed message

Fig. 3. General Architecture

Realisation of the New Gateway

Referring to the statistic of used web servers within the internet of April 2009 [8] there are most commonly used 2 web service infrastructures in current environments. In particular, those are the Apache Tomcat server with a contingent of 45.95% and Microsoft Internet Information Service (IIS) with a contingent of 29.97%. The remaining 24.06% are distributed over more than 30 other web server solutions, so they are not being taken into account for the following technical analysis considering in how far the service virtualization manager can be realized with existing and mainly used web services infrastructure solutions.

In the following it will be shown, how such a service virtualization manager can be realized with the mostly used web server solutions, namely the Apache Tomcat Server with AXIS and the IIS with WCF [11].

To provide a service virtualization manager, an ideally transparent intermediary service is needed acting as a message interceptor und as a message transformer. In particular, in the area of web services a HTTP router is needed doing this transformation without affecting the client calling the corresponding service as well as the underlying service implementation. Figure 4 illustrates an example of this processing:

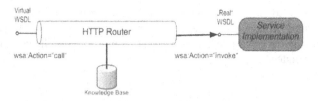

Fig. 4. Technical Realization

In particular, the HTTP router tunnels a request from a virtual WSDL to a concrete service call of a "real" service interface. Therefore in this example the virtual WSDL provides a method with the name "wsa:Action='call'. The HTTP router now maps this web service call to the corresponding "wsa:Action='invoke'" method call of the underlying service implementation. This is done completely transparent to the invoking client as well as to the service implementation.

Within the IIS / WCF realization the gateway infrastructure exposes virtual endpoints (URLs) similar to the (IIS) and may even be hosted inside the IIS like a simple service. The service administrator uses the capabilities of the virtualization gateway / IIS to decide which resources / services / workflows are exposed under which URL – all other services either remain hidden in the infrastructure or are exposed without a virtualization gateway intermediary. This way, the administrator can specify concretely which services are exposed in which manner (cp. Figure 5).

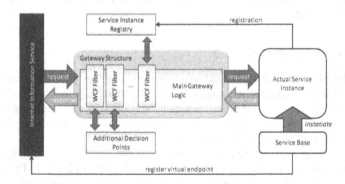

Fig. 5. Gateway Structure and its Relationship to IIS and Service Instances

Policy handlers can be registered at the virtualization gateway using the according management interface and the identifier of the specific gateway structure. Each service instance can thus principally be associated with its own gateway and policy handler chain, allowing for maximum flexibility.

The Service Instance Registry is a specific type of policy decision point that identifies the actual endpoints on basis of the transaction metadata (sender, related VO, addressed endpoint etc.). It will instruct the message chain about the next endpoint to forward the message to.

Axis [12] provides with the Handler concept an approach that allows to plug-in applications between the web server and the corresponding application services.

Therefore so called handler-chains can be realized describing a list of operations that can be executed on arriving messages for a specific service or for all web services being hosted on the corresponding web server. Figure 6 shows the general overview of the Axis architecture:

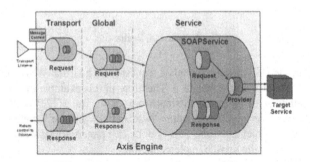

Fig. 6. Axis Engine Overview [12]

In particular, incoming messages are stored in a request queue. Before these messages are processed and forwarded to the corresponding service implementation the handlers being defined for this service are executed. These handlers are able to modify the incoming and outgoing messages, so at this point it is possible to plug in the knowledge support doing the mapping and the necessary transformations of the corresponding messages.

4 Trust Management

In distributed-system scenarios, the main security problem is cross-organizational authorization. Most identity and access systems available today provide flexible solutions for authorization-related problems within the boundaries of a single organization. Still, IT professionals who need security solutions for cross-organizational collaboration typically need to develop their own custom solutions.

The BREIN project extends the security work done in former projects, such as TrustCoM, MOSQUITO [6], NextGRID [5] or MYCAREVENT [7]. The security research in these projects addressed problems such as human-supported federation establishment and enactment, VO-centric identity and claims management, and authorization for cross-organizational service invocation. While that led to many insights into the VO security area, the BREIN project identified a couple of issues that needed further research: One open question is how to leverage the human user for context provisioning, such as why a particular service interaction happens, and subsequently utilizing that context for security decisions. The second broader issue for which a solution is needed is the access management for resources located outside of the data owner's organizational trust boundary. The third topic is related to the support for claims-based security in protocols that do not support WS-Security, such as MTOM-based streaming.

In the BREIN architecture, security-related implementation artifacts are located at various places and layers, so that BREIN can scale the flexibility of the solution depending on the concrete security requirements of the respective scenario. For example, it is clear that cross-organizational message exchanges always have to be integrity and confidentiality protected, and that the requestor needs to be authenticated and authorized. Depending on the capabilities and features of the web services stacks of both clients and application services, either the end-nodes take care of handling the cross-organizational security themselves, or big parts of that responsibility are factored into infrastructure components such as the gateway service. For example, if a web services-based client application cannot encrypt and sign SOAP messages using the appropriate cross-organizational security tokens, then that responsibility has to be handled by the gateway service which is sitting in the message path, on behalf of the client.

The Security Token Service (STS) issues claim-based tokens to authenticated users (or a gateway acting on behalf of the user) and is also involved in the process of establishing federations with other STSs'. Similarly to the gateway, the STS component needs to be installed within the security domains of the entities that want to communication and depending on the role they hold they perform different functions. Therefore the STS can play both the role of the client side STS as well as the server side STS performing different functions. The client-side role of the security token service issues tokens that are necessary to pass the access check on the service side. The tokens are generated based on the information that is extracted from the service call message. The Service-side role of the security token service performs an authorization decision on the ultimate service and issues a security token that will be understood by the service. It hence has the role of a policy decision point (PDP). The STS is a middleware component and is configured using its policy store. The policy store contains both the attribute information about clients in the own organization (i.e. the claims that can be issued), the capabilities of partner organizations (i.e. claims that the STS accepts from other issuers), and access policy for local resources, such as web services:

- User attributes and claims can be stored either within the STS' own configuration, or in external attribute stores such as Active Directory.
- The trust relationships with partner organizations describe e.g. which roles a partner company assumes in a given virtual organization, i.e. which statements and claims the partner is authorized to issue. Essentially this is similar to SecPAL's 'can-say' verb.
- The access policy for local services describes claim requirements for local services, i.e. which claims need to be present in the client's security token to access a particular service.

The STS will be queried for security token issuing by the *security handler*. This handler resides inside the Gateways and protects message that is about to be sent, and requests access control decisions for incoming messages.

The STS is implemented using .NET and WCF. The interaction will be through WS-* message. Most likely the component needs a network connection, although it could (theoretically) also communicate by local inter-process communication like named pipes. The WCF-based client-side security handler is implemented as a special SIR binding, which fetches the routing, security and binding information from the local SIR, creates the 'real' cross-organizational binding based on that endpoint information, and dispatches the message though this cross-organizational binding.

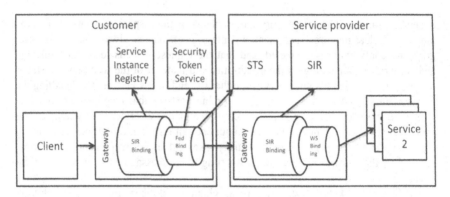

Fig. 7. SIR Binding Interactions

5 Brave New World

In order to evaluate the conceptual approach of the introduced virtualization infrastructure the WCF gateway prototype integrated within the Integrated Projects (IP) CoSpaces and BREIN [4], considering different of the mentioned benefits of such a virtualization infrastructure.

The IP CoSpaces is facing the challenging task in providing an infrastructure allowing for the support of collaboration of worldwide distributed engineering teams. Therefore CoSpaces aims to develop a framework that supports dynamic, ad-hoc collaborative working sessions [14]. This infrastructure stresses, beside the consideration of dynamic aspects within collaborations, security issues to be of the utmost priority and importance. Since security aspects usually affects every involved component within such a collaboration session, a new approach has been considered to allow application developers as well as collaboration participants to concentrate on their original tasks, e.g. the provision of a specific functionality within an application or the solving of a specific problem within a collaboration, without having to consider security aspects whilst being involved in a collaboration.

Since within collaborations between industrial partners often beside services also business critical data has to be shared, authentication, authorization and secure communication between participants has been determined as one of the most critical aspects that need to be considered by such a framework. Within CoSpaces Shibboleth has been chosen as the best suitable solution for providing an authentication infrastructure for authorization issues whilst considering dynamic aspects of such collaborations [15]. Therefore, the virtualization approach being presented within this paper is going to be used to transparently integrate an authentication and authorization infrastructure within the entire framework without affecting the underlying steering and coordination infrastructure components as well as the corresponding shared services and data. Consequently, the users as well as the application providers do not have to consider security aspects within their tasks whilst the framework ensures that only foreseen partners are allowed to access the corresponding services and data sets.

The IP BREIN faces the challenge that in today's world, enterprises, independent of their size, have to cooperate closely with other companies to keep their competitiveness, as no company is capable of fulfilling all requirements alone. But setting up these collaborations is still difficult and extremely costly. Especially for SMEs these collaborations are not really cost-efficient, as they have to put in high efforts to be able to compete on the market with other players. Therefore BREIN will enable service providers to reduce costs whilst maximizing profit by providing a framework that will automatically adapt to changes in individual business needs and/or environment in an intelligent manner. Cost and effort for service provisioning will be greatly reduced by simplifying business goal definition, intelligent optimization and decision making support. Therefore, BREIN is going to support the integration of "virtual" resources in workflows in order to achieve a higher degree of flexibility. This approach allows for both, an easier and more abstract usage of resources (e.g. a customer just invokes a "simulation" service without considering technical details) as well as an increased support of dynamism in such environments by easing the replacement of service providers (e.g. the customer still invokes a "simulation" service whilst his own company gateway redirects this request to a new service provider).

The "classical" WSDL approach would affect in such a dynamic environment that every client of a specific service provider has to adapt their applications to new service interfaces in case of any modification of the corresponding service provider infrastructure or in the case of a service provider change. Additionally a lot of added effort has to be spent for the corresponding service setup. But with the new gateway the client does not need to update his code, although the syntactical interface may have changed, since the messages of the calls via the old interface are mapped or, if needed, transformed, to the interface of the new service.

With this gateway the service provider is now able to implement any adoption needed, even regarding changes in inter-communication standards. Now it is possible to provide several interfaces for the same service, each adapting to another interface. E.g. one customer needs a secure connection to the service because sensible data has to be transferred while another one uses another version of WS-Addressing [9] or WS-Security [10].

eBusiness and the New Gateway

This approach introduces a new abstraction layer for SOAs facing the needs of eBusiness environments. In particular the main benefit is an *increment of flexibility*: Both, for the technical as well as for the business perspective, flexibility has been increased. From a technical point of view it is now possible to bind services statically in application codes while the corresponding service implementation can be migrated. Additionally the service provider can announce the available services independently from the protocol the potential service consumer are going to use. This way of announcing services allows the service provider to use and re-use already existing services in a very easy way. Beside this, the composition of services in a workflow has also been improved: Depending on the target outcome of a workflow services can now be combined regarding the announced contract. The service provider is consequently able to provide "new" products depending on the currently available resources, services and their current payload.

Resulting from this increase of flexibility, the main benefits of this approach are

- Increased customers satisfaction: service providers are now able to adapt very fast to different customers' needs.

- Easy and improved maintenance of provided services
- Efficient development since the customers' technical point of view does not need to be considered within a concrete service implementation.
- Easy adaptation of provided services to changing web standards. Since web standards in the area of security, addressing, reliable message transfer, etc. are continuously under development and improvement, the corresponding service provider has to support as most of these standards as possible.
- Decreased costs
- loose coupling can be better realised with such an approach
- Monitoring and logging in abstraction layer: enables the administrator to see which versions of a specific service are mostly used
- Governance guidelines force the realisation of specific functionality which is often not conforming with the current service realisation. The presented approach can realise this requirement without affecting the service implementation.
- Service consumer may use different end user systems to consume the corresponding services
- Many "grown" SOA infrastructures available are already existing and need to be integrated. This can be realised with an extremely reduced effort with the presented approach.

6 Conclusions

In this paper we presented an approach towards a "real" SOA paradigm and how this can only be realized with a corresponding support of a service virtualization infrastructure. We also presented a conceptual approach to realize this service virtualization taking into account the already existing, partly grown SOA realization with web service technologies. Finally we presented how this concept can be realized in principle taking into account the most common used web services infrastructures. The latter presentation showed that the current available concepts of these web service infrastructure implementations allows an adaptation of the "intelligence" of a service virtualization infrastructure in the sense that the corresponding knowledge support can be added in such a way that incoming messages of a virtual service definition can be mapped to a concrete service implementations.

Actually a first prototype of the WCF approach is available and in the testing phase within CoSpaces and BREIN. This first prototype actually allows the mapping of virtual EPRs to concrete EPRs including enhancements regarding security, policy enforcement, etc. The mentioned plug-in approach makes the introduced concept quite flexible regarding new requirements. A first prototype supporting the Shibboleth infrastructure is also be available. Additionally, the AXIS gateway is currently under development and will be available soon allowing a comparison of these two realizations.

We strongly believe in the success of SOA. The presented approach describes a necessary step towards an entire, SOA enabled infrastructure.

Acknowledgements

The results presented in this paper are partially funded by the European Commission under contract IST-5-034245 through the project CoSpaces as well as through the project BREIN under contract number IST-034556. This paper expresses the opinions of the authors and not necessarily those of the European Commission. The European Commission is not liable for any use that may be made of the information contained in this paper. The authors want to thank all who contributed to this paper, especially all members of the corresponding consortiums.

References

[1] Nash, A.: Service Virtualization – Key to Managing Change in SOA (01.06.2006), http://www.bitpipe.com/detail/RES/1130171201_512.html (30.04.2009)

[2] CoSpaces – EU IST Project (IST-5-034245), http://www.cospaces.org (30.04.2009)

[3] TrustCoM – EU IST Project (IST-2003-01945), http://www.eu-trustcom.com (30.04.2009)

[4] BREIN - EU IST Project (IST- 034556), http://www.gridsforbusiness.eu (30.04.2009)

[5] NextGRID - EU IST Project, http://www.nextgrid.eu/ (30.04.2009)

[6] MOSQUITO - EU IST Project (IST-004636), http://www.mosquito-online.org/ (30.04.2009)

[7] MYCAREVENT - EU IST Project (IST-04402), http://www.mycarevent.com/ (30.04.2009)

[8] Netcraft –Web server statistic (April 2009), http://news.netcraft.com/archives/2009/04/ (30.04.2009)

[9] Box, D., et.al.: WS-Addressing (10.08.2004), http://www.w3.org/Submission/ws-addressing/ (30.04.2008)

[10] Nadalin, A., Kaler, C., Monzilo, R., Hallam, Baker, P.: WS-Security (01.02.2006), http://www.oasisopen.org/committees/download.php/16790/wss-v1.1-spec-os-SOAPMessageSecurity.pdf (30.04.2009)

[11] WCF – Windows Communication Foundation, http://msdn.microsoft.com/wcf/ (30.04.2009)

[12] Axis Architecture Guide, http://ws.apache.org/axis/java/architecture-guide.html (30.04.2009)

[13] Schubert, L., Kipp, A., Wesner, S.: From Internet to Cross-Organisational Networking. In: Proceedings of the 15th ISPE International Conference on Concurrent Engineering: CE 2008, Belfast, Northern Ireland (August 2008)

[14] Kipp, A., Schubert, L., Assel, M.: Supporting Dynamism and Security in Ad-Hoc Collaborative Working Environments. In: Proceedings of the 12th World Multi-Conference on Systemics, Cybernetics and Informatics (WMSCI 2008), Orlando, USA (July 2008)

[15] Assel, M., Kipp, M.A.: A Secure Infrastructure for Dynamic Collaborative Working Environments. In: Proceedings of the International Conference on Grid Computing and Applications 2007, Las Vegas, USA (June 2007)

[16] Schubert, L., Wesner, S., Dimitrakos, T.: Secure and Dynamic Virtual Organizations for Business. In: Cunningham, P., Cunningham, M. (eds.) Innovation and the Knowledge Economy: Issues, Applications, Case Studies, pp. 1201–1208. IOS Press, Amsterdam (2005)

[17] Golby, D., Wilson, M.D., Schubert, L., Geuer-Pollmann, C.: An assured environment for collaborative engineering using web services. In: CE 2006 (2006)

[18] Wesner, S., Schubert, L., Dimitrakos, T.: Dynamic Virtual Organisations in Engineering. In: 2nd Russian-German Advanced Research Workshop on Computational Science and High Performance Computing, March 14-16 (2005)

Modeling Movable Components for Disruption Tolerant Mobile Service Execution

Rene Gabner[1], Karin Anna Hummel[2], and Hans-Peter Schwefel[1,3]

[1] Forschungszentrum Telekommunikation Wien, A-1220 Vienna, Austria
{gabner,schwefel}@ftw.at
[2] University of Vienna, A-1080 Vienna, Austria
karin.hummel@univie.ac.at
[3] Aalborg University, DK-9220 Aalborg, Denmark

Abstract. Software as a Service relies on ubiquitous network access which cannot be assured in mobile scenarios, where varying link quality and user movement impair the always connected property. We approach this challenge by utilizing movable service components between a remote cluster, cloud, or server and the client device using the service. To overcome connection disruptions, service components are moved to the client prior to connection loss and executed locally. Although the basic concept is a brute force approach, challenges arise due to best fitting service decomposition, accurate estimation of connection losses, and best trade-off between moving service components and the overhead caused by this proactive fault tolerance mechanism.

This paper contributes to the general approach by presenting a system architecture based on an extended client/server model which allows to move components. Additionally, an analytical model is introduced for analyzing where to place service components best and extended to investigate failure rates and average execution time in different system configurations, i.e., different placement of service components either on the server cloud or client side. The models presented are based on Markov chains and allow to analytically evaluate the proposed system. Applied to a specific use case, we demonstrate and discuss the positive impact of placing components temporarily at the client in terms of failure rate and mean service execution time.

Keywords: Mobile Computing, Software as a Service, Service Decomposition, Markov Model, Disruption Tolerance.

1 Introduction

Software as a Service (SaaS) [1] is a field in particular of interest for mobile computing scenarios, like support for mobile workers or mobile business in general. Instead of pre-installed software packages, software is hosted and maintained at a service provider and can be accessed by the user. In this vision, the burden of troublesome installing, updating, and maintaining is taken from the user. In mobile contexts, it is even more beneficial to access the software as a service to

D.R. Avresky et al. (Eds.): Cloudcomp 2009, LNICST 34, pp. 231–244, 2010.
© Institute for Computer Sciences, Social-Informatics and Telecommunications Engineering 2010

fulfill tasks without having pre-installed too many applications. Computing *cloud infrastructures* are enabling system architectures for supporting the envisioned SaaS solution.

In contrast to stationary scenarios, mobile networked systems are impaired by varying link conditions due to fading effects and environmental disturbances on the wireless medium, other devices competing for access to the wireless link, and moving in and out of the range of a wireless network. As a consequence, intermittent connectivity is likely to happen and has to be addressed to make *mobile SaaS* feasible.

Our approach addresses intermittent connectivity by considering different locations for service execution, i.e., at the (remote) server cloud or the mobile client. In case of stable connectivity, service parts may remain at the server and classical client/server communication will be efficient to assure fastest service execution. In situations of weak connectivity and frequent disconnections, service parts have to be moved to the client to remain operational which will lead to increased service execution times at the low performance mobile device. We see four major challenges of the approach: First, the best fitting granularity of service decomposition and dependencies between service components have to be found. Second, detecting best time periods for placing service components have to be detected, e.g., predicting disconnects in advance. Third, determining optimized allocations of service components for a certain predicted network behavior. Fourth, moving software service parts causes overhead and the trade-off between availability and networking overhead has to be considered.

In this paper, we approach the third research question, as it is a motivating prerequisite for the other challenges, by modeling a service as a composition of parts, i.e., service components, and analyzing how the allocation of these components to client or server side influences certain performance or reliability metrics. Successful service execution means that the components can be accessed and used. Intermittent connectivity now leads either to completely failed services or delayed service execution. We consider both cases and present *(i)* an *analytical model for service failure/success* evaluating the failure rate of services and *(ii)* an *analytical model for service execution time analysis* for different component placement configurations. Hereby, our fault model consists of network disconnection failures only.

The paper is structured as follows: After presenting a survey on related concepts for disconnected service operation in Section 2, we describe the system architecture for movable service components in Section 3. In Section 4 we introduce the analytical model based on Markov chains. Service invocations are modeled as transitions which may succeed or fail due to network failures. In Section 5, we introduce the editor use case and present results for this particular service to demonstrate the potential of both the general concept of meaningful placement of service components for tolerating disconnections and the insights gained by using the analytical models introduced. Section 6 summarizes the work and presents an outlook on future work planned.

2   Related Work

Allowing services to be allocated and executed at different distributed locations was a hot topic in the past years. Fuggetta et al. [4] address the increased size and performance of networks as a motivator for mobile code technologies. Different mobility mechanisms like migration, remote cloning, code shipping, and code fetching are utilized to meet a diversity of requirements. We conceive temporary proactive code migration to support our architecture best. However the main focus is the analysis of impacts of code migration and optimization of component location to achieve best service execution with a minimum of interruption and delay.

When mobile communications became popular, the research area expanded and mobile computing introduced challenges different from traditional distributed computing. These challenges are related to mobile data management, seamless mobile computing, and adaptations due to limited mobile device capabilities. Imielinski et al. [5] describe the implications and challenges of mobile computing from a data management perspective. Important aspects are *(i) management of location dependent data, (ii) disconnections, (iii) adaptations of distributed algorithms for mobile hosts, (iv) broadcasting over a wireless network*, and *(v) energy efficient data access*. While mobile networks grew rapidly, a diversity of different mobile devices were pushed to the market, running different operating systems and execution environments. Because of many different mobile platforms, service development becomes complex and costly, as each platform needs its own implementation of a service.

The SaaS approach can help to overcome multi implementations of services. Instead it is possible to run a service on an execution platform within the network. Every mobile client with access to the network's application server can use such services. Our architecture benefits from the SaaS approach as it overcomes complicated installations on the client and keeps the solution flexible to reconfiguration and component migration at runtime. To execute such SaaS services which support movable components, special execution environments at the client are required. One possible solution is presented by Chou and Li [2]. They adapted an Android based mobile platform for distributed services, and show one way to execute SOA based applications. This architecture supports also access to services deployed in a SaaS environment. Because such SaaS models depend on reliable network connectivity, disruption tolerant networks are also of particular importance for mobile scenarios.

There are various researchers investigating in disruption tolerance. For example, Chuah et al. [3] investigate network coding schemes for disruption tolerant mobile networks. They compare the performance of different schemes and message expiration times to enhance network connections between mobile nodes suffering from intermittent connectivity. Another approach introduced by Ott and Xiaojun [9] is based on the application layer and introduces end-to-end disconnection detection and recovery schemes for mobile wireless communication services. Such end-to-end solutions take advantage of the fact, that the observation of the network is not based on information from the underlying transport and physical layers, which are not available in all cases. The network prediction function proposed by our architecture could benefit from such end-to-end network state detection solutions.

An approach to deal with interrupted connections is discussed by Su et al. [10]. They propose an architecture for seamless networking utilizing specialized application proxies at the client. Those proxies are tuned to serve a special service like SMTP. In our proposed execution environment, proxies will only be used to support the migration of service components.

3   System Description

We propose an architecture which supports mobile, wireless service execution on thin-clients, based on the Software as a Service (SaaS) paradigm [1]. One major constraint of SaaS is the availability of a stable, *always-on* network connection to the host running the service. Applied in a mobile context, intermittent connectivity caused by disrupted transmissions at the air interface is a major challenge. To overcome this issue we propose to split the service into several service parts (service components) applying service decomposition techniques. Selected service components are moved proactively from the service execution platform to the thin-client in case of estimated bad network quality. The service execution platform is expected to run on a server cloud, in this paper also simply referred to as *server*.

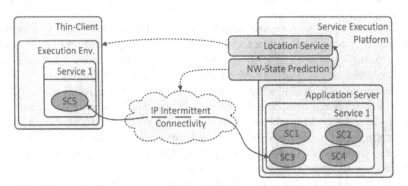

Fig. 1. Overall system architecture

Figure 1 shows a service *Service 1* which has been decomposed into five *service components* (*SC*1, *SC*2, *SC*3, *SC*4, and *SC*5). Each component is responsible for a well defined task. After it has finished, the execution flow is passed to another service component. This concept is sometimes termed *component chaining model*. The subsequently executed component may however depend on the result of the previous computation, which is modeled probabilistically for the component chaining description in Section 4.1.

The *Network State Prediction* (NSP) function collects and holds information about the current state of the network connection between the server and the thin-client. Additionally, it interfaces a couple of different data sources to predict the network state condition. For instance, the observation of the network state over a longer time period combined with additional geo-location information can be evaluated in this component. The location data can be requested directly from the thin-client if a GPS receiver is available or, otherwise, from a mobile operator. Of course there are other possible data sources which can be integrated by expanding the interface of the NSP. In case we expect network connection degradation, the NSP triggers the application server to move components which are essential for the execution within the next time periods to the client. If the service components have been moved successfully to the client, it is possible to continue service execution even if the connection is lost. In case a component is unreachable caused by a suddenly broken network link there are two possibilities to handle the situation: As described later in Section 4.2, the execution fails in case of an unreachable service component. The other approach modeled in Section 4.3 has an additional *network down* state to delay the whole service execution. After reconnecting to the service execution platform, the application server might decide to fetch back any of the service components to take over execution again.

In order to support the decision which components should be migrated in a specific network environment, the remainder of the paper focuses on component placement and analyze the impact of different *static* component placement configurations for an example service.

4   Service Component Model

In Section 3 we discussed the system architecture including the view of a service being decomposed into components some of which can be migrated between client and server. In order to make substantiated choices on which configuration to apply in a given setting, this section comes up with different Markov models that allow to analyze the consequence of a certain static placement of service components on client and server side.

4.1   Markov Model for Service Component Flow

An application consists of service components which may reside on the cloud (here referred to as a single application server) or on the (thin) client. The sequence of service components that is invoked in the course of a service execution is modeled as deterministic Markov chain. The service components are thereby assumed to be completely autonomous and are executed sequentially; as a consequence the only interaction between service components occurs when passing the execution flow from component i to component j, where $i, j = 1, ...N$. The transition probabilities between states in the Markov chain model (which correspond to service components) depend on the service type, usage patterns, and input objects. Those transition probabilities are collected in the stochastic matrix $\mathbf{P}$.[1] The Markov chain model contains exactly one absorbing state, whose

---

[1] Note, that we use bold fonts for matrices and vectors to improve readability.

meaning is a successful service completion. Without loss of generality, we order the states in this paper in a way that state N is always the absorbing success state. The initial state, i.e., first service component called, can be probabilistically described by an 'entrance vector' $\mathbf{p_0}$. The examples discussed later in this paper always assume state 1 as the single entrance state, hence $\mathbf{p_0} = [1, 0, ..., 0]$.

As the application model described by the transition probability matrix $\mathbf{P}$ (and the entrance vector $\mathbf{p_0}$) only describes the probabilistic sequence of component executions, it has to be slightly modified to allow for notions of execution time. Namely mean state-holding times $T_1, T_2, ...T_{N-1}$ for the $N-1$ states (the absorbing success state, here assumed state N, does not require an associated state-holding time) need to be defined which then allow to transform the discrete model into a continuous time Markov chain where the generator matrix $\mathbf{Q}$ is just obtained via correct adjustment of the main-diagonal of the matrix

$$\mathbf{Q^*} = \mathrm{diag}\,(1/T_1, ..., 1/T_{N-1}, 0) \cdot \mathbf{P},$$

such that the row-sums of $\mathbf{Q}$ are all equal to zero.

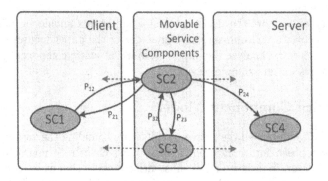

Fig. 2. Decomposed service with movable components

Some of the service components cannot be freely migrated between server and client side. Typical examples include user-interface components that naturally have to reside on the client, or service completion states that require centralized storage of the result in the application server, hence are fixed to reside on server side. See Section 5.1 for an example. Other service components can be migrated between client and server side, as illustrated in Figure 2. The vector $\mathbf{c} \in [0, 1]^N$ represents a specific placement of components on client and server side; here we use $c(i) = 0$ for a client-side placement of component i. If the service execution flow passes from a component i to another component j, this transition requires network communication, if and only if these two components are located on different physical entities, i.e., $c(i) \neq c(j)$.

The goal of this section is to come up with quantitative models that allow to calculate application reliability and performance for specific static configurations $\mathbf{c}$; the process of how such configurations are created, e.g., the download of the component to the client, is not considered. These models are developed in the following subsections.

4.2 Service Success/Failure Model

In the first scenario, we describe a modification of the discrete time Markov chain $\mathbf{P}$ such that the modified model $\mathbf{P}'(\mathbf{c})$ allows to compute the probability that the application is successfully completed given a certain component placement described by $\mathbf{c}$. As we consider the modified model for a specific given configuration, we drop the dependence on $\mathbf{c}$ in the following for notational convenience. The properties of the communication network are assumed to be described by a simple Bernoulli process, i.e., whenever network communication is needed upon transitions of the execution flow to a component placed on the different physical entity, the network is operational with probability $1 - p_f$ and the transition to the new service component succeeds. If network communication is not successful, the new service component cannot be executed and service execution fails.

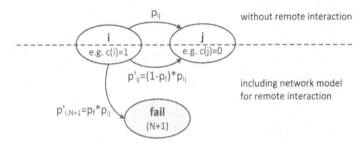

Fig. 3. Extended service component model including network failure

The modifications of the Markov chain to capture such behavior in the extended model $\mathbf{P}'$ are illustrated in Figure 3. The matrix $\mathbf{P}'$ contains one more state, state number $N+1$, which resembles an absorbing service failure state. Every transition $i \rightarrow j$, where $i, j = 1, ..., N$ between service components placed on different entities is partially forked off to the fail state with probability p_f. The probability of a service failure can be computed as the probability of reaching the absorbing fail state, i.e.,

$$Pr(\text{service failure}) = \left(\lim_{k \to \infty} \mathbf{p_0} \cdot \mathbf{P}'^k \right) \mathbf{e}'_{N+1},$$

where $\mathbf{e}'_{N+1}$ is a column vector with all components set to 0 except component $N + 1$ which is set to 1. The service failure probability can hence be computed numerically, see Section 5.2 for examples.

4.3 Execution Time Model

The Markov model in the previous section allows to calculate service success probabilities defined by the probability that the network communication is available for remote component interactions in a probabilistically chosen execution sequence of service components. If the network is not available (which occurs according to a Bernoulli experiment with probability p_f when the execution flow is migrated to a remotely placed component), the service execution is stopped and considered failed. There are however cases of elastic or delay-tolerant services in which a temporarily unavailable network connection just creates additional delay. Another variant is that the network connectivity is not completely unavailable but rather in a degraded state which leads to longer communication delays. In the following, we describe a Markov model transformation which allows to analyze the impact of such additional network disruption delay on the distribution of the service execution time for different placements of the components.

We use the continuous time version of the service model, i.e., a Continuous Time Markov Chain (CTMC), described by the generator matrix $\mathbf{Q}$, see Section 4.1. The service execution time without considering component placement and network interaction is then the phase-type distribution [7,8] described by the first $N - 1$ states.

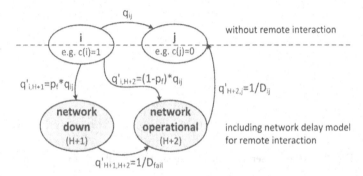

Fig. 4. Extended service component model including network failure and execution time

The following model of the execution time behavior for the client-server configuration $\mathbf{c}$ of the service components is employed: First all software components that are executed on the client side are assumed to execute more slowly by a factor of k_{client}. This is reflected by scaling all corresponding rows of $\mathbf{Q}$ by a factor of $1/k_{client}$. For the communication behavior, the following two input parameters are required in addition to the network failure probability p_f: *(i)* A matrix $\mathbf{D}$, whose elements $D_{i,j}$ specify the mean communication delay for the activation of component j from the remote component i. *(ii)* The mean time until network recovery D_{fail}. The generator matrix of the CTMC for the distributed client-server implementation under such assumptions on the remote communication delays is then obtained by adding two additional delay states for each transition $i \rightarrow j$ with $Q_{i,j} \neq 0$ and $c(i) \neq c(j)$. Let's assume these two additional delay states obtain labels $H+1$ and $H+2$, then the following modified transition rates are employed in the extended matrix $\mathbf{Q}'$ (illustrated in Figure 4):

$$Q'(i,j) = 0; \quad Q'(i, H+1) = p_f Q(i,j); \quad Q'(i, H+2) = (1 - p_f)Q(i,j)$$

$$Q'(H+1, H+2) = 1/D_{fail}, \quad Q'(H+2, j) = 1/D_{i,j}.$$

The diagonal elements of $\mathbf{Q}'$ need to be adjusted accordingly. If component i and j are placed on the same entity ($c(i) = c(j)$), then $Q'(i,j) = Q(i,j)$. Note that using a matrix for the remote communication delays allows to distinguish between components that may have different sizes of parameters/data associated with their remote call. For the numerical examples in Section 5.3, we however employ $D_{i,j} = 1$ for all i,j.

The extended generator matrix $\mathbf{Q}'$ then contains the phase-type distribution (time until reaching state N, which is assumed to be the service success state), for which the standard matrix calculations for moments, tail probabilities, or density values can be applied, see [7,8]. Numerical results are presented in Section 5.3.

Note, that many variants of the Execution Time Model can be defined: For instance, the current approach in Figure 4 assumes that the network is operational with probability $1 - p_f$ and in that case the remote component call can be successfully finalized. One could of course also consider the case that the network connection can fail during the remote component call, which would correspond to a transition from state $H + 2$ to state $H + 1$ in the figure. Similarly, more general network down times than exponential can be represented by replacing state $H + 1$ by a phase-type box of states.

5   Numerical Results

In the following we present numerical results to illustrate the service failure and execution time models for the example of a text editor service.

5.1   Text Editor Example Service

The editor example described below is used in Sections 5.2 and 5.3 to exemplify results of the introduced Markov models. Figure 5 shows the discrete time Markov model of the editor, including the values of the transition probabilities.

The transition probabilities are chosen so that they approximately resemble average user behavior: Component 2, the *Editing Framework*, is used most frequently as it processes the input of the user. Any key press or menu bar activity is communicated from the *UI* to the *Editing Framework*. Thus, the transitions between *UI* and *Editing Framework* component are most frequently taken. Creating, opening, or saving a document (components 3 to 5) are less likely operations compared to keystrokes. Components 1 (user interface) and 6 (service success) are special with respect to placement in the client/server architecture. The user interface needs to be executed on the client, and the final success operation is assumed to include storage of the document in the server cloud, hence must be located at the server. This fixes two of the components in the configuration vector $\mathbf{c}$.

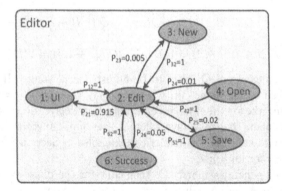

Fig. 5. Example use case text editor service

	1: UI	2: Edit	3: New	4: Open	5: Save	6: Success
config 1	client	server	server	server	server	server
config 2	client	server	server	server	client	server
config 3	client	client	server	server	server	server
config 4	client	client	client	client	client	server

Fig. 6. Editor example configurations

We consider four different static configurations to analyze the execution characteristics of the editor as summarized in Figure 6. For configuration 1, everything expect the UI is located at the server. This is a pure SaaS configuration. For configurations 2 and 3, exactly one component in addition to the UI is placed on the client (note, that the selected components are used with different frequencies). Configuration 4 is placing all movable components on the client, hence, this configuration puts the highest resource requirements to the client.

5.2   Numerical Results for Service Success Probability

The editor example service is now used to exemplify the Markov model capabilities and to show the type of analysis and conclusions that can be obtained from the service success model in Section 4.2. Figure 7 shows the calculated service failure probabilities for the four different placement configurations of service components (Figure 6). The probability of network failure upon remote component interaction, p_f, is varied along the x-axis. The best possible scenario results when all editor components are placed on the client (solid line), so that only a single network interaction is necessary, namely the one connected to the transition to the success state (at which the edited file is stored at the server). As there is exactly one network interaction necessary in this case, the service failure probability is equal to p_f in this case.

At the other extreme, the full SaaS configuration in which only the user-interface is placed on the client (dashed-dotted line), frequent network

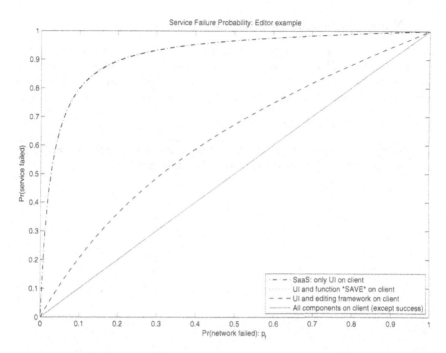

Fig. 7. Service failure probability of the editor service in four different component placement configurations

interactions are necessary in particular for transitions between the *UI* and *Editing Framework* component leading to a rapid increase of service failure probability already for very small parameter ranges of p_f. Hence, the SaaS approach is in this example only useful for scenarios of good network connectivity (p_f well below 5%). Moving the service component *Save* to the client actually increases the service failure probability slightly due to the necessary interactions between editing (remaining on server) and saving (moved to the client), however hardly visible in Figure 7. Placing the *Editing Framework* instead on the client leads to a dramatic improvement: For instance, a service failure probability below 40% can be achieved also for network failure probabilities up to more than 20%.

Due to the simple structure of the editor example, the qualitative superiority of the configuration placing *UI* and *Editing Framework* both on the client is intuitively clear. However, the Markov model can be used to substantiate such choices with quantitative results and it can be argued whether moving a component might even worsen the failure rate. In particular for more complex service component interactions the Markov model can be used to make optimized choices about which component to place on client-side.

Note, that the four curves in Figure 7 never cross. Hence, when purely optimizing placement choices based on minimizing service failure probability, the network quality (expressed by p_f) does not influence the 'ranking' of the different placements.

5.3   Numerical Results for Execution Time Analysis

In the following we present numerical results to illustrate the application of the execution time CTMC from Section 4.3. The results use the same modular text editor service as previously for the service failure probability analysis. The mean state-holding time for the different states (assuming execution on the server) are:

$$T_{UI} = 1, T_{edit} = 0.1, T_{new} = T_{open} = T_{save} = 1.$$

Due to the possibility of rescaling time, we use configurable *units of time* in the investigations below; for illustration, seconds can be assumed.

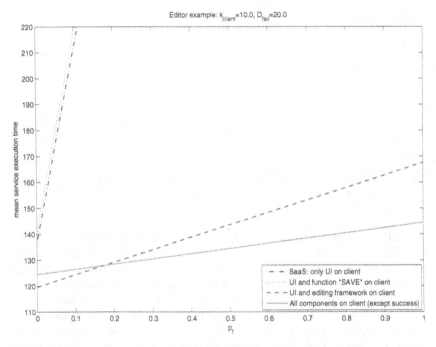

Fig. 8. Mean service execution time [units of time] of the editor example in four different configurations

The execution of the service component on the client is assumed to take $k_{client} = 10$ times as long as the execution on the server. The remote call of another module is for all module pairs the same, $D_{ij} = 1$. If the network connection is down (with probability p_f), the mean time to recovery is exponentially distributed with mean $D_{fail} = 20$. Figure 8 shows the mean application execution times for the same four component placement configurations as in the previous section. The full SaaS approach leaving all components on the server (dashed-dotted line) requires frequent network interactions, which degrades application execution time dramatically already for rather small probabilities p_f. When moving the *Save* component to the client, the execution time even increases showing that this configuration is not beneficial. Installing all components on the client (solid line) minimizes the impact of the network quality (as expressed by p_f). However, for parameter ranges of p_f smaller than approx. 15% in the calculated example, the solution of having both the *UI* and the *Editing Framework* executed locally on the client performs best. The latter is a consequence of the slow-down factor k_{client} of the processing at the client.

In summary, the calculation model can here be used to dynamically optimize the execution times via changes of the component placement depending on network quality. Note that the execution times grow linearly with p_f; as the network functionality does not change the execution flow through the modules (only its timing), the number of remote component invocations stays the same, hence p_f linearly scales into mean service execution times.

The representation of the execution time as phase-type distribution also allows to calculate numerically the density, tail probabilities, and higher moments of the execution time distribution. For the example configurations, we calculated the coefficient of variation (variance normalized by the square of the mean) of the execution time distribution for all configurations. The results showed that placing all components on the server not only dramatically increases the mean time, but also shows a higher variability in the application execution time. (The variance can be a useful input for an M/G/1 queuing type of analysis, as then the mean queue-length and system time only depend on the first two moments of the service time, e.g., P-K formula [6]).

6   Conclusions

In this paper, an architecture and modeling approach for movable service components has been presented targeting the Software as a Service paradigm. Moving service components from a server cloud to the mobile clients allows to tolerate disconnection periods, which are likely to occur in mobile scenarios. First, we described the concept of moving crucial service components from the server cloud to the client. Second, we presented analytical models to investigate the potentials of proactive placement of components. The models are generic for disruption tolerant computing based on movable components and allows to give insights for various, even complex services.

The usefulness of the analytical models has been demonstrated for a sample editor use case service, consisting of network intensive and non-network intensive components. In this use case and realistic parameter settings, evaluation results in terms of failure rate and mean service execution time showed indeed the potential benefits of moving service components to the client in case of expected frequent networking failures. These results are encouraging for extending the approach in future work both in terms of proposing means for triggering proactive service component migration and investigating the trade-off between messaging overhead and decreased service failure rate.

Acknowledgments. This work has been supported by the Austrian Government and by the City of Vienna within the competence center program COMET.

References

1. Bennett, K., Layzell, P., Budgen, D., Brereton, P., Munro, M., Macaulay, L.: Service-based Software: The Future for Flexible Software. In: 7th Asia-Pacific Software Engineering Conference, pp. 214–221. IEEE Computer Society Press, Los Alamitos (2000)
2. Chou, W., Li, L.: WIPdroid – A Two-way Web Services and Real-time Communication Enabled Mobile Computing Platform for Distributed Services Computing. In: International Conference on Services Computing, pp. 205–212. IEEE Computer Society Press, Los Alamitos (2008)
3. Chuah, M., Yang, P., Xi, Y.: How Mobility Models Affect the Design of Network Coding Schemes for Disruption Tolerant Networks. In: 29th International Conference on Distributed Systems Workshop, pp. 172–177. IEEE Computer Society Press, Los Alamitos (2009)
4. Fuggetta, A., Picco, G.P., Vigna, G.: Understanding Code Mobility. IEEE Transactions of Software Engineering 24(5), 342–361 (1998)
5. Imielinski, T., Badrinath, B.R.: Mobile Wireless Computing: Challenges in Data Management. Communications of the ACM 37(10), 18–28 (1994)
6. Kleinrock, L.: Queueing Systems. Theory, vol. I. John Wiley & Sons, New York (1975)
7. Lipsky, L.: Queueing Theory: A Linear Algebraic Approach, 2nd edn. MacMillan Publishing Company, New York (2009)
8. Neuts, M.: Matrix-Geometric Solutions in Stochastic Models, Revised Edition. Dover Publications, London (1995)
9. Ott, J., Xiaojun, L.: Disconnection Tolerance for SIP-based Real-time Media Sessions. In: 6th International Conference on Mobile and Ubiquitous Multimedia. ACM Press, New York (2007)
10. Su, J., Scott, J., Hui, P., Crowcroft, J., de Lara, E., Diot, C., Goel, A., Lom, M.H., Upton, E.: Haggle: Seamless Networking for Mobile Applications. In: Krumm, J., Abowd, G.D., Seneviratne, A., Strang, T. (eds.) UbiComp 2007. LNCS, vol. 4717, pp. 391–408. Springer, Heidelberg (2007)

Cloud Computing Applications

Track Session 1

Virtual Distro Dispatcher: A Light-Weight Desktop-as-a-Service Solution

S. Cristofaro, F. Bertini, D. Lamanna, and R. Baldoni

Dipartimento di Informatica e Sistemistica "Antonio Ruberti"
"Sapienza" Università di Roma, Italy
{cristofaro,flavio.bertini,davide.lamanna,
roberto.baldoni}@dis.uniroma1.it
http://www.vdd-project.org

Abstract. Utility computing can occur at different levels. From Software-as-a-Service (SaaS) paradigm, Desktop-as-a-Service (DaaS) paradigm can be derived: desktops can be transformed into a cost-effective, scalable and comfortable subscription service. In VDD, desktop virtual machines are instantiated on a server and then provided to clients as a whole, on demand, across a network. Since the first release and publication, new features have been implemented and performance improvements achieved. As virtualization holds a critical role in the system, research and tests have been done for implementing the best virtualization solution. A comprehensive performance analysis is presented, depicting results that encourage to go on with the research and towards a real-life use. Operational costs analysis showed further economic and ecological advantages. The possibility to project operating systems not natively supporting the Xorg X11 has been introduced, opening the way to the projection of widespread though proprietary operating systems.

Keywords: XEN, UML, LTSP, Trashware, VDD-Project, Utility computing.

1 Introduction

Cloud computing architectures are rapidly spreading over the world of IT, supporting the idea of provisioning various computing capabilities"as-a-service", in a transparent way for users. Information is stored in servers on a network and cached temporarily on clients, such as desktops, entertainment centers, table computers, notebooks, wall computers, handhelds, etc. [7]. Reliable services are delivered to clients from next-generation data centers based on virtualization technologies. Some of the most relevant issues brought about by this paradigm are whether or not this is really feasible on a geographical scale, where network latency matters, and, more generally, whether or not a browser can really substitute every kind of computer application. Finally, big privacy issues rise: users data and work are given away in the hands of third parties, without any control and any real guarantee. Without necessarily dealing with these"cloudy" aspects,

D.R. Avresky et al. (Eds.): Cloudcomp 2009, LNICST 34, pp. 247–260, 2010.
© Institute for Computer Sciences, Social-Informatics and Telecommunications Engineering 2010

it is always possible to reason about the more general concept of Utility computing, according to which computing resources, such as computation and storage,
can be precisely metered and packaged, similarly to what happens with a traditional public utility, apart from the fact that the distribution of such a service
happens to be in "The Cloud". Utility computing can occur at different levels. As long as applications are concerned, one talks about Software-as-a-Service
(SaaS): applications are hosted as a service provided to users across a network
(e.g., the Internet). If systems are concerned, one can talk about Desktop-as-a-
Service (DaaS): desktops can be transformed into a cost-effective, scalable and
comfortable subscription service. Desktops are instantiated on a server and then
provided to clients on demand across a network. Virtual Distro Dispatcher [1] is
a distributed system whose aim is to project virtual, fully operational operating
system instances on terminals.

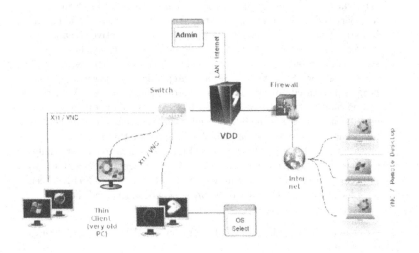

Fig. 1. Virtual Distro Dispatcher general scheme

The VDD architecture is represented in the Figure 1. More detailed information of the whole system are widely discussed in [1].

Client terminals can be obsolete PCs or energy saving thin clients (such as
mini-ITX) managed by a powerful, multiprocessor (and possibly clustered) central system. The previous version of VDD, presented in [1], has got many limitations: Performances were still weak; Virtualization was performed only through
UML[2] instances; Only Linux kernel based distributions could be projected on
terminals. The new implementation of VDD hereby presented has focused in
particular on performance improvements (as described in Section V). Moreover,
operating systems other than Linux (e.g., Open Solaris, ReactOS, Microsoft
Windows®...) can be accessed from terminals, thanks to the introduction of
XEN[3] virtualization system. VDD gives users the possibility to enjoy their own
favorite operating systems, including those that are not Open Source, possibly

at the same time, on each single thin client. It is important to remember (see [1] for details) that thin clients are interfaces to proper and isolated machines, that can be made to measure for whatever need and in whatever number (within server limits, of course). This is completely transparent to users, who, even from an obsolete machine, can select a particular machine with certain characteristics and then do absolutely everything they would do on such a machine as if it was physical and with its performance. Another dutiful remark regards licensing. Virtual Distro Dispatcher uses Open Source/GPL software and free communication protocols and it is released as Free Software. The infrastructure allows to run proprietary operating systems as guests and this is regulated by specific licenses, costs and limitations, that should be taken into account by VDD users.

2   Related Work

Using the taxonomy in [6], it is possible to identify three types of virtualized client computing (VCC):

1. **Application:** Encapsulating and isolating a specific application from its underlying host operating system and running it in the client environment, isolated from other applications running locally. Examples: Citrix Presentation Server (version 4.5+), Altiris Software Virtualization Suite, Thinstall, Microsoft SoftGrid, Trigence AE, Endeavors;
2. **Desktop:** Using virtualization to decouple the client environment (including operating system, application and data) from its host hardware and isolating it from other software or systems running on the client. It can be server-hosted or client-hosted. Server-hosted examples: VMware VDI, Virtual Iron VDI, Citrix XenDesktop, Qumranet Solid ICE. Client-hosted examples: VMware ACE/Player/Workstation/Fusion, SWsoft Parallels, Kidaro Managed Workspace, Sentillion;
3. **Virtual user session:** Creating multiple user sessions on the server, within a single operating system, that can be accessed concurrently. Examples: Citrix Presentation Server, Microsoft Terminal Services, Sun Secure Global Desktop Software.

Within these three types of VCC, two delivery models can be adopted (again in [6]):

- **Remote interaction:** I/O operations between a client device and a server through specific (and sometimes proprietary) protocols and software;
- **Remote streaming:** delivering executable blocks of data from a server to a client device, through specific (and sometimes proprietary) protocols and/or software.

VDD is in between type 2 and 3, as desktop virtualization software is used to host multiple unique and isolated client environments aboard a single server (or a group of servers in a cluster). Interaction with these remote virtual desktops is performed through virtual user (graphical) sessions. VDD exploits network transparency of X-Window-System: the machine where an application program (the client application) runs can differ from the user's local machine (the display server). X-Window-System clients run on virtual servers and create multiple user sessions within multiple virtual environments. X-Window-System display servers run on thin clients (terminals). VNC protocols can be used for OSs which lack of X11 server (e.g. Windows and ReactOS), so both delivery models listed above are available.

The need for multiple development environments, especially in research laboratories, but also in teaching or developing circumstances, made the study of heterogeneous systems integration quite important. The availability of different operating systems at the same time, give users the possibility to develop software applications and to test them in several environments directly from their terminal, pursuing software portability. Other products supplying for this kind of service started to be developed. For example, an interesting DaaS system, Cendio Thin Linc[1], that is a LTSP based architecture like VDD, allows users to access remote desktops from everywhere[2]. Another example is NoMachine NX[3], which virtualizes desktops over the Internet too. VDD's main advantage is that only Free/OpenSource Software has been used, this being one requirement of our research. Another advantage is the extreme lightness, as highlighted in Section V. Development of virtualization systems plays a fundamental role in our research, mainly for performance issues. This is highlighted in section III, where more related work on this matter is cited.

3 Virtualization

Virtualization holds a critical role in VDD, as it enables the possibility to run multiple and diverse operating system instances to be projected to each thin client. The present piece of research focused on performance issues, hence several considerations and tests have been done in order to choose the best virtualization solution.

Unfortunately, the x86 architecture is more difficult to virtualize with respect to others, due to the presence of some particular instructions, such as the ones related to memory segmentation [5]. Even though, its large diffusion stimulated the development of many techniques to overcome such architecture limitations.

One of the most used virtualization techniques is the *binary rewriting* (also known as binary translation) which consists in scanning the code of the running guest with the aim of intercepting and modifying privileged instructions in order to fit in the virtualization system. Therefore, there is no need to modify the operating system source code, since all changes are made at run-time. On the

---

[1] http://www.cendio.com/products/thinlinc

[2] VDD is focused on projecting different operating system instances in the same LAN at the moment. Dispatching Linux on terminals over the Internet is technically possible, but not considered as something to deal with, at the moment (see also Section VII).

[3] http://www.nomachine.com/

other hand, there is a loss of performance, especially where the code contains several privileged instructions. The most popular virtualization systems using binary rewriting are VMware[4] and VirtualBox[5].

Another important technique is *paravirtualization*. It modifies privileged instructions, but at compile time instead of run-time. Even though modifying the guest operating systems source code implies an extra effort, one may notice a considerable performance increase, getting very close to an unvirtualized system (see Section V). Xen is one of the most powerful and famous virtualization system using mainly such a technique.

A more recent solution is the *Hardware Assisted Virtualization*. The last generation of AMD and Intel CPUs, have been developed with different virtualization extensions for x86 architecture[6]. The main purpose of these extensions, is to speed up the whole virtualization process and to make it easier for x86. Performance are in between the binary rewriting and paravirtualization techniques.

The choice of the virtualization system is fundamental to make VDD as performant as possible. Since the previous version of VDD uses User Mode Linux to dispatch Linux on terminals (for that reason, it was possible to emulate only Linux distributions), in order to make the right choice of a valid alternative and to add new functionalities, it has been useful to delineate a new list of constraints for our purposes (Table 1):

C1 - Open Source Software
C2 - Support for OS guest virtualization other than Linux (e.g. Microsoft Windows®)
C3 - Quick and easy to restore
C4 - Symmetric Multi Processing (SMP) OS guest support
C5 - User level kernel execution
C6 - Integrated VNC Server

Table 1. List of main VDD constraints

	C1	C2	C3	C4	C5	C6
VMWare		$\checkmark$	$\checkmark$	$\checkmark^7$		$\checkmark^8$
VirtualBox	$\checkmark^9$	$\checkmark$	$\checkmark$			
UML	$\checkmark$		$\checkmark$		$\checkmark$	
Qemu	$\checkmark$	$\checkmark$	$\checkmark$	$\checkmark$		$\checkmark$
XEN	$\checkmark$	$\checkmark^{10}$	$\checkmark$	$\checkmark$		$\checkmark$

---

[4] Since the version 5.5, Vmware Workstation also supports the Hardware Assisted Virtualization technique. The 6.0 version and above, supports also Linux guest paravirtualization.

[5] VirtualBox also supports Hardware Assisted Virtualization.

[6] AMD introduced the AMD-V extension (also known as Pacifica) whereas the technology used by Intel is called VT-x.

[7] VMware supports a maximum of two virtual processors per guest. VMware ESX Enterprise edition, supports up to four virtual processors.

Both Qemu and XEN satisfy most of the above main constraints, but tests showed that XEN is absolutely more performant than Qemu, mainly due to its use of paravirtualization for the guest OS supporting it[11].

4   Extension of Functionalities

The aim of VDD is to project virtual Operating Systems instances on thin clients. Unlike LTSP-only based architectures, offering only the host operating system to thin clients, VDD uses virtualized guest systems like sandboxes to prevent users from breaking into the central server. The isolation conditions produce an high security level both for the user and the overall system.

Since the beginning of the project, the utilization of UML allowed to run many different Linux distributions in user space. The next step was to introduce XEN as an alternative to UML. Although using XEN implies not to use completely user space virtualized systems, it is now possible to support much more operating systems other than Linux.

The introduction of advanced virtualization techniques made the system more performant as a consequence of both Hardware Assisted Virtualization and paravirtualization support. A further advantage comes from the possibility to assign many virtual CPUs to the guest systems, granting the symmetric multi processing to CPU-bound multi-threading tasks.

In the previous VDD version, UML was the only virtualization system, so the graphical subsystem was constituted only by Xorg X11 client/server model as the session projecting vehicle. The possibility to project operating systems not natively supporting the Xorg X11, brought to the need to set up a VNC client/server architecture. This has been possible thanks to the integration of a native VNC server inside XEN. In fact, a custom VNC client bash script has been added to LTSP [4] (running on Gentoo GNU/Linux) so that it could be possible to use it on thin clients, even if they are obsolete hardware.

Another strong point of this new release of VDD is to go over the technological gap due to the Trashware [8]. It is now possible to run a last generation operating system on an obsolete PC, like if it was running on a last generation computer, with negligible performance drop. For example, granting just for the sake of argument that it can be considered an actual bargain, it is now possible to run Microsoft Windows Vista®on a very old PC with a few memory resources.

5   Performance Analysis

A massive number of tests have been carried out in order to stress in depth system resources, such as CPU, memory, storage and network. For each such

---

[8] Only for the Server Edition.

[9] VirtualBox Open Source Edition has less functionalities respect of the closed source edition.

[10] XEN needs the VT-x or AMD-V technology to run unmodifiable Operating Systems.

[11] For non paravirtualizable OS guests, XEN uses a customized Qemu version.

system resource, one particularly significant test is hereby presented. The aim of the performance analysis is to understand as deeply as possible what happens at a system level in order to make then considerations about how this affects the desktop level. Tests have been performed on two architectures, 32 bit and 64 bit[12], using *LMbench* as the principal benchmark suite. In order to publish such tests, the LMbench license requires that the benchmark code must be compiled with standard gcc *compilation flags*. Furthermore, some standard applications, like Linux kernel compilation or John The Ripper benchmark have been used in tests. The testbed has got the following characteristics:

- Intel Core 2 Quad 6600
- RAM 4GB (667 Mhz Dual Channel)
- 2 SATA 500 GB Hard Disks (RAID 0)
- 2 1000Mbps Ethernet switches
- 10 diskless thin clients
- 14 1000Mbps Ethernet cards
- Cat. 6 FTP Ethernet cables

All tests have been carried out on the host system and inside the virtual machines, both for XEN and UML, in 32 and 64 bits both for the host and the guest systems. By *host*, the real host system is meant, i.e. an unpatched standard Gentoo Linux distribution, without any modification. Confusion should not be made with the XEN or the UML host, whose benchmarks are not relevant for comparisons. Hence, all tests have been performed on the standard host and within XEN and UML virtual machines. The following cflags have been used to compile[13] the analyzed systems:

Table 2. CFLAGS for VDD circumstances (host, UML and XEN)

Standard host system	-march=native -fomit-frame-pointer -pipe -O2
Host and guest UML systems	-march=native -fomit-frame-pointer -pipe -O2
Host and guest XEN systems	-march=native -fomit-frame-pointer -pipe -O2 -mno-tls-direct-seg-refs

Since the vanilla Linux kernel already includes virtualization patches[14] (paravirt-ops), tests have been performed both using the XEN source patches and vanilla Linux kernel, as regards guest tests.

In order to make a CPU-bound test, John The Ripper has been used. It includes benchmarks for all supported hashing algorithms. Such benchmarks are particularly suitable for the purpose of this investigation, since they make it possible to precisely evaluate the overhead introduced by virtual machines. Even though the two machines have a Core 2 Quad CPU, each test has been performed

---

[12] Two identical PCs have been used: one system has been compiled as 32 bit code, the other one as 64 bit code.

[13] Compiled using GNU gcc version 4.2.

[14] Since version 2.6.25 for 32 bit and since version 2.6.27 for 64 bit.

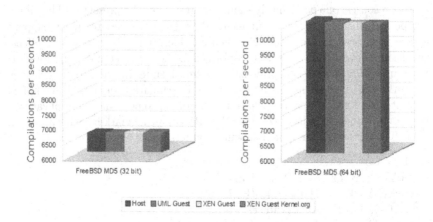

Fig. 2. Benchmark results for the John The Ripper test

only without Symmetric Multi Processing, in order to make comparisons with UML possible[15].

Thanks to paravirtualization, as expected, all results are quite close to each other. As it appears in the charts above (Figure 2), the overhead introduced by virtualization systems is quite unimportant. In any case, 64 bit systems proved to be far more performant.

As regards the LMbench memory mapping benchmark, an interesting difference between host and guest, especially for UML, can be noticed. The benchmark showed in the chart below is *bw_mmap_rd*, using the *open2close* option. This benchmark measures the bandwidth used to map a segment of a file to the memory and read it. Function *mmap()* belongs to a category of functions that is one of the hardest to be managed by virtual machines. This happens because virtual machines can not access physical memory directly. Hence, analyzing its behavior represents an excellent way to test system call management performed by paravirtualized systems and, in particular, to test how efficient is the hypervisor in managing it. As a matter of fact, this test is one of those in which Xen and, even more, UML loose more with respect to the host.

As a comment to the charts (Figure 3), all guest virtualized systems are sensitive to system call management. This is true especially for UML, due to the fact that it manages all system calls in user space, through a set of data structures, and this makes it quite slower than Xen. It is then possible to state that memory mapping management is the Achilles' heel of virtualized systems, even if Xen can cope with it better than others.

The next test is about filesystem latency. The test intends to verify the performance of virtualized systems in managing loop files (as in virtualized systems loop files act as virtual disks). In particular, the number of files created/deleted

---

[15] UML does not support SMP in skas4 mode. It was supported only it in TT mode, but TT mode is no longer supported.

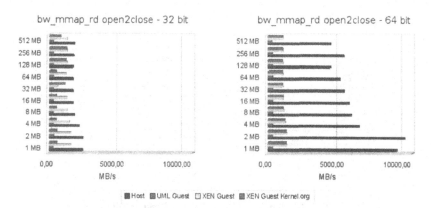

Fig. 3. Memory mapping benchmark results

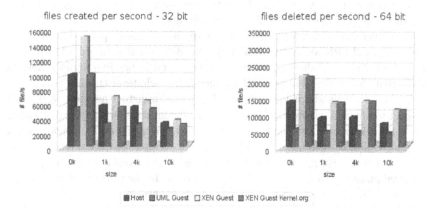

Fig. 4. Filesystem latency test results

per second is counted. The test has been repeated over files with different dimensions. Since guest systems are located into loop files, this may affect the test comparisons. In order to resolve this problem and to make tests comparable, a loop file have been generated also for the host system, which is so in exactly the same conditions of the guest. This test requires a destination directory where the system may create and delete files. So, each test has been performed inside each virtual machine. For the host system, the destination directory coincides with the loop file[16].

Results on Figure 4 show that the management of loop files in virtualized systems has reached an optimal level, especially for Xen. It is even better than the management of loop files made by the host system. This is because special functions have been developed in order to address such a critical issue. The test shown below is on memory again.

---

[16] All filesystems are ext3.

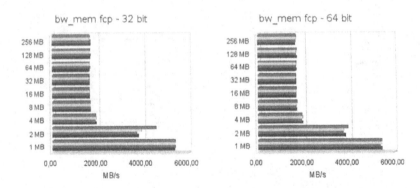

Fig. 5. Memory read/write speed test results

This test is useful to evaluate the overhead introduced for reading and writing in memory (Figure 5), after space is allocated, hence it does not take into account memory allocation, but only reading and writing speed. The test has been repeated with segments of memory with different size, in order to evaluate also the behavior of the system when cache is and is not functioning. Results show that the overhead is minimal and negligible, whatever the size is[17].

The next test is about performance decay due to virtual network cards with respect to physical network cards (Figure 6). The server is on a physical machine, while the client is on a virtualized machine. The two machines are connected via Gigabit Ethernet switches and cables. The test shows that virtual machines, on a physical network, do not introduce any significant overhead with respect to physical machines connected on the same network. In the picture below, the blue line represents the result of two physical hosts connected.

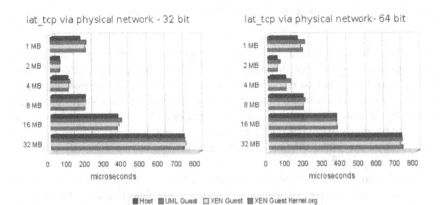

Fig. 6. Physical network latency test results

---

[17] Because of hierarchical memory (especially the 8MB L2 cache of the Q6600), results of reading small segments of memory are already in cache and hence obtained faster.

As it can be read in the man pages, lat_tcp is a client/server program that measures interprocess communication latencies. The benchmark passes a message back and forth between the two processes (this sort of benchmark is frequently referred to as a "hot potato" benchmark). No other work is done in the processes.

Another test could be the same of the previous, locally executed (i.e. both the client and the server are located within the localhost). There are no substantial differences for the systems involved in this test, apart from the fact that all data transfers are not conveyed through a physical local area network but through a virtualized network too. So, the whole network traffic is in the localhost.

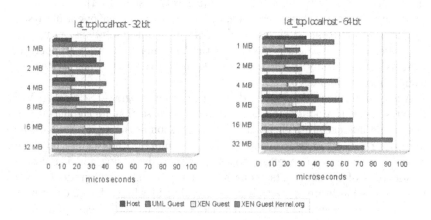

Fig. 7. Local host network latency test results

Test results on Figure 7 shows that the overhead is minimal and hence do not represent a bottleneck.

As a final remark, one can say that tests performed on VDD showed a negligible overhead introduced by the use of virtualization. This is true in particular for the tests hereby presented, which were selected based on the differences they are able to show in a more remarkable way with respect to others. The overhead may result significant only in particular situations (e.g., 3D graphic development), whereas performance at a desktop level is practically not affected. This is certainly encouraging for continuing the research, particularly if it succeed in showing more precisely the relation between system performance and desktop performance (see Section VII).

6   Operational Costs Analysis

VDD is an inexpensive solution born from the idea of Trashware [1],[8]. Research pushed forward from considering money saving for setting up a complete environment, to money saving for maintaining and operating it. For example, considering a LAN with 10 computers, three cases can be put to the test:

a) Buy 10 new PCs (no VDD)
b) Buy one new generation PC for the VDD server + 10 Trashware diskless thin clients for free
c) Buy one new generation PC for the VDD server + 10 mini ITX stations[18]

Solution a is far more expensive than the others, both for initial costs and for operational costs. In terms of initial costs, the cheapest solution is b, the only cost being the hardware for the VDD server management station, with money saving up to 83% with respect to a. This solution provides up to 18,5% for the energy saving[19]. Replacing obsolete and maybe cumbersome thin clients with mini-ITX terminals (solution c), money saving can be up to 72%. In this case, energy saving can arrive up to 71,4% (always with respect to a).

About the cost of a system upgrade, with solution a, a global operating system update has to be done on each PC, whereas with b and c solutions, an upgrade only involves the central server which is the VDD manager, since no operating systems resides in any diskless thin client. In this case, the whole system will result upgraded in one go.

A similar consideration can be done for hardware upgrade. Setting up VDD requires the central station to be powerful enough so that no significant overhead could influence thin clients utilization. As soon as the need for a hardware upgrade arises and/or more client stations are required, a more powerful central server could be needed. In regard to server-side hardware upgrade, it reflects to performance of all thin clients in one go, similarly to software upgrade. In regard to client-side hardware upgrade, instead, modifications for each thin client would be required. Economic-wise, this is not relevant, thanks to the reuse of hardware components refurbished through Trashware. This provides a practically unlimited amount of hardware dismissed too early by individuals or companies, and that are instead useful for building or upgrading VDD systems. In most cases, companies dismiss computers that are absolutely not obsolete as they consider[20]. Hardware reuse allows VDD thin clients to be upgraded and hence survive in pretty much all failure cases, by using the massive amount of spare hardware, produced by the current unsustainable production system, as a replacements resource.

7   Future Works

Setting up VDD may be rather demanding for people not so familiar with GNU/Linux and quite a high level of experience is required to manage all spare software components. One of the next step to further improve VDD is to develop a Graphical User Interface to make virtual machines dispatching as simple

---

[18] More generally, low energy systems such as mini/nano/pico-ITX.
[19] Considerations about energy cost analysis have been done consulting the http://www.eu-energystar.org/it/it_007c.shtml website. Each (thin client) station has been considered to be powered on for 6 hours per day.
[20] Social enterprises exist which work in refurbishing dismissed PCs thanks to Free Software. One of those is Binario Etico, www.binarioetico.org

as possible. Possible directions are: a web-based control panel, accessible from everywhere at any time and/or a host side interface to manage the whole environment from the central station. Code in Python has started to be written (having portability in mind).

As highlighted in Section V, it would be useful to explore more in depth relations between system level and desktop level regarding performance. Mapping application requirements to system specifications would help in designing and tuning the system for best desktop performance. Another interesting goal is to introduce High Availability Clusterization. VDD is managed by one central server at the moment. In [1], it was proposed to set up a HPC cluster like OpenMosix [8] to boost the core system. Unfortunately, HPC clustering does not have a wide interest any more, also due to the tremendous decrease of hardware price. Research interests are now focused on High Availability Clusters instead of HPC, in order to increase dependability and availability against failures [9].

As seen in Section 2, related work exists that consider dispatching desktops on the Internet an important characteristic. VDD can technically do that, even if this is not part of the research at the moment. It could be something to look at in the future, provided that the study on mapping system and network performance to desktop performance is carried out before. The high flexibility offered by the VNC protocol may allow to dispatch virtual Linux distributions over the Internet too. The only main difference is not to use obsolete computers as clients in this case, as data compression requires more performant PCs.

Privacy issues can easily be addressed by VDD, both at a local and at a global scale, simply by cyphering data. Although the whole system is quite safe, the utilization of encrypted volumes as filesystem partitions (using algorithms like AES-256), would give users the possibility to keep their data private and secure from intruders. Not even the administrator, who is in charge of managing such partitions, could be able to access data stored in them. This way, the well known privacy issue raised by cloud computing can be effectively addressed.

8   Conclusion

Intensely put to the test, VDD has proved to have wide margin to exploit as for system and network performance. VDD can open new frontiers of virtualization and distribution of resources by changing the way people resort to desktops. While the present paper was about to be finished, authors received news from NLnet foundation[21] regarding a request for funds to support the project, made by Binario Etico cooperative company[22]. NLnet decided to finance the project!

---

[21] http://www.nlnet.nl/ NLnet foundation financially supports organizations and people that contribute to an open information society, in particular it finances projects based on Free Software.

[22] http://www.binarioetico.org/ Binario Etico cooperative company sells products and services exclusively based on Free Software and reuse of obsolete PCs. It requested NLnet foundation for money to finance VDD project.

VDD emphasizes the importance of software over hardware. By using a new way of managing desktop environment software, VDD offers a technological point of view focused on ecology and saving, without renouncing to productivity and performance. Hardware development is closed to its saturation. VDD is the proof that software, in particular Free Software, can offer real ways to stimulate people creativity and reach new technological achievements.

References

1. Bertini, F., Lamanna, D., Baldoni, R.: Virtual Distro Dispatcher: A costless distributed virtual environment from Trashware. In: Stojmenovic, I., Thulasiram, R.K., Yang, L.T., Jia, W., Guo, M., de Mello, R.F. (eds.) ISPA 2007. LNCS, vol. 4742, pp. 223–234. Springer, Heidelberg (2007)
2. Dike, J.: User Mode Linux, April 22. Bruce Perens' Open Source Series, p. 352. Prentice Hall PTR, Englewood Cliffs (2006)
3. Chisnall, D.: The Definitive Guide to the XEN Hypervisor, 1st edn., p. 320. Prentice Hall PTR, Englewood Cliffs (November 19, 2007)
4. Linux Terminal Server Project, http://www.ltsp.org
5. Popek, G.J., Goldberg, R.P.: Formal Requirements for Virtualizable Third Generation Architectures. Communications of the ACM 17(7), 412–421
6. Rose, M.: (Industry Developments and Model) - Virtualized Client Computing: A Taxonomy (December 2007),
   http://www.idc.com/getdoc.jsp?containerId=209671
7. Hewitt, C.: ORGs for Scalable, Robust, Privacy-Friendly Client Cloud Computing. IEEE Internet Computing, 96–99 (September/October 2008)
8. Russo, R., Lamanna, D., Baldoni, R.: Distributed software platforms for rehabilitating obsolete hardware. In: OSS 2005: Proceedings of The First International Conference on Open Source Systems, pp. 220–224 (2005)
9. Cully, B., Lefebvre, G., Meyer, D., Feeley, M., Hutchinson, N.: Remus: High Availability via Asynchronous Virtual Machine Replication. In: Proceedings of the 5th USENIX Symposium on Networked System design and implementation, pp. 161–174 (Awarded Best Paper)

On Cost Modeling for Hosted Enterprise Applications

Hui Li and Daniel Scheibli

SAP Research, Vincenz-Priessnitz-Str. 1, 76131 Karlsruhe, Germany
hui.li@computer.org

Abstract. In enterprises nowadays typical business-critical processes rely on OLTP (online transaction processing) type of applications. Offering such applications as hosted solutions in Clouds rises many technical and non-technical challenges, among which TCO (Total Cost of Ownership) is one of the main considerations for most on-demand service/Cloud providers. In order to reduce TCO, a first step would be to analyze and study its cost components in depth. In this paper we adopt a quantitative approach and model two tangible cost factors, namely, server hardware and server power consumption. For server hardware, on one hand, a pricing model for CPU is proposed as a function of per-core performance and the number of cores, which also manifests the current multi-/many-core trend. Server power consumption, on the other hand, is modeled as a function of CPU utilization (as a main indication of system activity). By using published results from both vendor-specific and industry-standard benchmarks such as TPC-C, we show that a family of *Power functions* is successfully applied in deriving a wide range of cost models. Such analytic cost models, in turn, prove to be useful for the Cloud providers to specify the Service Level Agreements (SLAs) and optimize their service/infrastructure landscapes.

1   Introduction

Cloud computing represents the next wave of IT industry transformation by delivering services and computing as utilities over the Internet [1]. When the services and infrastructure are available in a pay-as-you-go manner to the general public, it is called a *Public Cloud*. The *Private Cloud*, on the other hand, refers to the internal services and resources of ITO (IT Organization) in a business which are not available to the public. Public cloud, such as Amazon Web Services, proves to be a sustaining business model for applications such as Web 2.0, testing and development, and certain data-intensive/HPC applications. ITOs can also outsource some of its non-critical processes from its Private Cloud to a Public one for elasticity and cost-saving considerations.

Despite the success of on-demand solutions for certain functionalities such as HR and CRM, business/mission critical applications remain largely to be deployed on-premise, especially for large organizations. For small and medium enterprises (SMEs), however, there is a market that the whole suite of business

D.R. Avresky et al. (Eds.): Cloudcomp 2009, LNICST 34, pp. 261–269, 2010.
© Institute for Computer Sciences, Social-Informatics and Telecommunications Engineering 2010

applications be offered as hosted solutions. Apart from the challenges arise from security and multi-tenancy, TCO (Total Cost of Ownership) is one of the main considerations for any on-demand provider for such applications. This applies to both SaaS/Public Clouds for general offerings and Private Clouds that serve the LoBs (Line of Business).

For the Cloud providers to specify the Service Level Agreements (SLAs) and optimize their service/infrastructure landscapes [4], it is of crucial importance to analyze, understand, and model cost components within the TCO. This paper focuses on the cost modeling for hosted OLTP applications on both public and private Clouds. TCO is intrinsically complex and involves a great deal of tangible/intangible factors. Rather than providing a comprehensive TCO model, this paper focuses mainly on the quantitative aspects and models two tangible cost components, namely, server hardware and server power consumption. Firstly, a pricing model for CPU is proposed as a function of per-core performance and the number of cores. The per-core performance is based on the published results of industry-standard OLTP benchmark TPC-C [11] on Intel DP/MP platforms. The fitted CPU pricing model also manifests the current multi-/many-core trend. Secondly, server power consumption is modeled as a function of CPU utilization using a customized Power function. By combining the fitted models for both CPU costs and power consumption, we have developed a simplified analytic model for hosted OLTP applications that incorporates hardware and operation costs.

The rest of the paper is organized as follows: Section 2 develops a CPU cost model based on the certified results of TPC-C benchmarks on Intel DP/MP platforms. Section 3 conducts customized performance tests and models the server power consumption in relationship to the CPU utilization as the main indicator for system activity. Section 4 presents the combined cost model for OLTP applications in a hosted environment, and discusses its context and applicability. Conclusions and future work are presented in Section 5.

2   Modeling CPU Costs for OLTP Applications on Multi-core Platforms

Among the many components of server hardware, namely CPU, memory, storage, and network, we focus on the CPU costs in this paper and make simplified assumptions that costs of other components remain constants or scale with the CPU costs. We are particularly interested in the price-performance relationship on multi-/many-core platforms, as the general trend in processor development has been from single-, multi-, to many cores. Our goal is to investigate and model the relationship between the objective, namely the price per-CPU (C_{cpu}) or price per-core (C_{core}), and the two related parameters: number of cores (N_{core}) and benchmark results per-core (T_{core}). T_{core} also corresponds to the processing speed of the core, and thus the resource demands of the measured OLTP applications. If we model the application system as a closed multi-station queuing center, T_{core} is theoretically bounded by $1/D$, where D is the resource demand

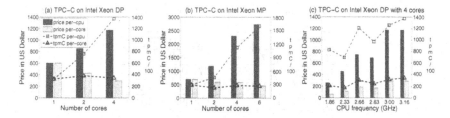

Fig. 1. 117 certified TPC-C benchmark results run on Intel Xeon DP/MP platforms within the timeframe between 7/2002 and 12/2008. TPC-C is measured in transactions per minute (tpmC). Such a throughput measure is defined as how many New-Order transactions per minute a system generates while executing other transactions types.

(minimum response time) of the application on the server. This gives a general idea on the relationship between the performance model and the cost model, whose objectives are conflicting with each other. In this section we focus on modeling the CPU costs P given the number of cores and benchmark results per-core for OLTP applications.

We examine the certified TPC-C [11] benchmark results on Intel DP/MP platforms and associate them with CPU price information [7], which are shown in Figure 1[1]. As there are two independent parameters (N_{core} and T_{core}) involved, we study one of them by fixing the value of the other, and vice versa.

Firstly let us look at the price versus the number of cores given a similar per-core performance. In 1(a), we can see that the per-core price decreases as the number of cores per CPU increases on the Intel Xeon DP platform. As the per-core performance of TPC-C remains the same, the price/performance ratio improves by adding more cores. Generally this trend also applies to TPC-C on Intel MP as shown in Figure 1(b). We notice that the per-core tpmC decreases slightly as the number of cores increases. This is because that the core frequency scales down as the number of cores scales up, which is shown in Table 1. Nevertheless, as the chip design becomes better and more efficient, the per-core performance/frequency ratio (r) improves along the evolution of generations. From a customer perspective this does not mean that the response time of a single application can improve as the resource demand decreases only by increasing the core speed. The main benefit is on the much improved throughput numbers per CPU price.

Secondly let us examine the price versus the per-core performance given the same number of cores. In Figure 1(c), as predicted, we can see that the price increases as the CPU frequency and throughput numbers increase. Some abnormal behavior happens between 2.33 GHz and 2.83 GHz. This may be explained

---

[1] Disclaimer: The performance in tpmC is influenced by additional factors like machine architecture, cache sizes, memory size/latency/bandwidth, operating system, storage system characteristics, DBMS, TPC-C version/settings as well as other factors not mentioned here. Vendor-specific benchmarks [9] and certified results [10] are also studied and the results are not published here.

Table 1. CPU frequency and the performance/frequency ratio: $r = T_{core}/GHz$

Benchmark	1-core	2-core	4-core	6-core
tpcc/DP (GHz)	3.4	3.0	3.16	-
tpcc/DP (r)	9.5	12.7	10.9	-
tpcc/MP (GHz)	3.33	3.0	2.93	2.66
tpcc/MP (r)	8.7	7.6	9.6	10.0

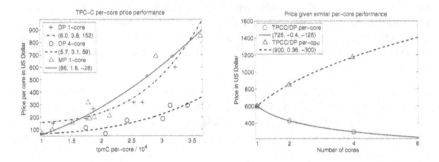

Fig. 2. Fitted power function parameters are (c_1, c_2, c_3) as appeared in Equation 1

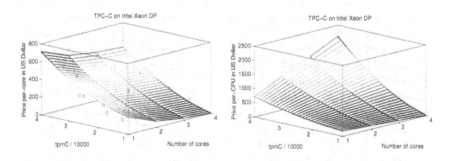

Fig. 3. The fitted cost models for price per-core (C_{core}) and price per-CPU (C_{cpu})

partially by the noise in the data as there is only one available measurement each for CPU frequency at 2.33 GHz and 2.83 GHz. Nevertheless, the general trend of price increasing with speed (core frequency) still holds. Figure 2 gives a better view on the pattern of how price changes with the per-core performance for TPC-C. On both DP and MP platforms with different cores, the per-core price scales with the per-core throughput like a power function. We studied different functions for curve fitting, including polynomial, exponential, power, and other custom functions. It is found that the power function, shown in Equation 1, gives the overall best fit for different data sets.

$$f(x) = c_1 x^{c_2} + c_3 \qquad (1)$$

Table 2. CPU cost model parameters for TPC-C on Intel Xeon DP (Equation 3)

model param.	c_1	c_2	c_3	c_4	c_5
TPCC/DP	36	2.0	261	-0.9	-105

Figure 2 also shows that the price per-core decreases like a power function while increasing the number of cores per-CPU. This indicates that the power function (Equation 1) can be used to model the relationships between price per-core and throughput performance/number of cores individually.

The next step is to study per-core performance (T_{core}) and number of cores (N_{core}) jointly and model their relationship with price. Since the power function is the best fitted model for T_{core} and N_{core} individually, we can extend this model to a multi-variable case[2]. A power function with two variables can be formulated as follows:

$$C_{core} = g(T_{core}, N_{core}) = \tag{2}$$
$$c_1 T_{core}^{c_2} + c_3 N_{core}^{c_4} + c_5,$$

where $(c_1, ..., c_5)$ are the parameters to be fitted. The price per-CPU C_{cpu} is readily obtained by multiplying price per-core with the number of cores:

$$C_{cpu} = N_{core} C_{core} = N_{core} g(T_{core}, N_{core}). \tag{3}$$

Figure 3 shows the fitting of TPC-C/DP data with the cost models C_{core} and C_{cpu}. A non-linear least-squares method in the Matlab Optimization toolbox is used for curve fitting, and the fitted parameters are shown in Table 2. We can see that the fitted model gives an overall good interpolation of real benchmark results. The trend/relationship between price and the two factors, namely performance per-core and number of cores, is well captured. Although different benchmarks on different platforms may yield different parameters[3], the model shown in Equation 3 is general and flexible enough for estimating a wide range of CPU cost information.

It should be noted that the power-function based model for CPU costs developed in this section depends on the Intel pricing schemes for its multi-/many-core platforms. Our contribution is to fit such price information with mathematical models, in relationship to real OLTP benchmark results. This gives the planners/architects at the provider side a convenient tool for estimating hardware costs given the desired performance level of their applications.

---

[2] An informal proof for this extension can be described as follows: When x or y is constant, either $f(x)$ or $f(y)$ takes the form $ax^b + c$. This means there is no x or y components of any form in the function other than x^b or y^d. So $f(x, y)$ can be written as $ax^b + cy^d + e$.

[3] There are no sufficient data for curve fitting of TPC-C benchmark on Intel MP platform.

Table 3. Power consumption model parameters for a customized OLTP application (Equation 5)

model param.	c_1	c_2	c_3	c_4	c_5
OLTP app.	276.7	15	7	2.1	1.1

3 Modeling Power Consumption

Power consumption and associated costs become increasingly significant in modern datacenter environments [6]. In this section we analyze and model the server power consumption of OLTP applications. We study the relationship between system power consumption (P_{sys}, measured in Watts) and CPU utilization (U), which is used as the main metric for system-level activity. Our experimental methodology and tooling are largely similar to the ones in [5,6], except that we focus on OLTP-like workloads. We run a customized OLTP application similar to sales and distribution business processes, on a 64-bit Linux server with 1 Intel dual-core CPU and 4 GB main memory. The system power is measured using a power meter connected between the server power plug and the wall socket. The CPU utilization data is collected using Linux utilities such as *sar* and *iostat*. Monitoring scripts in SAP performance tools are also used for correlating power and CPU utilization data.

Before data fitting and modeling we first perform a data pre-processing step called *normalization*. Instead of directly modeling P_{sys} we use a normalized power unit P_{norm}, which is defined as follows:

$$P_{norm} = \frac{P_{sys} - P_{idle}}{P_{busy} - P_{idle}}, \tag{4}$$

where the measured P_{idle} ($U = 0$) and P_{busy} ($U = 1$) for our test system are 42W and 84W, respectively. The normalized measurement results are shown in Figure 4.

Generally speaking the server power consumption increases as the CPU utilization grows. One particular important finding from the measurement data is the so-called power capping behavior [6], which means there are few times that the highest power is consumed by the server. Additionally we find that such highest power points are drawn mostly when the CPU utilization is higher than 80% and they have very similar peak values. Most of the common functions, such as quadratic polynomial, power, exponential, and Gaussian, cannot fit such flat curve of power values in the high-utilization interval (see the quadratic fitting in Figure 4).

We developed a model that can fit such power-capping behavior well. The model is inspired by the frequency response curve of a linear filter called Butterworth filter. It has such desired "flat" behavior in the passband of the frequency. We replace the polynomial part of the transfer function with the following customized power function which has two U components:

$$h(U) = c_1 U^{c_2} + c_3 U^{c_4} + c_5, \tag{5}$$

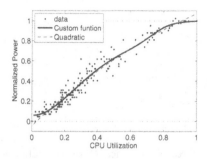

Fig. 4. Normalized system power relates to CPU utilization. The custom function is shown in Equation 6.

where $(c_1, ..., c_5)$ are the parameters to be fitted. The model that relates normalized power (P_{norm}) and CPU utilization U can be formulated as follows:

$$P_{norm}(U) = 1 - h(U)^{-1}. \tag{6}$$

The fitting result is shown in Figure 4 and the fitted model parameters are listed in Table 3. We can see that the proposed power model fits the measurement data well, especially during the high utilization period. Given the measurements for P_{idle} and P_{busy}, the overall system power consumption P_{sys} can be obtained by substituting P_{norm} (Equation 6) in Equation 4.

4 A Cost Model for Enterprise Applications

By combining the cost models for CPU and power consumption in previous sections (equations (3), (4), and (6)), we developed a cost model for business applications:

$$Cost(T_{core}, N_{core}, U, I) = \tag{7}$$
$$p_0 + p_1 C_{cpu} + p_2 \int_{t \in I} P_{sys}(U(t))dt,$$

where t is the measurement time, I is the measurement period $(t \in I)$, p_0 is an adjusting constant, p_1, and p_2 are the weighting parameters that scale the individual model outputs. If during the measurement period only average utilization is available, the output can be written as $P_{sys}(\overline{U})I$. The model in (7) uses an additive form to combine server hardware costs and operational costs, in which parameters p_1 and p_2 have to be set properly to reflect different cost structures.

To summarize from a mathematical modeling perspective, we can conclude that the power function $(c_1 x^{c_2} + c_3)$ and its variants have attractive properties for fitting a wide range of curves, including both single- and multi-variable case. Thus, the power function family represents a general and flexible modeling library from which different cost models can be fitted and derived.

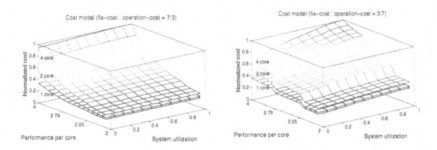

Fig. 5. Cost model structures: For a typical "classical" data center, the ratio of fixed cost versus operational cost (r) is set to 7 : 3. For a modern commodity-based data center, the ratio r is set to 3 : 7

In practice when using the cost model for the optimization of enterprise systems, we need to determine the weighting parameters p_1 (fixed cost) and p_2 (operational cost). These parameters are chosen in a way to reflect the real numbers obtained in case studies in [3]. There are two situations under study in this paper. On one hand, for a typical "classical" data center the ratio of fixed cost versus operational cost (r) is set to 7 : 3, which indicates that the high server capital costs dominate overall TCO by 70%. For a modern commodity-based data center, on the other hand, the ratio r is set to 3 : 7. This means operational costs including power consumption and cooling become the dominating factor. The cost model outputs of (7) for these two situations are illustrated in Figure 5, where differences can be clearly identified. For instance, the total cost increases significantly with the increasing system utilization for the high operational cost situation ($r = 3 : 7$), which is not the case for the high fixed cost counterpart($r = 7 : 3$). We also observe that the discontinuity of cost model outputs along the performance/core axis in the $r = 3 : 7$ situation. This is because the settings of P_{idle} and P_{busy} take discrete values like a piecewise constant function. The CPU performance per core is divided into three ranges and the values of P_{idle} and P_{busy} are set accordingly. For instance, for a 2-core system from low to high performance, P_{idle} and P_{busy} have been set to $[40, 60, 80]$ and $[65, 95, 150]$, respectively. Such settings are made in accordance to the CPU power consumption characteristics on Intel platforms. In the $r = 7 : 3$ situation, however, such effects is dramatically reduced as the operational cost is no longer dominant. In our ongoing research we investigate both situations in the optimization phase to see how different cost structures impact the SLA-driven planning on the service provider side.

5   Conclusions and Future Work

In this paper we developed a analytic cost model that consists of two tangible cost components: server hardware and power consumption. The CPU price is modeled as a function of number of cores and per-core throughput performance for OLTP applications. The server power consumption is modeled as a function of CPU utilization. Both models include Power function or its variants as components, which indicates that Power function as a mathematical form is suitable to fit a wide range of cost structures.

Cost modeling is one important enabling component in our ongoing work on SLA-driven planning and optimization of hosted business applications [8]. Service-Level Agreements (SLA) are bidding contracts between service consumer and service provider on guarantee terms such as performance and cost. In our view well-specified SLAs are important, even indispensable components for making utility-driven SOA and Cloud computing a success. SLAs can also be applied between layers and IT stacks in a provider's landscape. For enabling SLA-aware planning and optimization studies on the provider side, practical models are needed to encapsulate performance information, cost information, and other factors. The proposed cost model is utilized in our studies in optimizing a system landscape running OLTP applications by taking multiple conflicting objectives into account.

References

1. Above the clouds: A berkeley view of cloud computing. Tech. Rep. UCB/EECS-2009-28, University of California, Berkeley (2009)
2. Barroso, L.: The price of performance: An economic case for chip multiprocessing. ACM Queue 3(7), 48–53 (2005)
3. Barroso, L.A., Hölzle, U.: The Datacenter as a Computer: An Introduction to the Design of Warehouse-Scale Machines. Morgan & Claypool, San Francisco (2009)
4. Chase, J.S., Anderson, D.C., Thakar, P.N., Vahdat, A., Doyle, R.P.: Managing energy and server resources in hosting centres. In: Proc. of SOSP, pp. 103–116. ACM, New York (2001)
5. Economou, D., Rivoire, S., Kozyrakis, C., Ranganathan, P.: Full-system power analysis and modeling for server environments. In: Proc. of Workshop on Modeling, Benchmarking and Simulation, MOBS (2006)
6. Fan, X., Weber, W.-D., Barroso, L.A.: Power provisioning for a warehouse-sized computer. In: Proc. of the 34th Intl. Sym. on Computer Architecture (ISCA 2007), pp. 13–23. ACM Press, New York (2007)
7. INTEL. Intel processor pricing, 2007-2009, http://www.intc.com/priceList.cfm (accessed March 2009)
8. Li, H., Theilmann, W., Happe, J.: SLA Translation in Multi-layered Service Oriented Architectures: Status and Challenges. Tech. Rep. 2009-08, University of Karlsruhe, Germany (2009)
9. Marquard, U., Goetz, C.: SAP Standard Application Benchmarks - IT Benchmarks with a Business Focus. In: Kounev, S., Gorton, I., Sachs, K. (eds.) SIPEW 2008. LNCS, vol. 5119, pp. 4–8. Springer, Heidelberg (2008)
10. SAP. The Sales and Distribution (SD) Benchmark, Two-tier Internet Configuration (2009), http://www.sap.com/solutions/benchmark/sd.epx (accessed March 2009)
11. TPC. TPC-C: on-line transaction processing benchmark V5 (2009), http://www.tpc.org/tpcc/ (accessed March 2009)

Author Index